JASOTRON: '012

Jasontron: 2012

Other *FoxTrot* Books by Bill Amend

FoxTrot • Pass the Loot • Black Bart Says Draw • Eight Yards, Down and Out
Bury My Heart at Fun-Fun Mountain • Say Hello to Cactus Flats • May the Force Be with Us, Please
Take Us to Your Mall • The Return of the Lone Iguana • At Least This Place Sells T-shirts
Come Closer, Roger, There's a Mosquito on Your Nose • Welcome to Jasorassic Park
I'm Flying, Jack . . . I Mean, Roger • Think iFruity • Death by Field Trip
Encyclopedias Brown and White • His Code Name Was The Fox
Your Momma Thinks Square Roots Are Vegetables • Who's Up for Some Bonding?
Am I a Mutant or What! • Orlando Bloom Has Ruined Everything
My Hot Dog Went Out, Can I Have Another? • How Come I'm Always Luigi?
Houston, You Have a Problem • And When She Opened the Closet, All the Clothes Were Polyester
Math, Science, and Unix Underpants • FoxTrot Sundaes
AAAA! A FoxTrot Kids Edition

Anthologies

FoxTrot: The Works • FoxTrot *en masse* • Enormously FoxTrot • Wildly FoxTrot
FoxTrot Beyond a Doubt • Camp FoxTrot • Assorted FoxTrot • FoxTrot: Assembled with Care
FoxTrotius Maximus • Jam-Packed FoxTrot • Wrapped-Up FoxTrot • The Best of FoxTrot

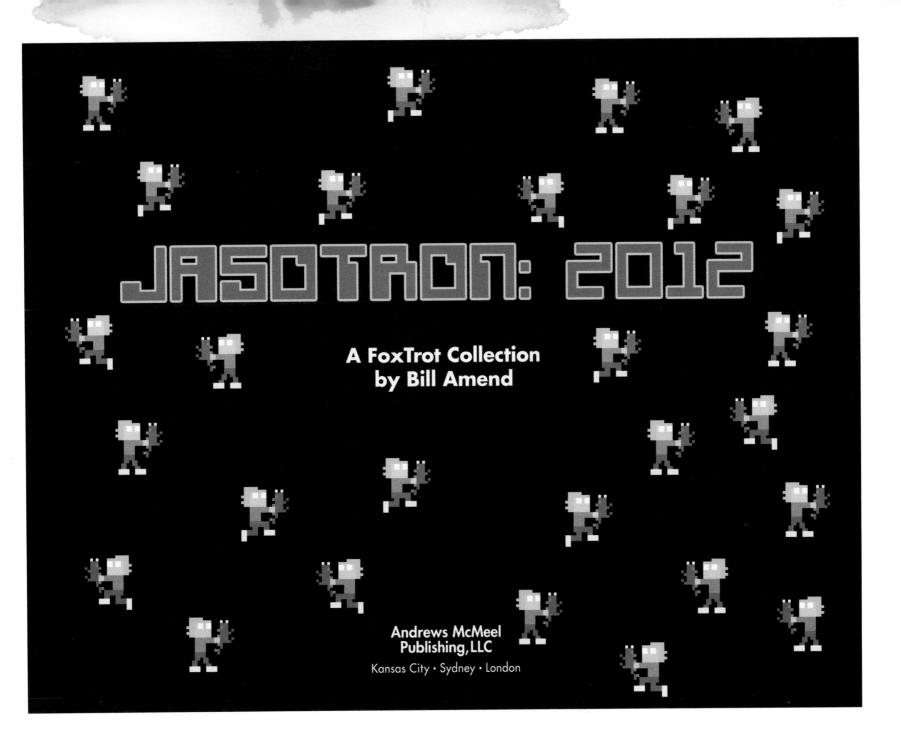

JASOTRON: 2012

**A FoxTrot Collection
by Bill Amend**

Andrews McMeel
Publishing, LLC

Kansas City · Sydney · London

Andrews McMeel Publishing, LLC
an Andrews McMeel Universal company
1130 Walnut Street, Kansas City, Missouri 64106

12 13 14 15 16 BAM 10 9 8 7 6 5 4 3 2 1

ISBN: 978-1-4494-2306-3
Library of Congress Control Number: 2012936750

www.andrewsmcmeel.com
www.foxtrot.com

ATTENTION: SCHOOLS AND BUSINESSES

Andrews McMeel books are available at quantity discounts with bulk purchase for educational, business, or sales promotional use. For information, please e-mail the Andrews McMeel Special Sales Department: specialsales@amuniversal.com.

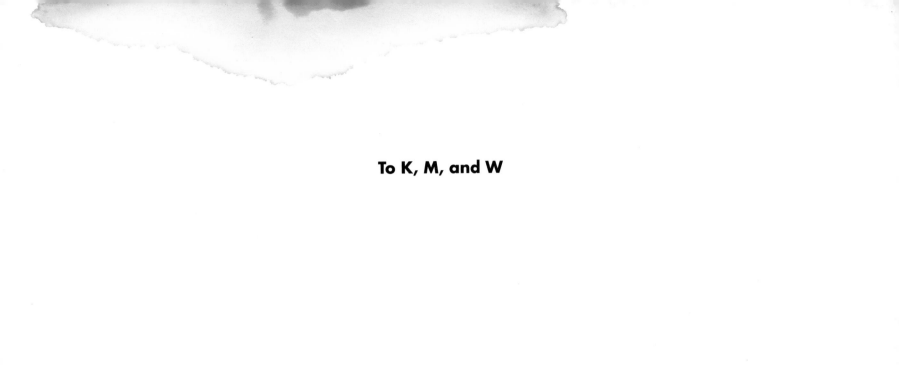

To K, M, and W

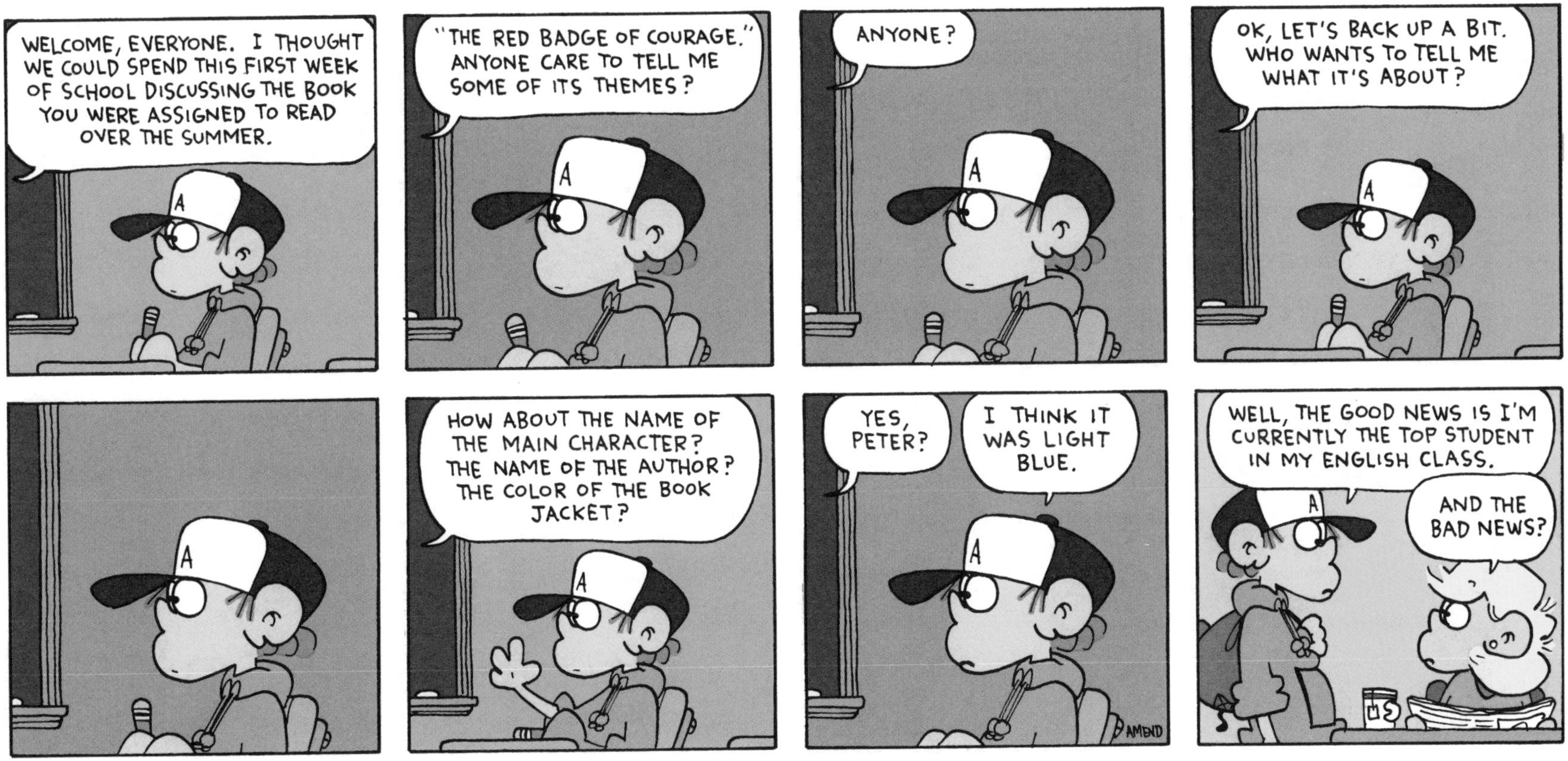
WELCOME, EVERYONE. I THOUGHT WE COULD SPEND THIS FIRST WEEK OF SCHOOL DISCUSSING THE BOOK YOU WERE ASSIGNED TO READ OVER THE SUMMER.
"THE RED BADGE OF COURAGE." ANYONE CARE TO TELL ME SOME OF ITS THEMES?
ANYONE?
OK, LET'S BACK UP A BIT. WHO WANTS TO TELL ME WHAT IT'S ABOUT?
HOW ABOUT THE NAME OF THE MAIN CHARACTER? THE NAME OF THE AUTHOR? THE COLOR OF THE BOOK JACKET?
YES, PETER?
I THINK IT WAS LIGHT BLUE.
AMEND
WELL, THE GOOD NEWS IS I'M CURRENTLY THE TOP STUDENT IN MY ENGLISH CLASS.
AND THE BAD NEWS?

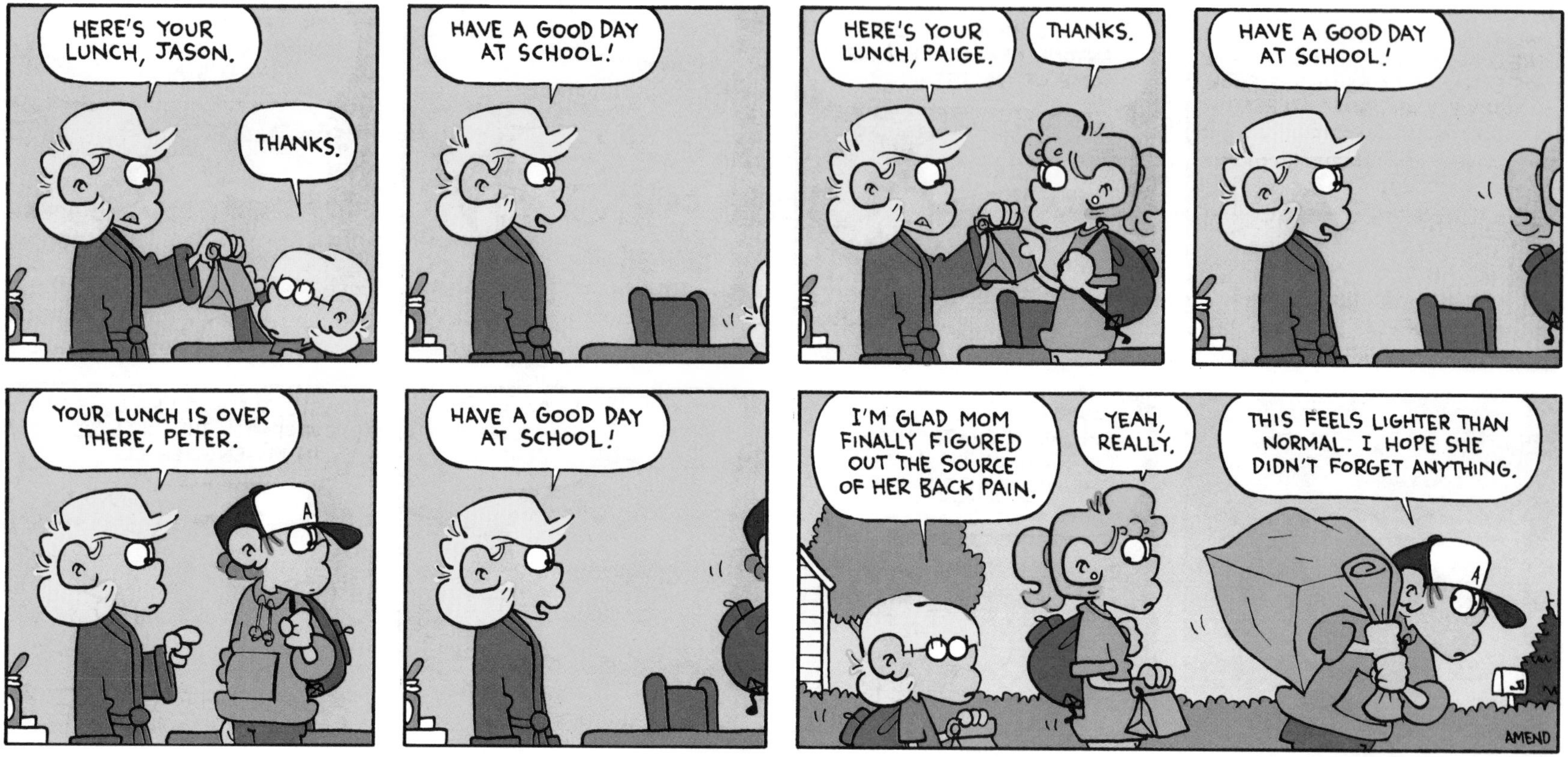
HERE'S YOUR LUNCH, JASON.
THANKS.
HAVE A GOOD DAY AT SCHOOL!
HERE'S YOUR LUNCH, PAIGE.
THANKS.
HAVE A GOOD DAY AT SCHOOL!
YOUR LUNCH IS OVER THERE, PETER.
HAVE A GOOD DAY AT SCHOOL!
I'M GLAD MOM FINALLY FIGURED OUT THE SOURCE OF HER BACK PAIN.
YEAH, REALLY.
THIS FEELS LIGHTER THAN NORMAL. I HOPE SHE DIDN'T FORGET ANYTHING.
AMEND

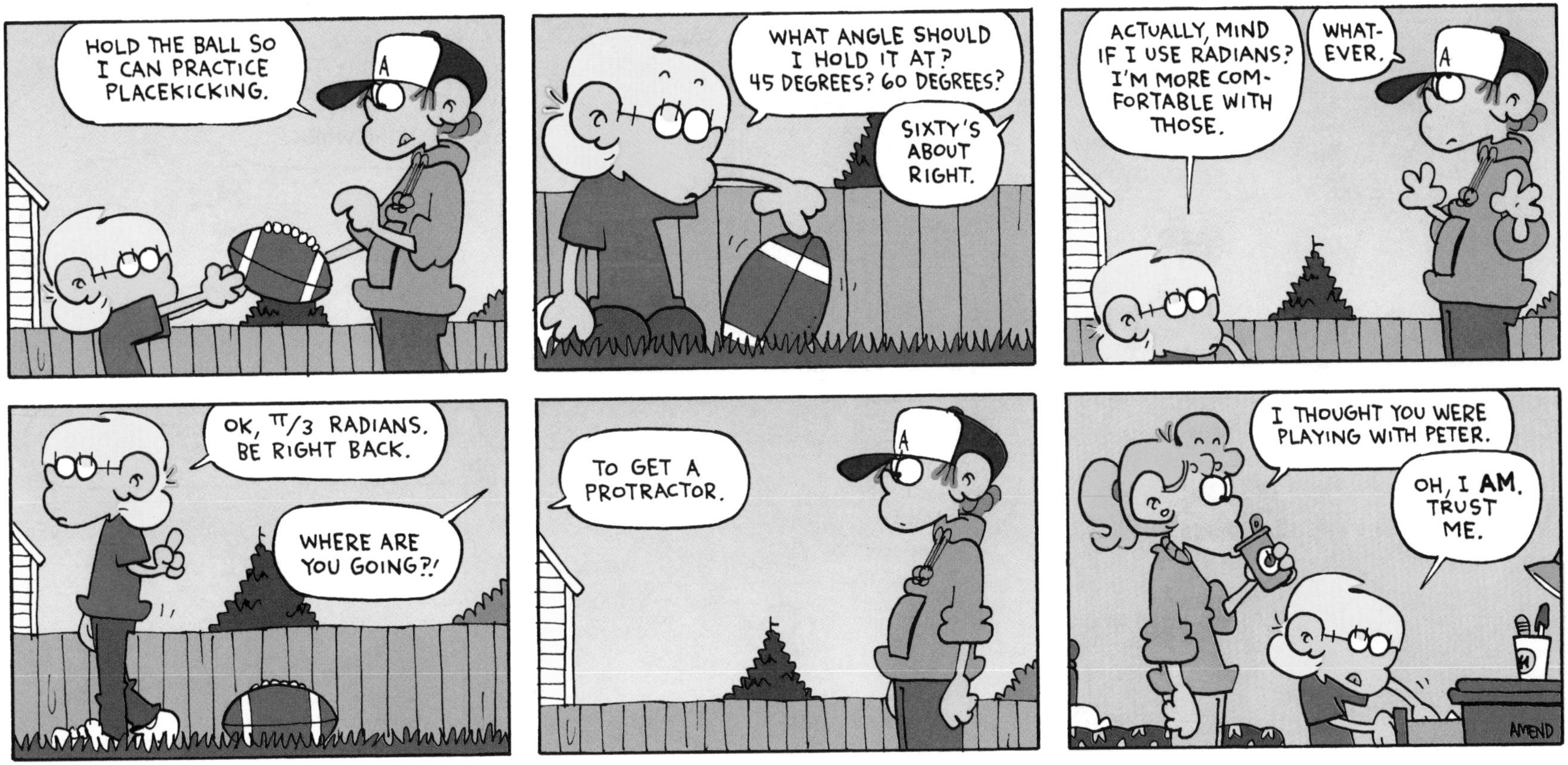
HOLD THE BALL SO I CAN PRACTICE PLACEKICKING.
WHAT ANGLE SHOULD I HOLD IT AT? 45 DEGREES? 60 DEGREES?
SIXTY'S ABOUT RIGHT.
ACTUALLY, MIND IF I USE RADIANS? I'M MORE COM-FORTABLE WITH THOSE.
WHAT-EVER.
OK, π/3 RADIANS. BE RIGHT BACK.
WHERE ARE YOU GOING?!
TO GET A PROTRACTOR.
I THOUGHT YOU WERE PLAYING WITH PETER.
OH, I AM. TRUST ME.
AMEND

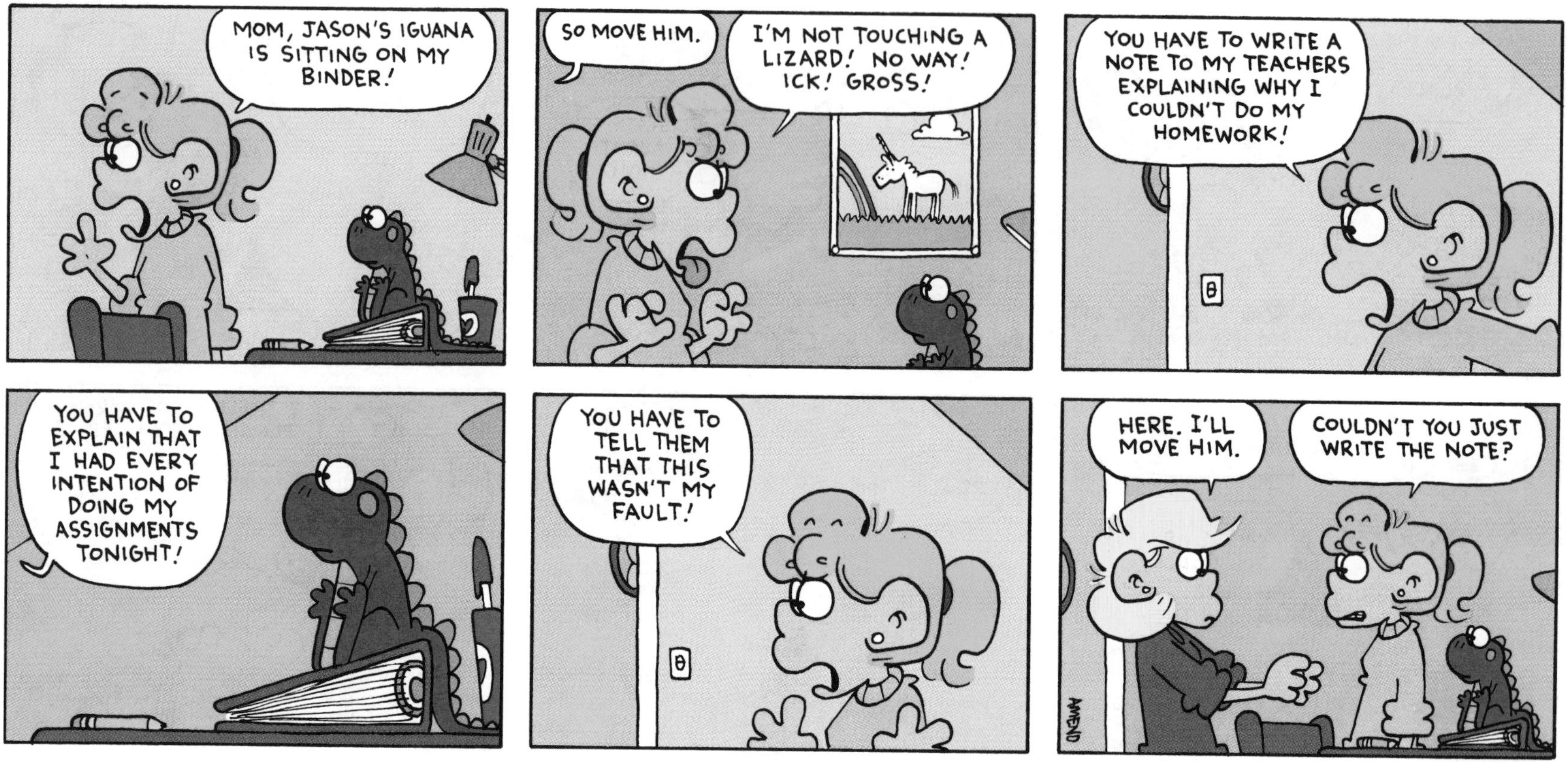
MOM, JASON'S IGUANA IS SITTING ON MY BINDER!
SO MOVE HIM.
I'M NOT TOUCHING A LIZARD! NO WAY! ICK! GROSS!
YOU HAVE TO WRITE A NOTE TO MY TEACHERS EXPLAINING WHY I COULDN'T DO MY HOMEWORK!
YOU HAVE TO EXPLAIN THAT I HAD EVERY INTENTION OF DOING MY ASSIGNMENTS TONIGHT!
YOU HAVE TO TELL THEM THAT THIS WASN'T MY FAULT!
HERE. I'LL MOVE HIM.
COULDN'T YOU JUST WRITE THE NOTE?
AMEND

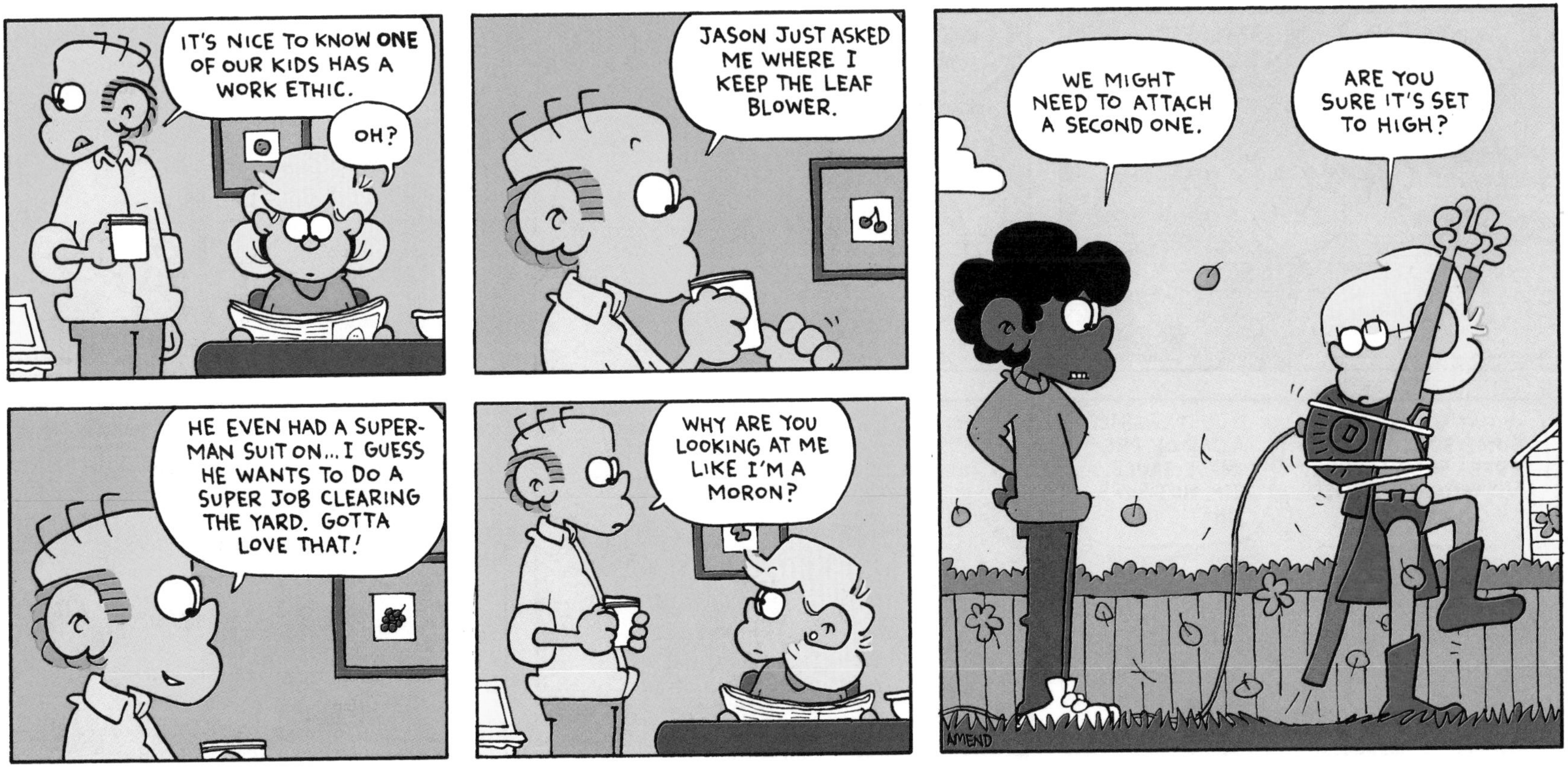
IT'S NICE TO KNOW ONE OF OUR KIDS HAS A WORK ETHIC.
OH?
JASON JUST ASKED ME WHERE I KEEP THE LEAF BLOWER.
HE EVEN HAD A SUPER-MAN SUIT ON... I GUESS HE WANTS TO DO A SUPER JOB CLEARING THE YARD. GOTTA LOVE THAT!
WHY ARE YOU LOOKING AT ME LIKE I'M A MORON?
WE MIGHT NEED TO ATTACH A SECOND ONE.
ARE YOU SURE IT'S SET TO HIGH?
AMEND

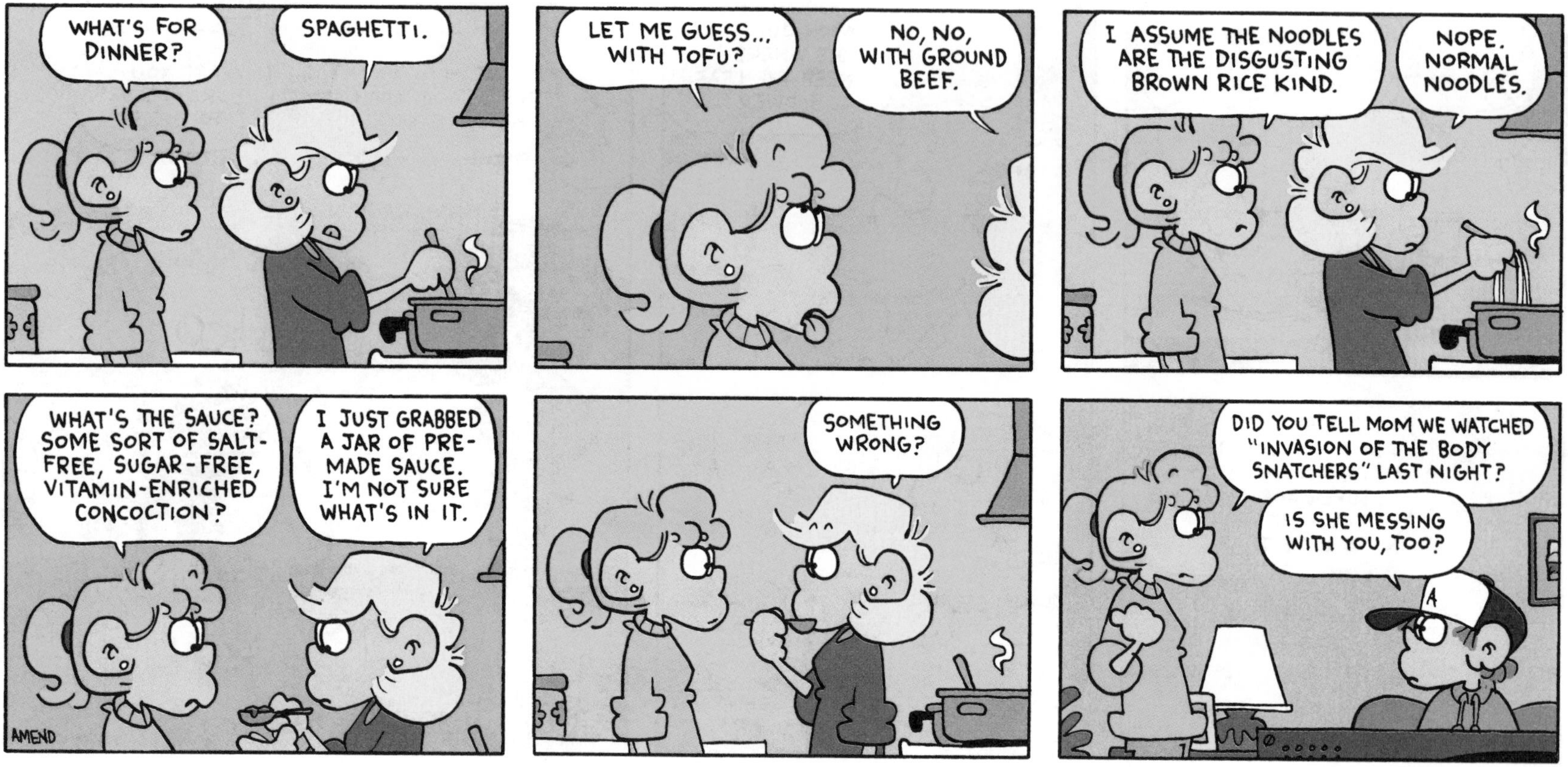
WHAT'S FOR DINNER?
SPAGHETTI.
LET ME GUESS... WITH TOFU?
NO, NO, WITH GROUND BEEF.
I ASSUME THE NOODLES ARE THE DISGUSTING BROWN RICE KIND.
NOPE. NORMAL NOODLES.
WHAT'S THE SAUCE? SOME SORT OF SALT-FREE, SUGAR-FREE, VITAMIN-ENRICHED CONCOCTION?
I JUST GRABBED A JAR OF PRE-MADE SAUCE. I'M NOT SURE WHAT'S IN IT.
AMEND
SOMETHING WRONG?
DID YOU TELL MOM WE WATCHED "INVASION OF THE BODY SNATCHERS" LAST NIGHT?
IS SHE MESSING WITH YOU, TOO?

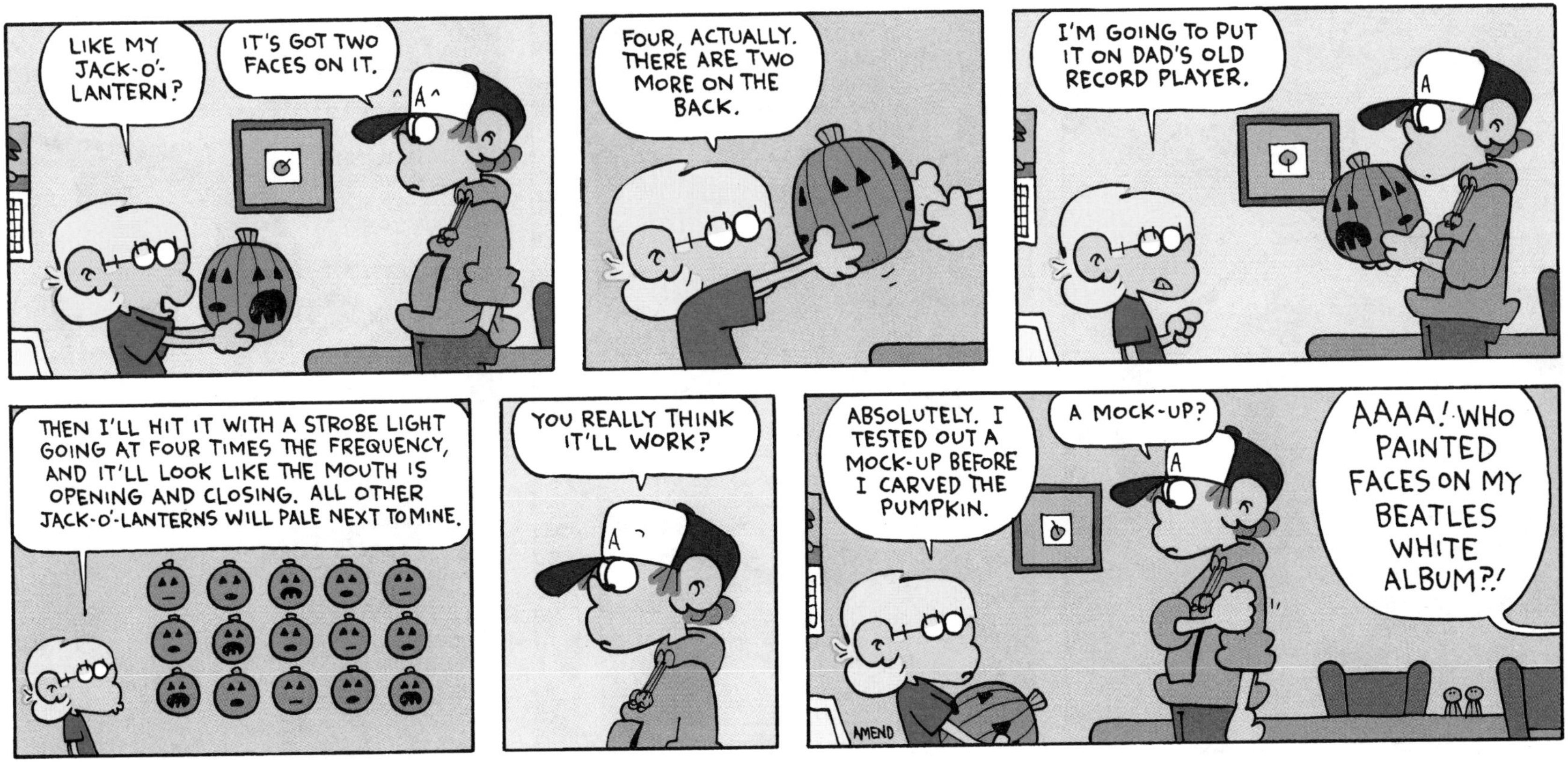
LIKE MY JACK-O'-LANTERN?
IT'S GOT TWO FACES ON IT.
FOUR, ACTUALLY. THERE ARE TWO MORE ON THE BACK.
I'M GOING TO PUT IT ON DAD'S OLD RECORD PLAYER.
THEN I'LL HIT IT WITH A STROBE LIGHT GOING AT FOUR TIMES THE FREQUENCY, AND IT'LL LOOK LIKE THE MOUTH IS OPENING AND CLOSING. ALL OTHER JACK-O'-LANTERNS WILL PALE NEXT TO MINE.
YOU REALLY THINK IT'LL WORK?
ABSOLUTELY. I TESTED OUT A MOCK-UP BEFORE I CARVED THE PUMPKIN.
A MOCK-UP?
AAAA! WHO PAINTED FACES ON MY BEATLES WHITE ALBUM?!
AMEND

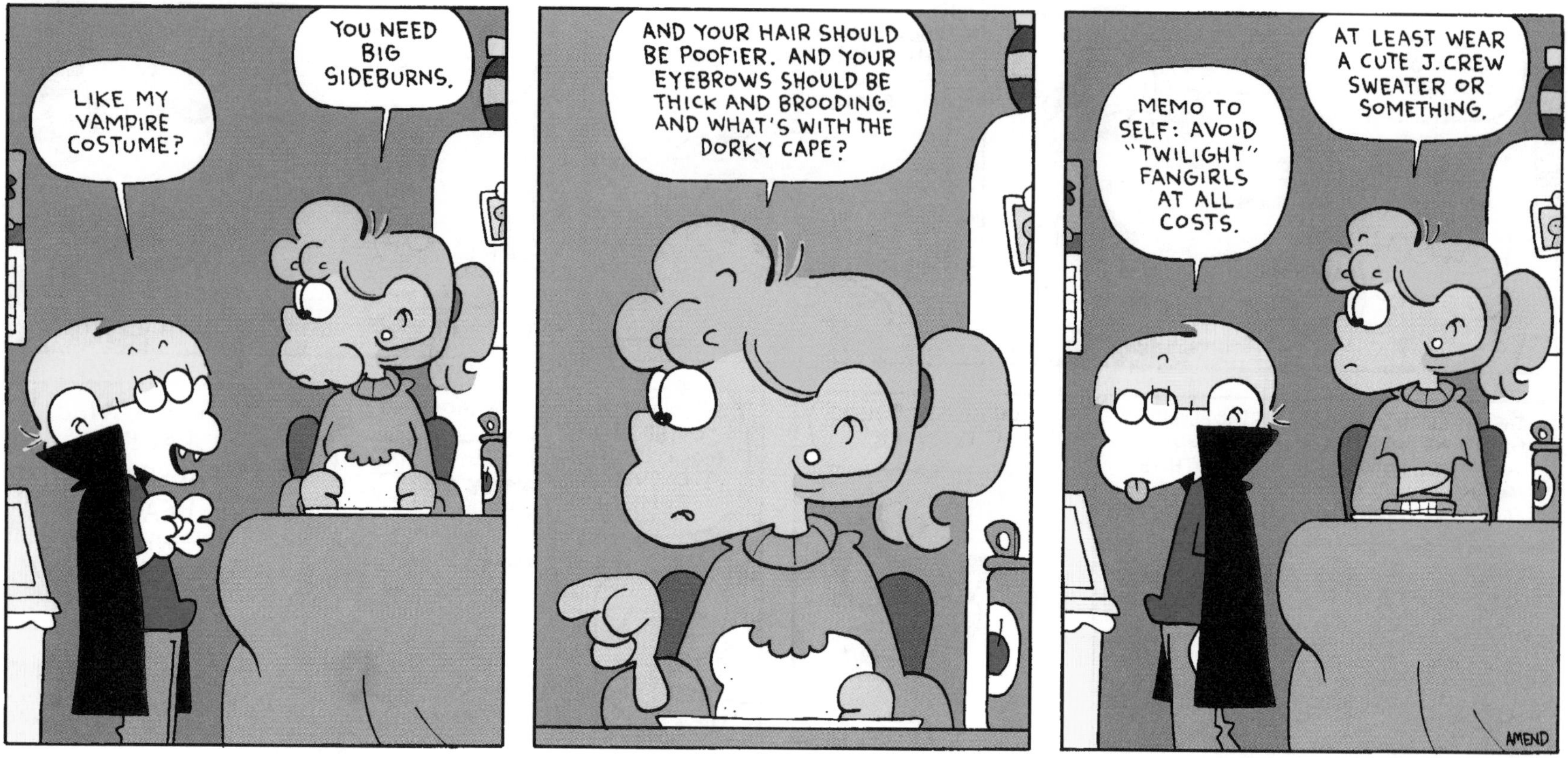
LIKE MY VAMPIRE COSTUME?
YOU NEED BIG SIDEBURNS.
AND YOUR HAIR SHOULD BE POOFIER. AND YOUR EYEBROWS SHOULD BE THICK AND BROODING. AND WHAT'S WITH THE DORKY CAPE?
AT LEAST WEAR A CUTE J.CREW SWEATER OR SOMETHING.
MEMO TO SELF: AVOID "TWILIGHT" FANGIRLS AT ALL COSTS.
AMEND

LET'S SEE... ONE FOOD CALORIE IS THE ENERGY REQUIRED TO HEAT ONE KILOGRAM OF WATER BY ONE DEGREE CELSIUS...
IF A CHILD WEIGHS 75 POUNDS, THAT'S 34 KILOGRAMS, OF WHICH ABOUT 60 PERCENT IS WATER...
NORMAL HUMAN BODY TEMPERATURE IS 37 DEGREES CELSIUS...
JASON, CAN YOU COME HERE FOR A SECOND?
WHATCHA NEED?
I'M TRYING TO GET A SENSE OF HOW MUCH HALLOWEEN CANDY YOU'VE EATEN.
AMEND

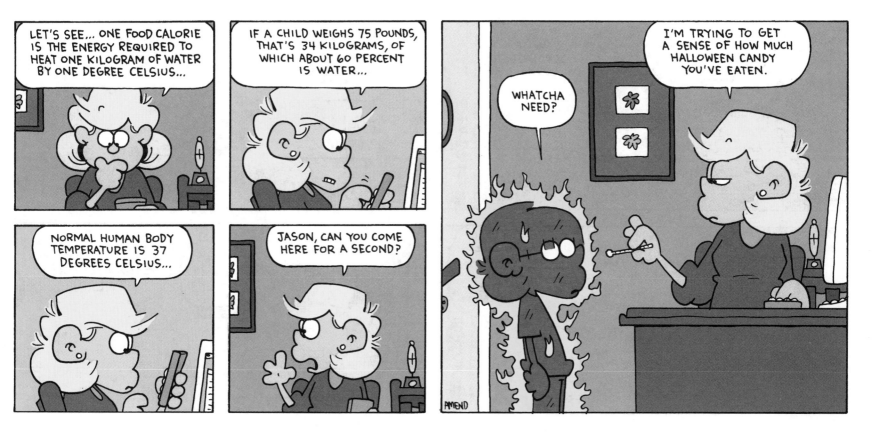

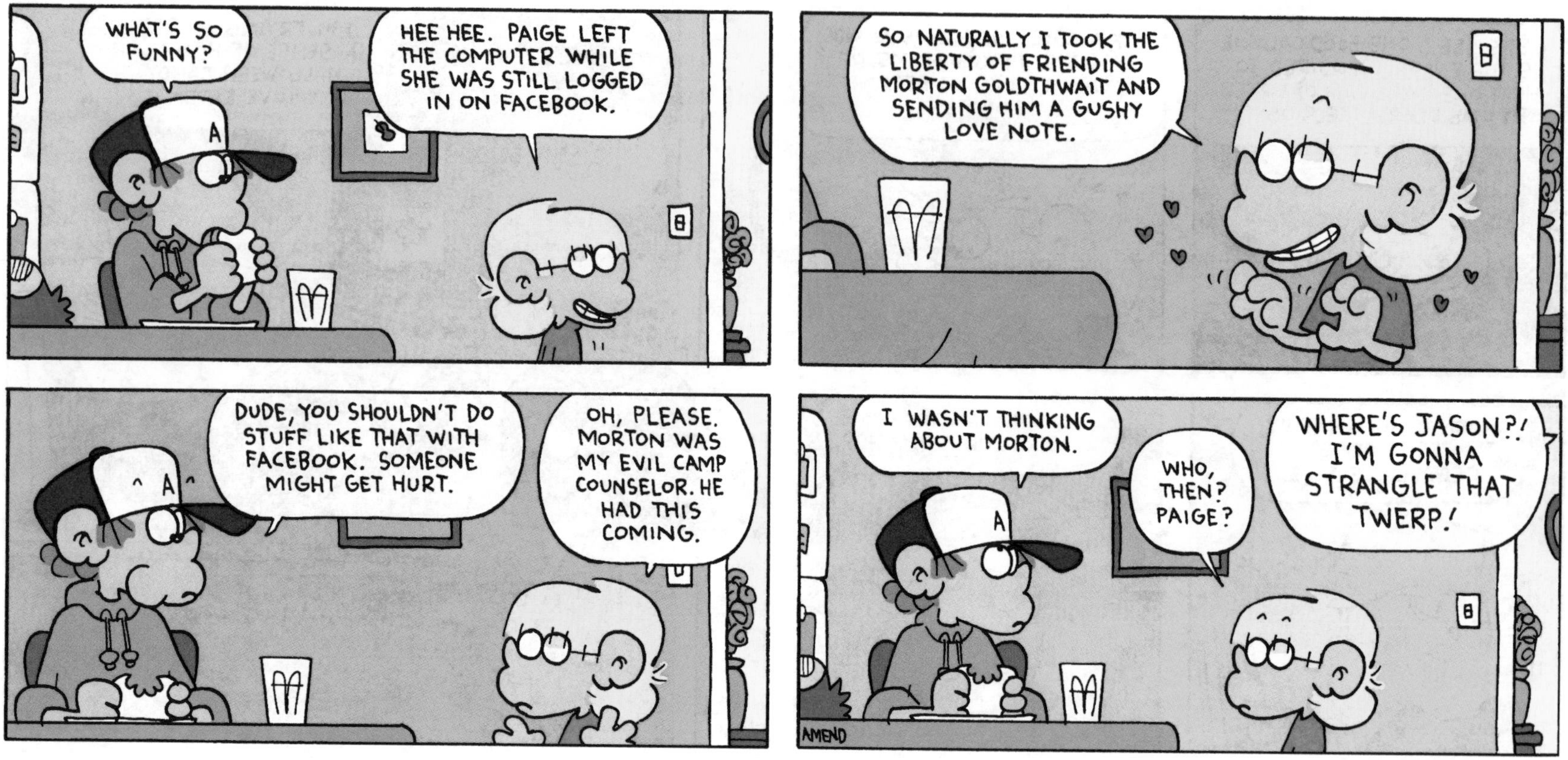
WHAT'S SO FUNNY?
HEE HEE. PAIGE LEFT THE COMPUTER WHILE SHE WAS STILL LOGGED IN ON FACEBOOK.
SO NATURALLY I TOOK THE LIBERTY OF FRIENDING MORTON GOLDTHWAIT AND SENDING HIM A GUSHY LOVE NOTE.
DUDE, YOU SHOULDN'T DO STUFF LIKE THAT WITH FACEBOOK. SOMEONE MIGHT GET HURT.
OH, PLEASE. MORTON WAS MY EVIL CAMP COUNSELOR. HE HAD THIS COMING.
I WASN'T THINKING ABOUT MORTON.
WHO, THEN? PAIGE?
WHERE'S JASON?! I'M GONNA STRANGLE THAT TWERP!
AMEND

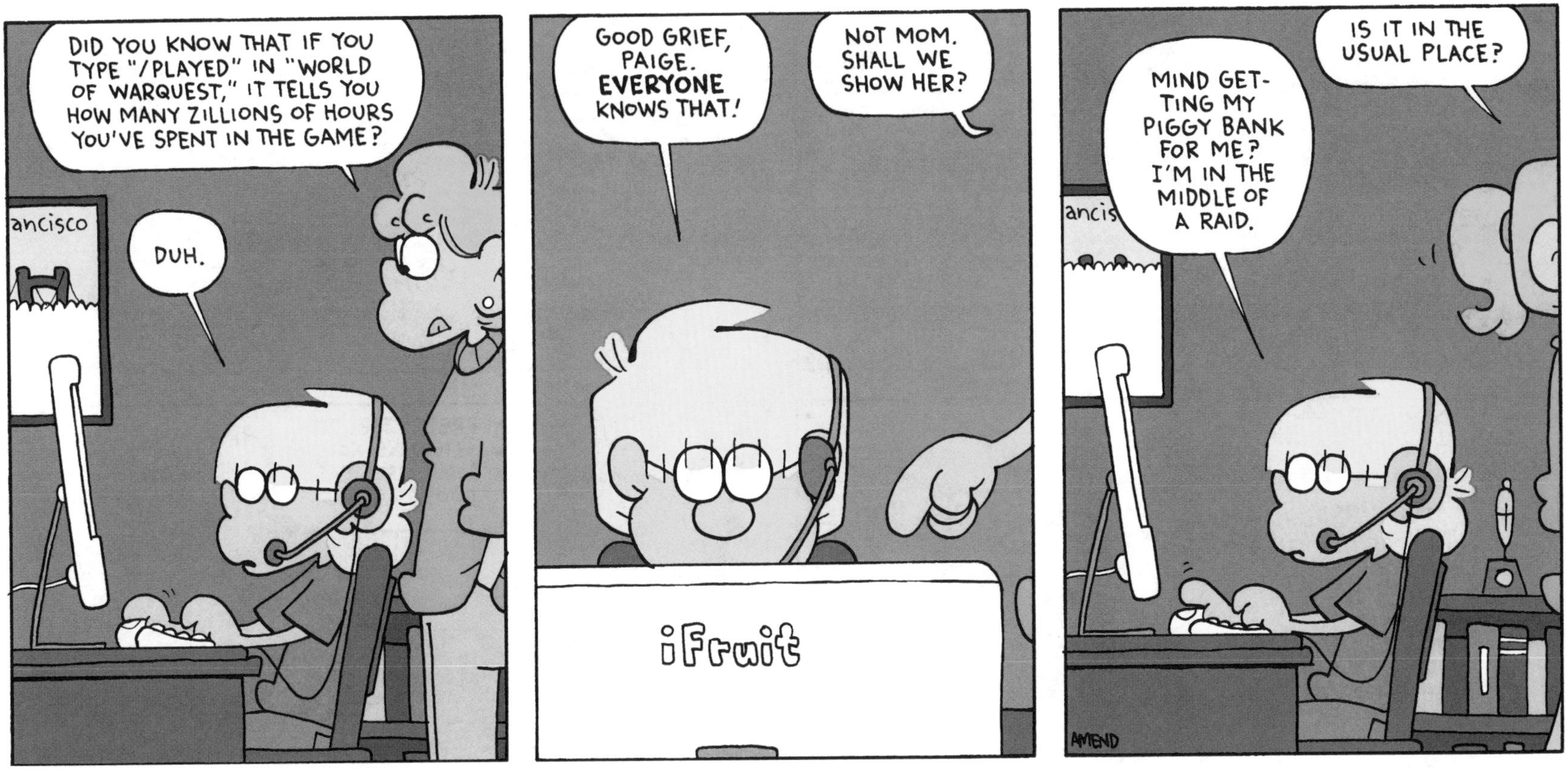
DID YOU KNOW THAT IF YOU TYPE "/PLAYED" IN "WORLD OF WARQUEST," IT TELLS YOU HOW MANY ZILLIONS OF HOURS YOU'VE SPENT IN THE GAME?
DUH.
ancisco
GOOD GRIEF, PAIGE. **EVERYONE** KNOWS THAT!
NOT MOM. SHALL WE SHOW HER?
iFruit
MIND GETTING MY PIGGY BANK FOR ME? I'M IN THE MIDDLE OF A RAID.
IS IT IN THE USUAL PLACE?
ancis
AMEND

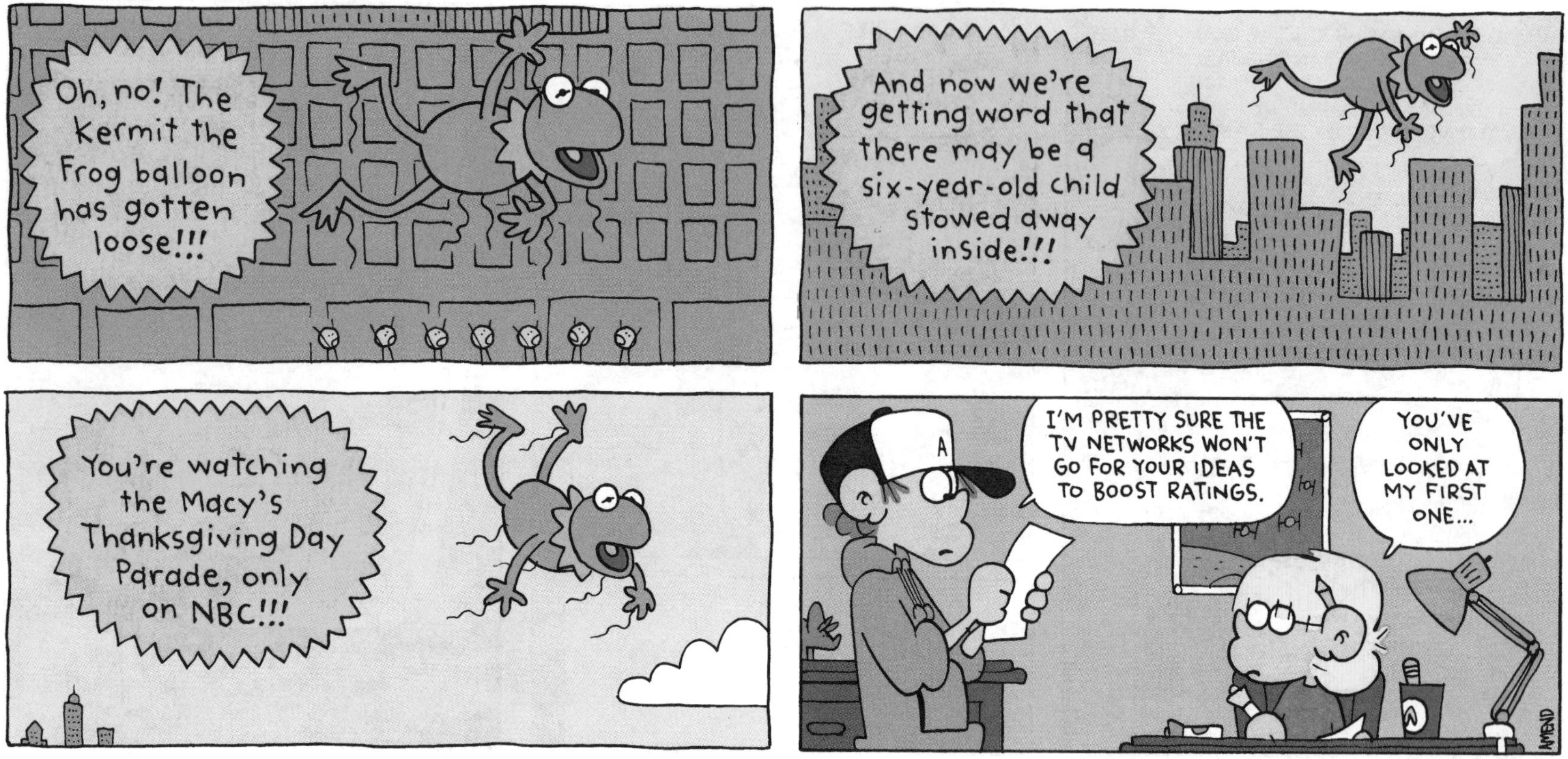
Oh, no! The Kermit the Frog balloon has gotten loose!!!
And now we're getting word that there may be a six-year-old child stowed away inside!!!
You're watching the Macy's Thanksgiving Day Parade, only on NBC!!!
A
I'M PRETTY SURE THE TV NETWORKS WON'T GO FOR YOUR IDEAS TO BOOST RATINGS.
YOU'VE ONLY LOOKED AT MY FIRST ONE...
AMEND

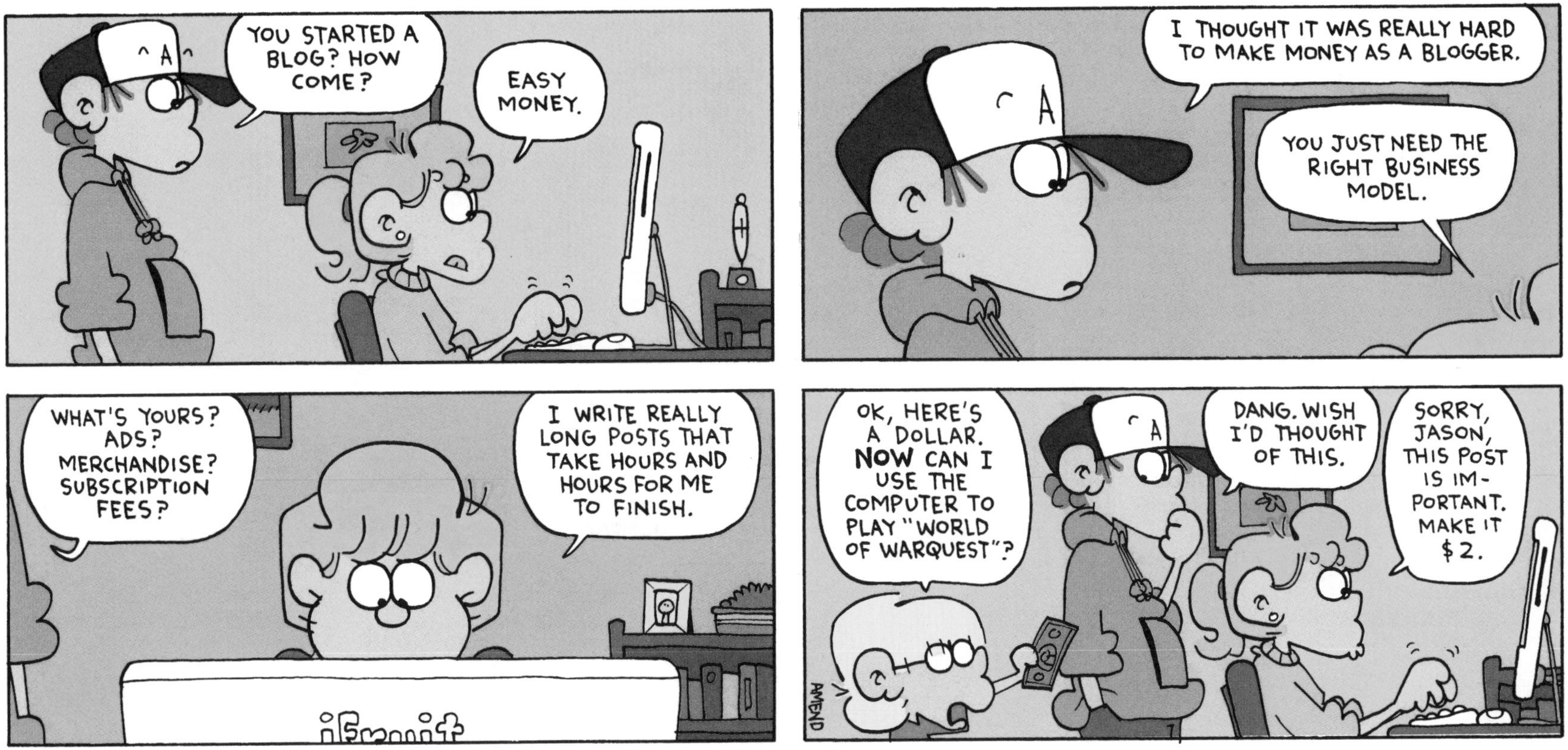
YOU STARTED A BLOG? HOW COME?
EASY MONEY.
I THOUGHT IT WAS REALLY HARD TO MAKE MONEY AS A BLOGGER.
YOU JUST NEED THE RIGHT BUSINESS MODEL.
WHAT'S YOURS? ADS? MERCHANDISE? SUBSCRIPTION FEES?
I WRITE REALLY LONG POSTS THAT TAKE HOURS AND HOURS FOR ME TO FINISH.
iFruit
OK, HERE'S A DOLLAR. **NOW** CAN I USE THE COMPUTER TO PLAY "WORLD OF WARQUEST"?
DANG. WISH I'D THOUGHT OF THIS.
SORRY, JASON, THIS POST IS IM-PORTANT. MAKE IT $2.
AMEND

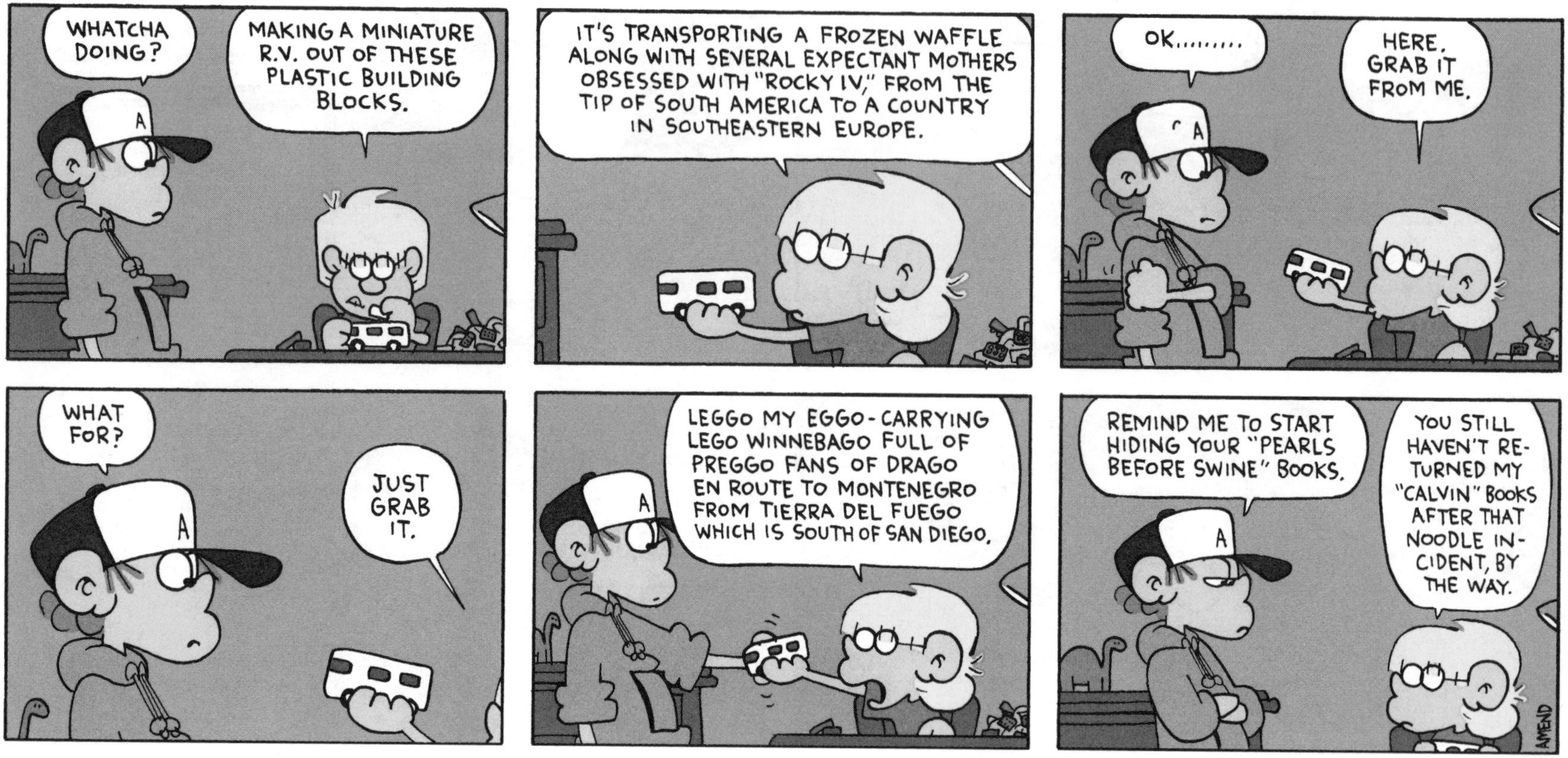
WHATCHA DOING?
MAKING A MINIATURE R.V. OUT OF THESE PLASTIC BUILDING BLOCKS.
IT'S TRANSPORTING A FROZEN WAFFLE ALONG WITH SEVERAL EXPECTANT MOTHERS OBSESSED WITH "ROCKY IV," FROM THE TIP OF SOUTH AMERICA TO A COUNTRY IN SOUTHEASTERN EUROPE.
OK.........
HERE. GRAB IT FROM ME.
WHAT FOR?
JUST GRAB IT.
LEGGO MY EGGO-CARRYING LEGO WINNEBAGO FULL OF PREGGO FANS OF DRAGO EN ROUTE TO MONTENEGRO FROM TIERRA DEL FUEGO WHICH IS SOUTH OF SAN DIEGO.
REMIND ME TO START HIDING YOUR "PEARLS BEFORE SWINE" BOOKS.
YOU STILL HAVEN'T RE-TURNED MY "CALVIN" BOOKS AFTER THAT NOODLE IN-CIDENT, BY THE WAY.
AMEND

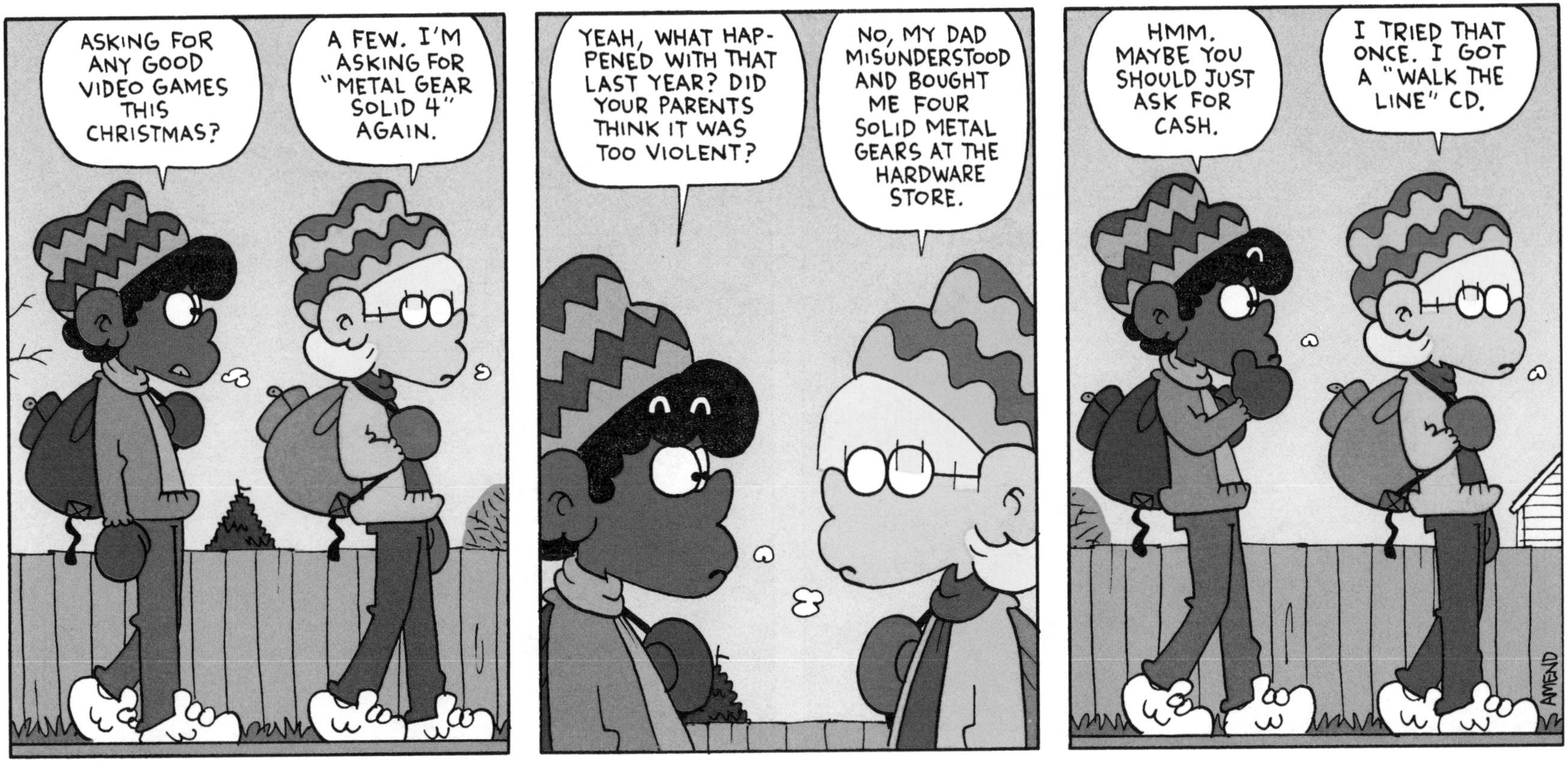
ASKING FOR ANY GOOD VIDEO GAMES THIS CHRISTMAS?
A FEW. I'M ASKING FOR "METAL GEAR SOLID 4" AGAIN.
YEAH, WHAT HAPPENED WITH THAT LAST YEAR? DID YOUR PARENTS THINK IT WAS TOO VIOLENT?
NO, MY DAD MISUNDERSTOOD AND BOUGHT ME FOUR SOLID METAL GEARS AT THE HARDWARE STORE.
HMM. MAYBE YOU SHOULD JUST ASK FOR CASH.
I TRIED THAT ONCE. I GOT A "WALK THE LINE" CD.
AMEND

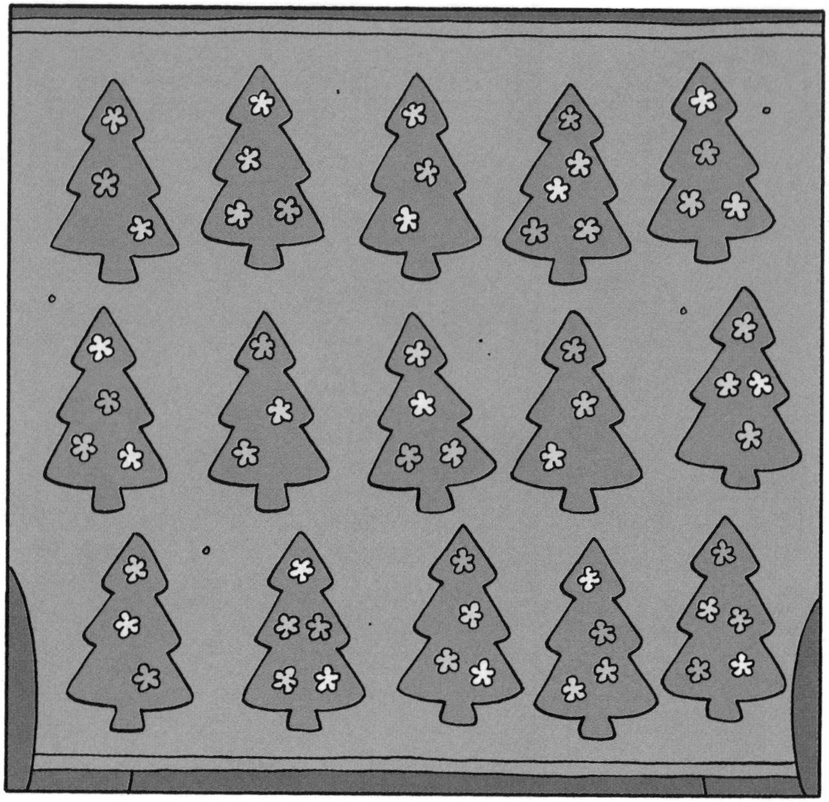

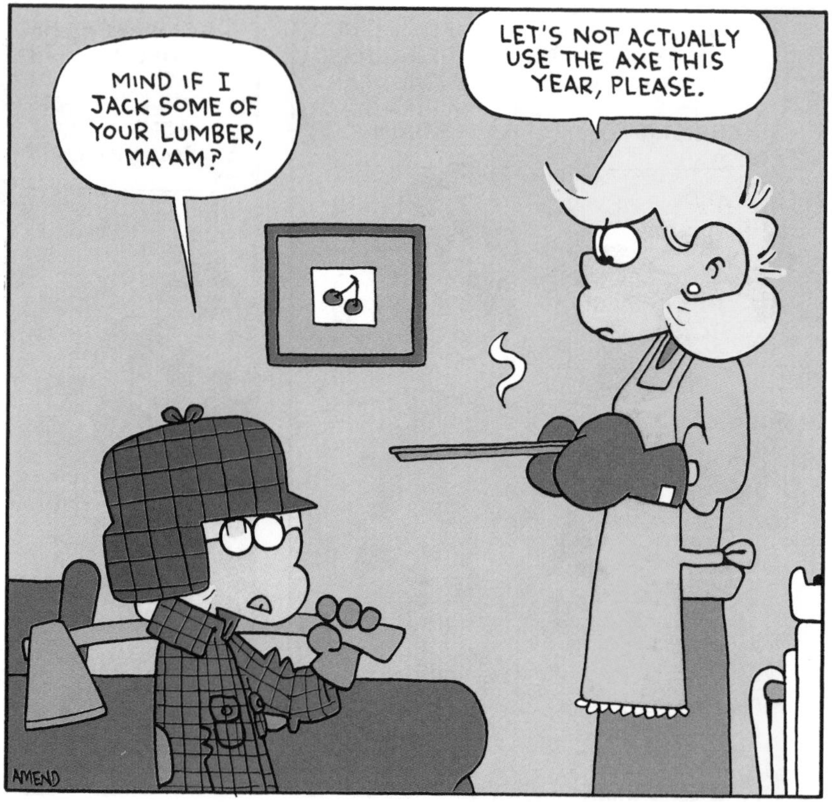
MIND IF I JACK SOME OF YOUR LUMBER, MA'AM?
LET'S NOT ACTUALLY USE THE AXE THIS YEAR, PLEASE.
AMEND

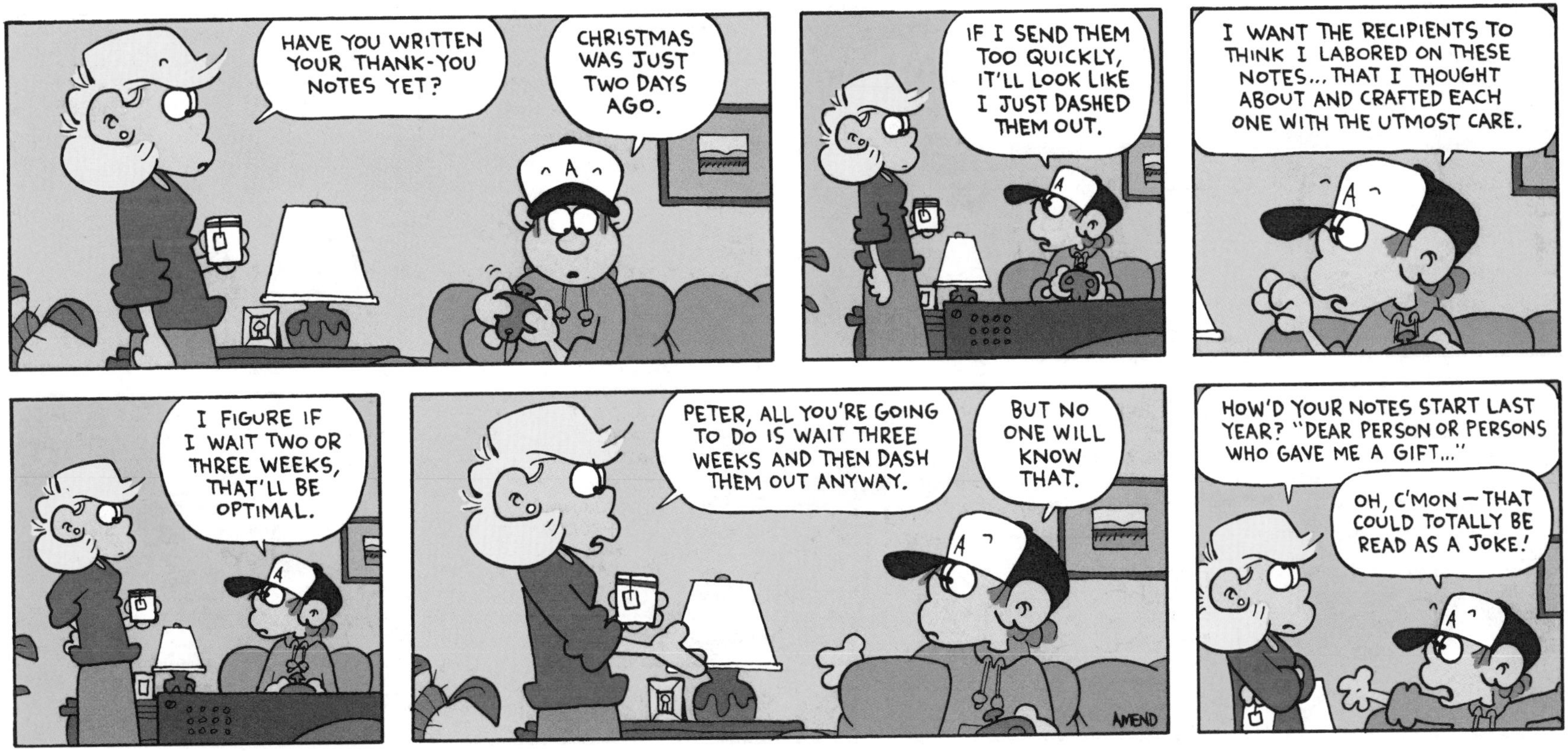
HAVE YOU WRITTEN YOUR THANK-YOU NOTES YET?
CHRISTMAS WAS JUST TWO DAYS AGO.
IF I SEND THEM TOO QUICKLY, IT'LL LOOK LIKE I JUST DASHED THEM OUT.
I WANT THE RECIPIENTS TO THINK I LABORED ON THESE NOTES... THAT I THOUGHT ABOUT AND CRAFTED EACH ONE WITH THE UTMOST CARE.
I FIGURE IF I WAIT TWO OR THREE WEEKS, THAT'LL BE OPTIMAL.
PETER, ALL YOU'RE GOING TO DO IS WAIT THREE WEEKS AND THEN DASH THEM OUT ANYWAY.
BUT NO ONE WILL KNOW THAT.
AMEND
HOW'D YOUR NOTES START LAST YEAR? "DEAR PERSON OR PERSONS WHO GAVE ME A GIFT..."
OH, C'MON — THAT COULD TOTALLY BE READ AS A JOKE!

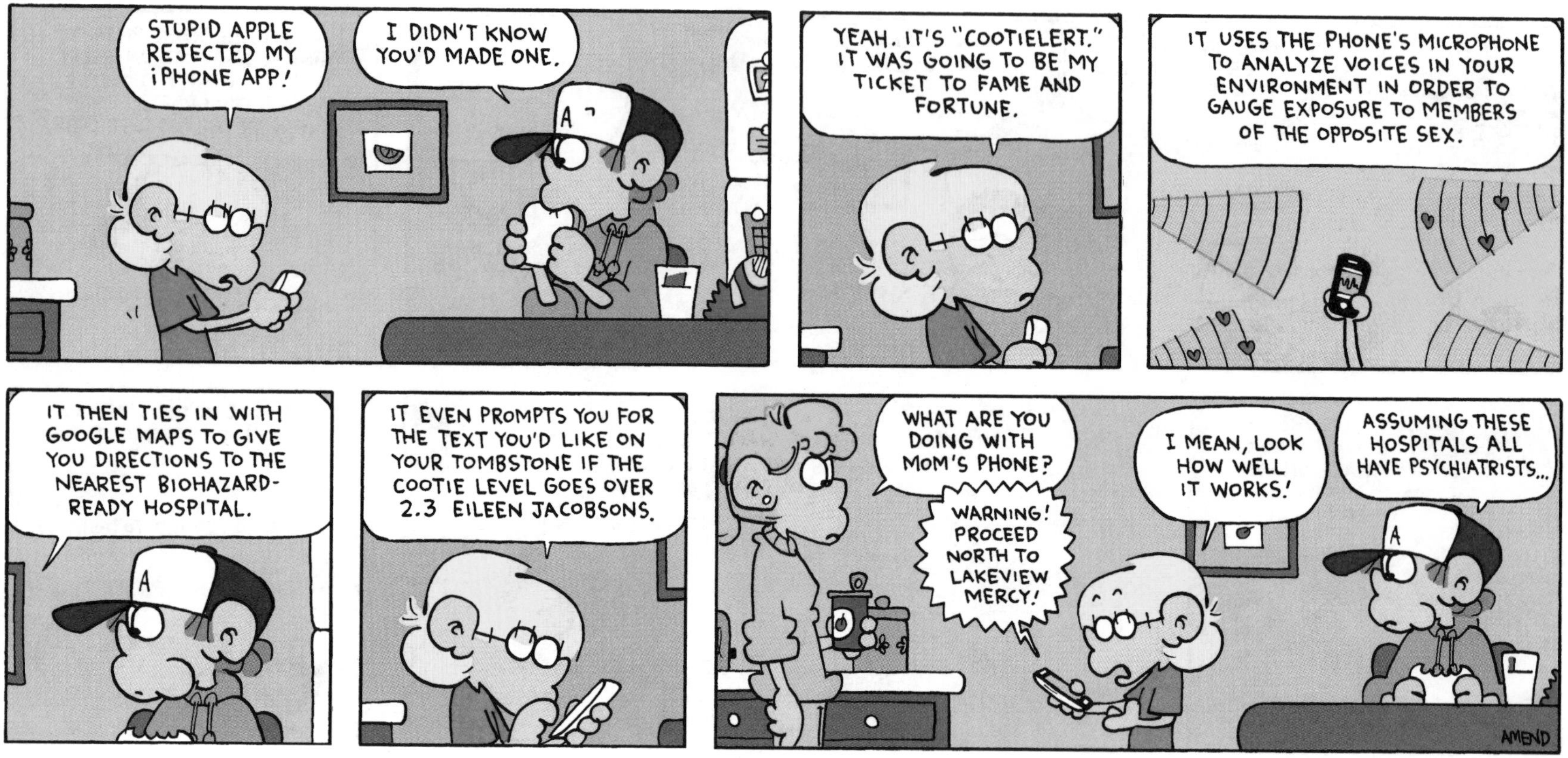
STUPID APPLE REJECTED MY iPHONE APP!
I DIDN'T KNOW YOU'D MADE ONE.
YEAH. IT'S "COOTIELERT." IT WAS GOING TO BE MY TICKET TO FAME AND FORTUNE.
IT USES THE PHONE'S MICROPHONE TO ANALYZE VOICES IN YOUR ENVIRONMENT IN ORDER TO GAUGE EXPOSURE TO MEMBERS OF THE OPPOSITE SEX.
IT THEN TIES IN WITH GOOGLE MAPS TO GIVE YOU DIRECTIONS TO THE NEAREST BIOHAZARD-READY HOSPITAL.
IT EVEN PROMPTS YOU FOR THE TEXT YOU'D LIKE ON YOUR TOMBSTONE IF THE COOTIE LEVEL GOES OVER 2.3 EILEEN JACOBSONS.
WHAT ARE YOU DOING WITH MOM'S PHONE?
WARNING! PROCEED NORTH TO LAKEVIEW MERCY!
I MEAN, LOOK HOW WELL IT WORKS!
ASSUMING THESE HOSPITALS ALL HAVE PSYCHIATRISTS...
AMEND

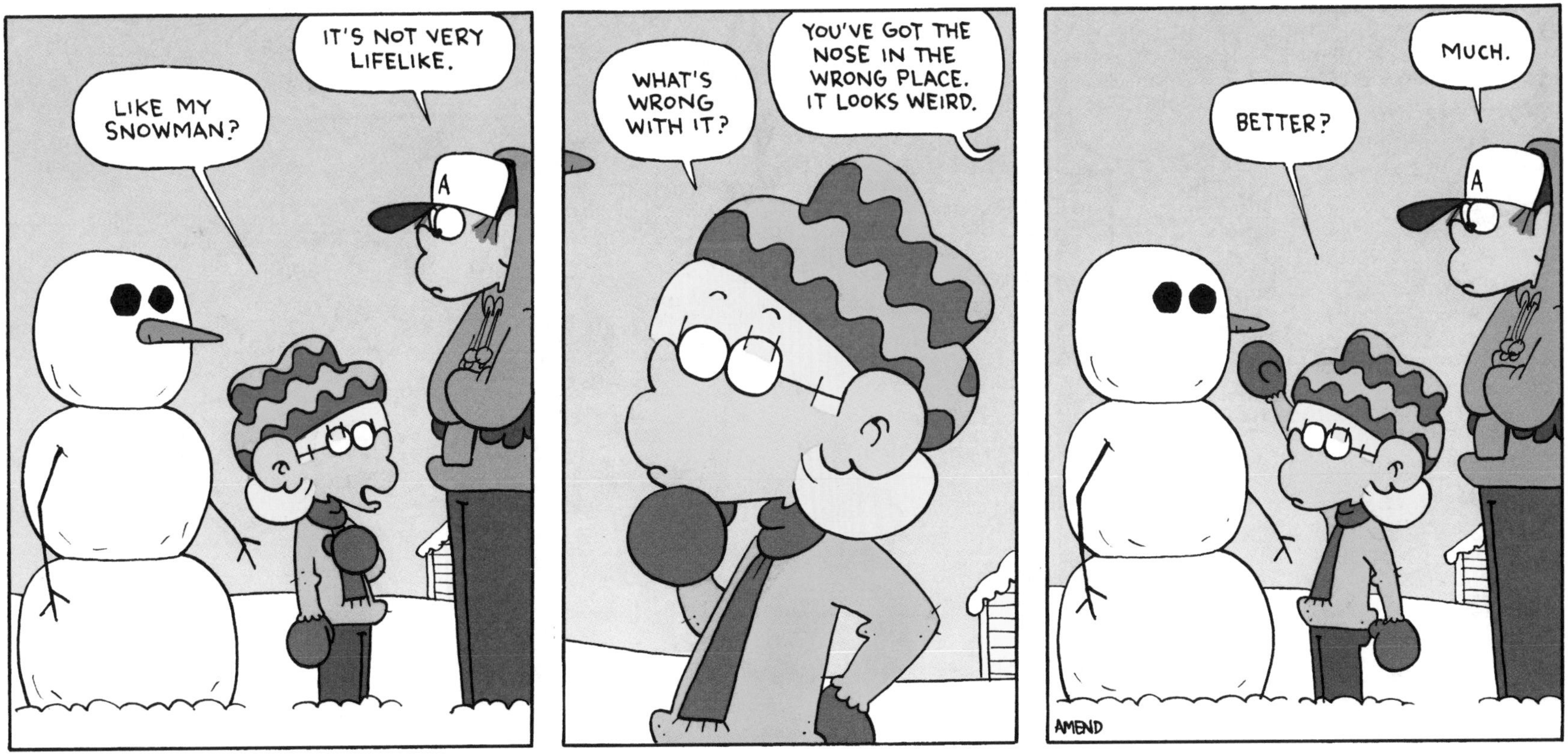
LIKE MY SNOWMAN?
IT'S NOT VERY LIFELIKE.
WHAT'S WRONG WITH IT?
YOU'VE GOT THE NOSE IN THE WRONG PLACE. IT LOOKS WEIRD.
BETTER?
MUCH.
AMEND

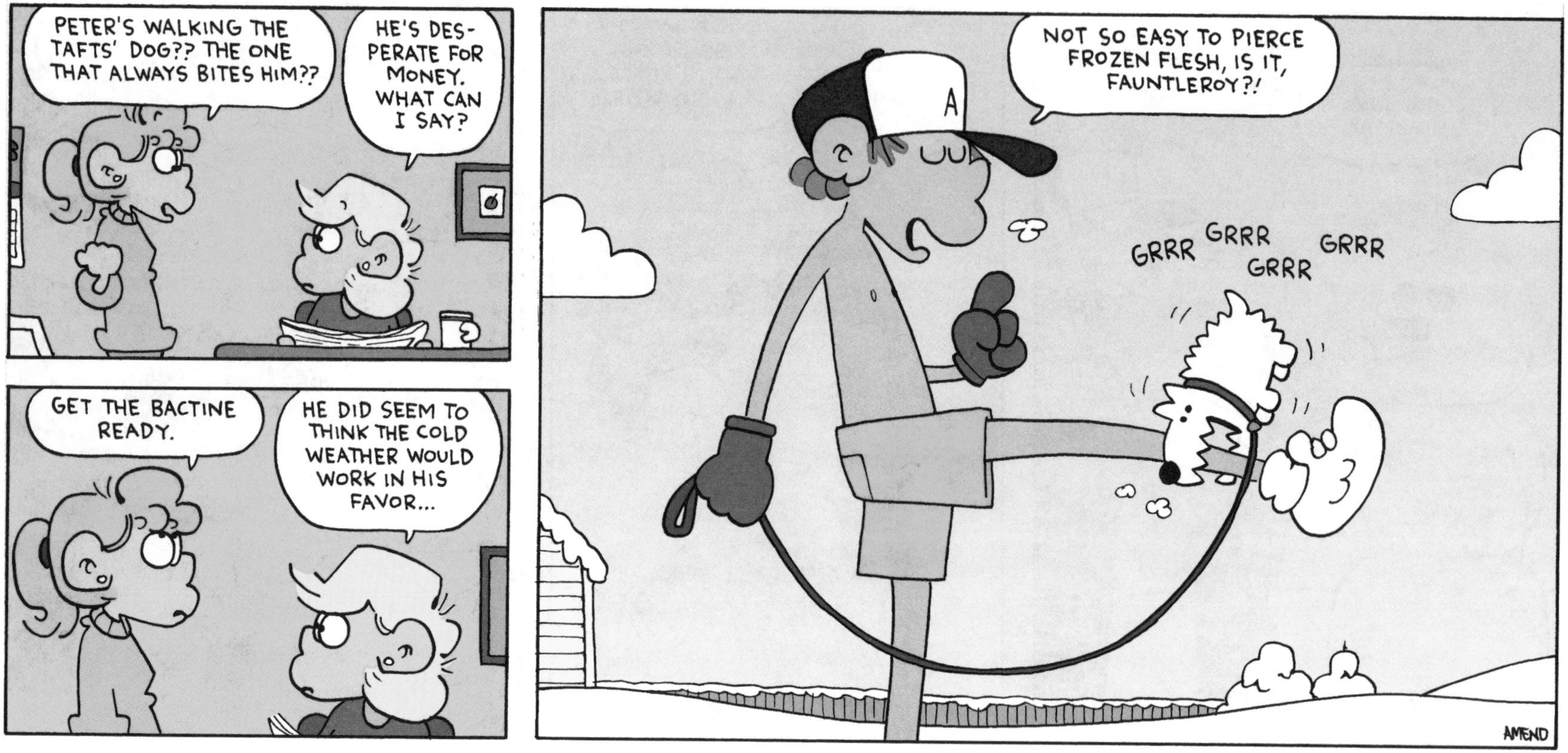
PETER'S WALKING THE TAFTS' DOG?? THE ONE THAT ALWAYS BITES HIM??
HE'S DES-PERATE FOR MONEY. WHAT CAN I SAY?
GET THE BACTINE READY.
HE DID SEEM TO THINK THE COLD WEATHER WOULD WORK IN HIS FAVOR...
NOT SO EASY TO PIERCE FROZEN FLESH, IS IT, FAUNTLEROY?!
GRRR GRRR GRRR GRRR
A
AMEND

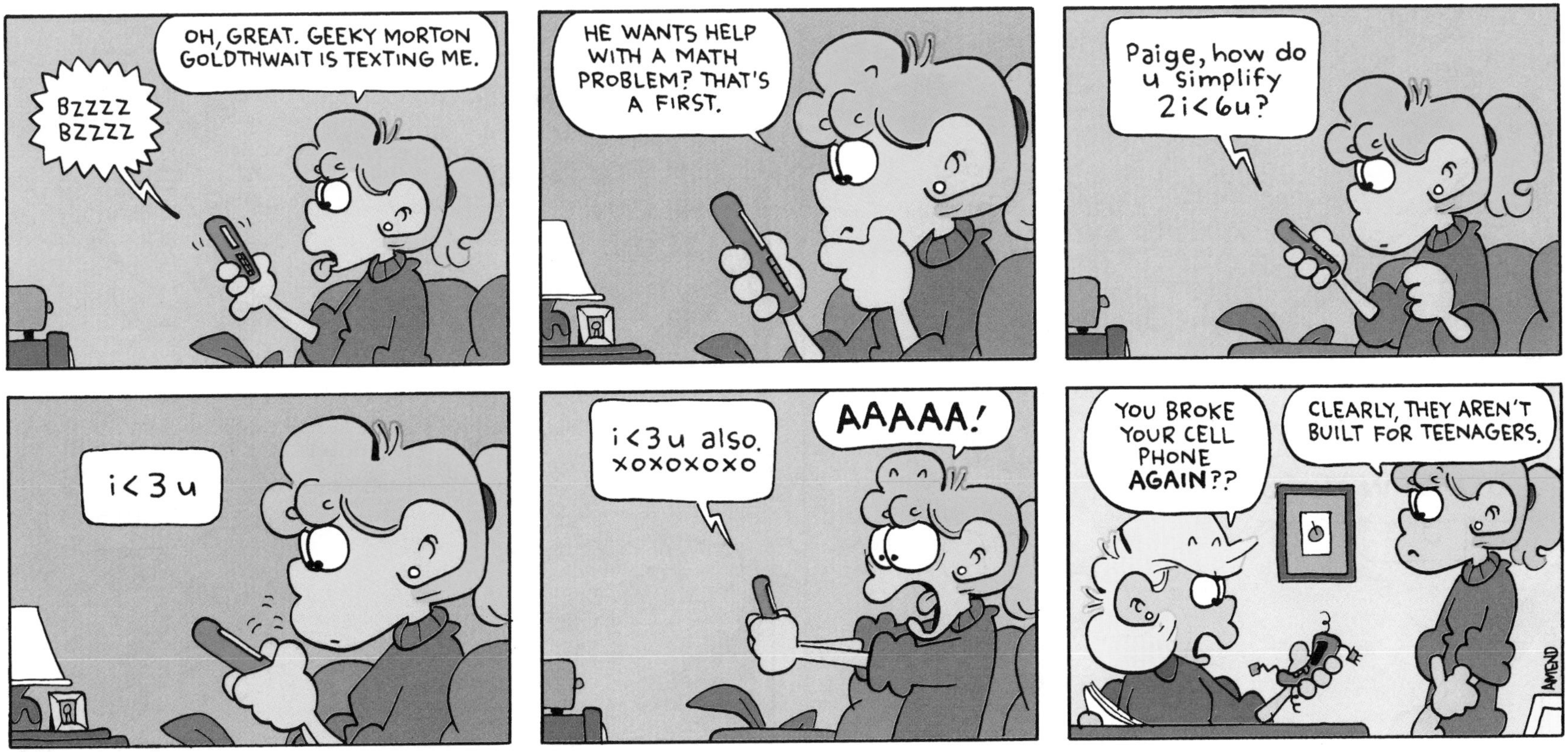
OH, GREAT. GEEKY MORTON GOLDTHWAIT IS TEXTING ME.
BZZZZ BZZZZ
HE WANTS HELP WITH A MATH PROBLEM? THAT'S A FIRST.
Paige, how do u simplify 2i<6u?
i<3 u
i<3 u also. xoxoxoxo
AAAAA!
YOU BROKE YOUR CELL PHONE AGAIN??
CLEARLY, THEY AREN'T BUILT FOR TEENAGERS.
AMEND

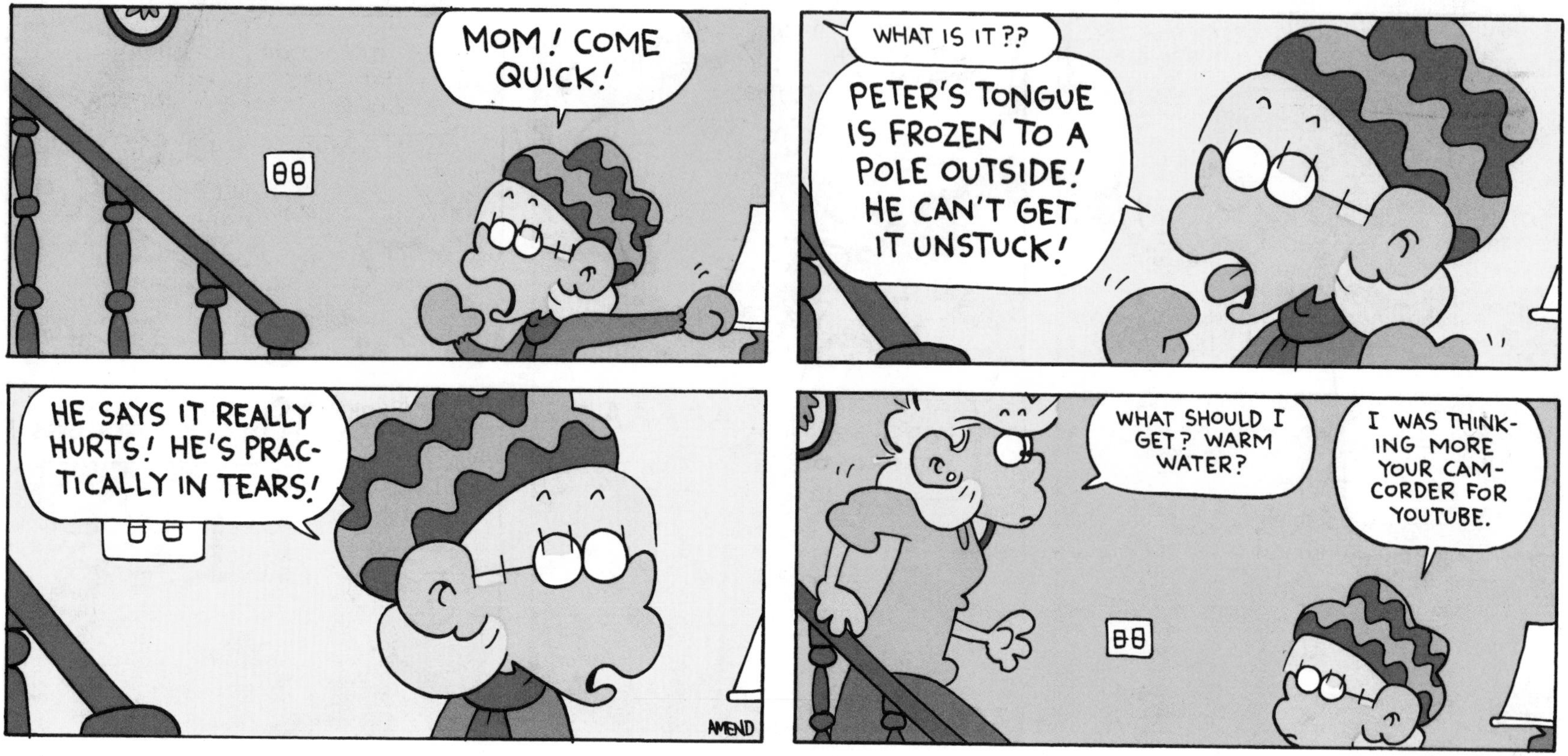
MOM! COME QUICK!
WHAT IS IT??
PETER'S TONGUE IS FROZEN TO A POLE OUTSIDE! HE CAN'T GET IT UNSTUCK!
HE SAYS IT REALLY HURTS! HE'S PRAC-TICALLY IN TEARS!
AMEND
WHAT SHOULD I GET? WARM WATER?
I WAS THINK-ING MORE YOUR CAM-CORDER FOR YOUTUBE.

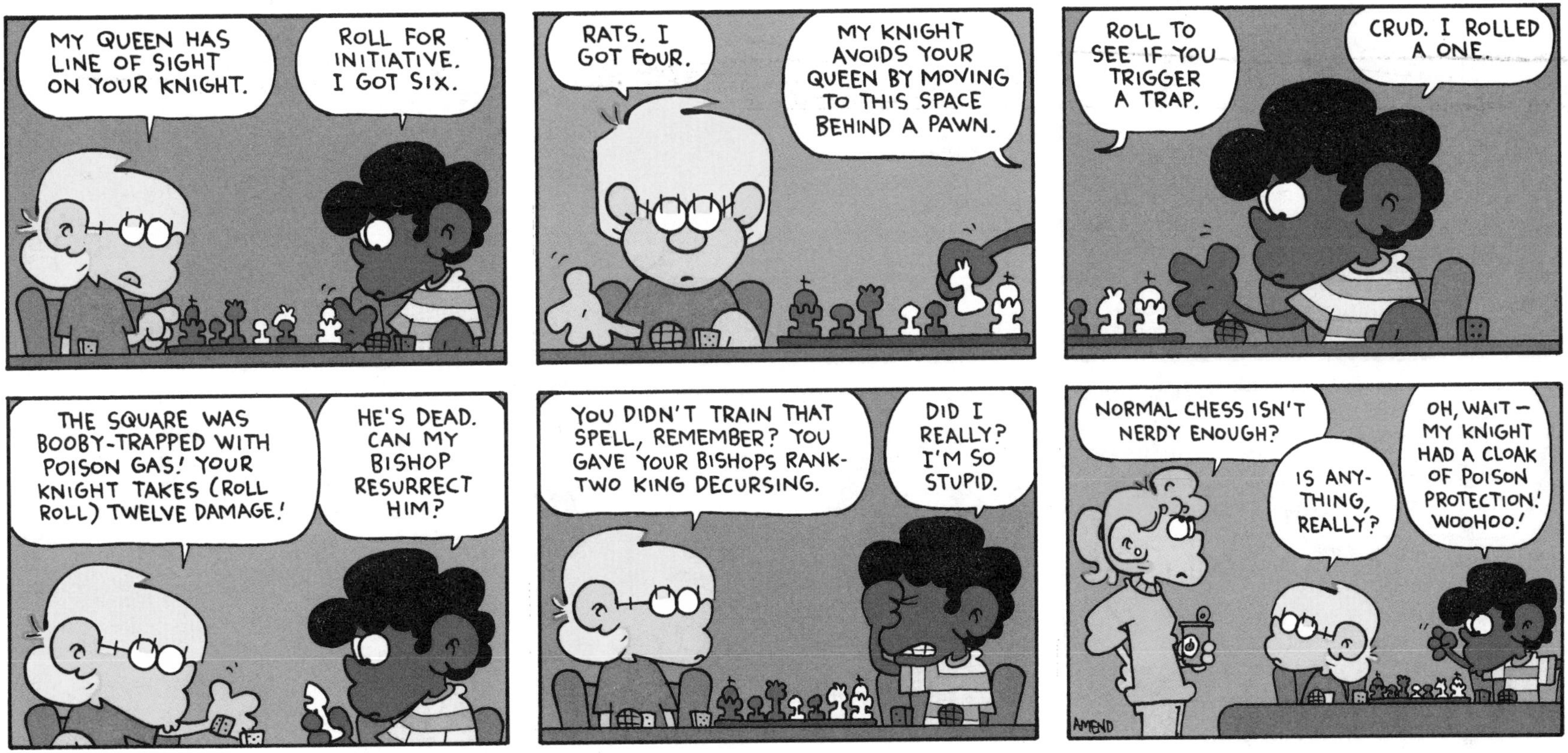
MY QUEEN HAS LINE OF SIGHT ON YOUR KNIGHT.
ROLL FOR INITIATIVE. I GOT SIX.
RATS. I GOT FOUR.
MY KNIGHT AVOIDS YOUR QUEEN BY MOVING TO THIS SPACE BEHIND A PAWN.
ROLL TO SEE IF YOU TRIGGER A TRAP.
CRUD. I ROLLED A ONE.
THE SQUARE WAS BOOBY-TRAPPED WITH POISON GAS! YOUR KNIGHT TAKES (ROLL ROLL) TWELVE DAMAGE!
HE'S DEAD. CAN MY BISHOP RESURRECT HIM?
YOU DIDN'T TRAIN THAT SPELL, REMEMBER? YOU GAVE YOUR BISHOPS RANK-TWO KING DECURSING.
DID I REALLY? I'M SO STUPID.
NORMAL CHESS ISN'T NERDY ENOUGH?
IS ANY-THING, REALLY?
OH, WAIT — MY KNIGHT HAD A CLOAK OF POISON PROTECTION! WOOHOO!
AMEND

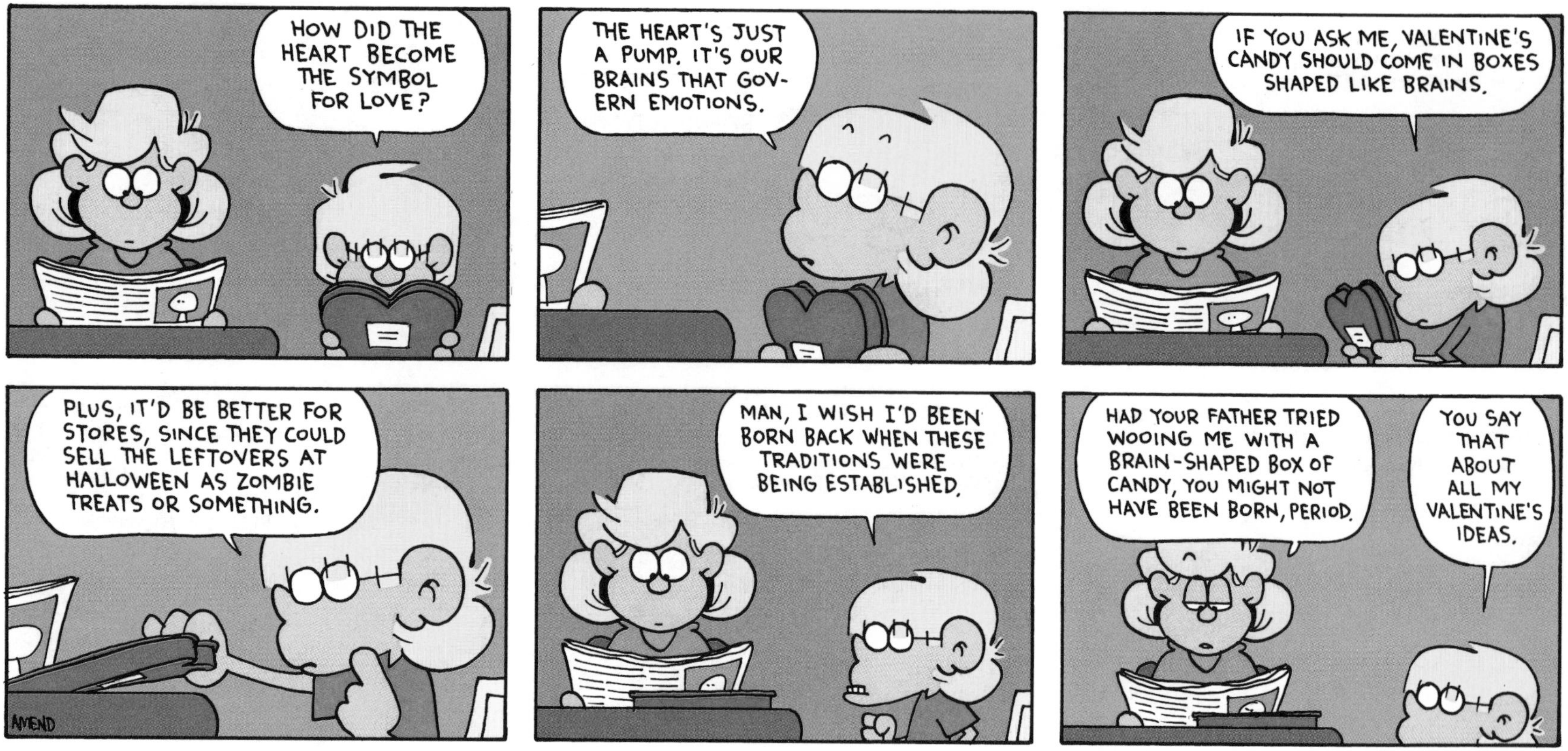
HOW DID THE HEART BECOME THE SYMBOL FOR LOVE?
THE HEART'S JUST A PUMP. IT'S OUR BRAINS THAT GOV-ERN EMOTIONS.
IF YOU ASK ME, VALENTINE'S CANDY SHOULD COME IN BOXES SHAPED LIKE BRAINS.
PLUS, IT'D BE BETTER FOR STORES, SINCE THEY COULD SELL THE LEFTOVERS AT HALLOWEEN AS ZOMBIE TREATS OR SOMETHING.
AMEND
MAN, I WISH I'D BEEN BORN BACK WHEN THESE TRADITIONS WERE BEING ESTABLISHED.
HAD YOUR FATHER TRIED WOOING ME WITH A BRAIN-SHAPED BOX OF CANDY, YOU MIGHT NOT HAVE BEEN BORN, PERIOD.
YOU SAY THAT ABOUT ALL MY VALENTINE'S IDEAS.

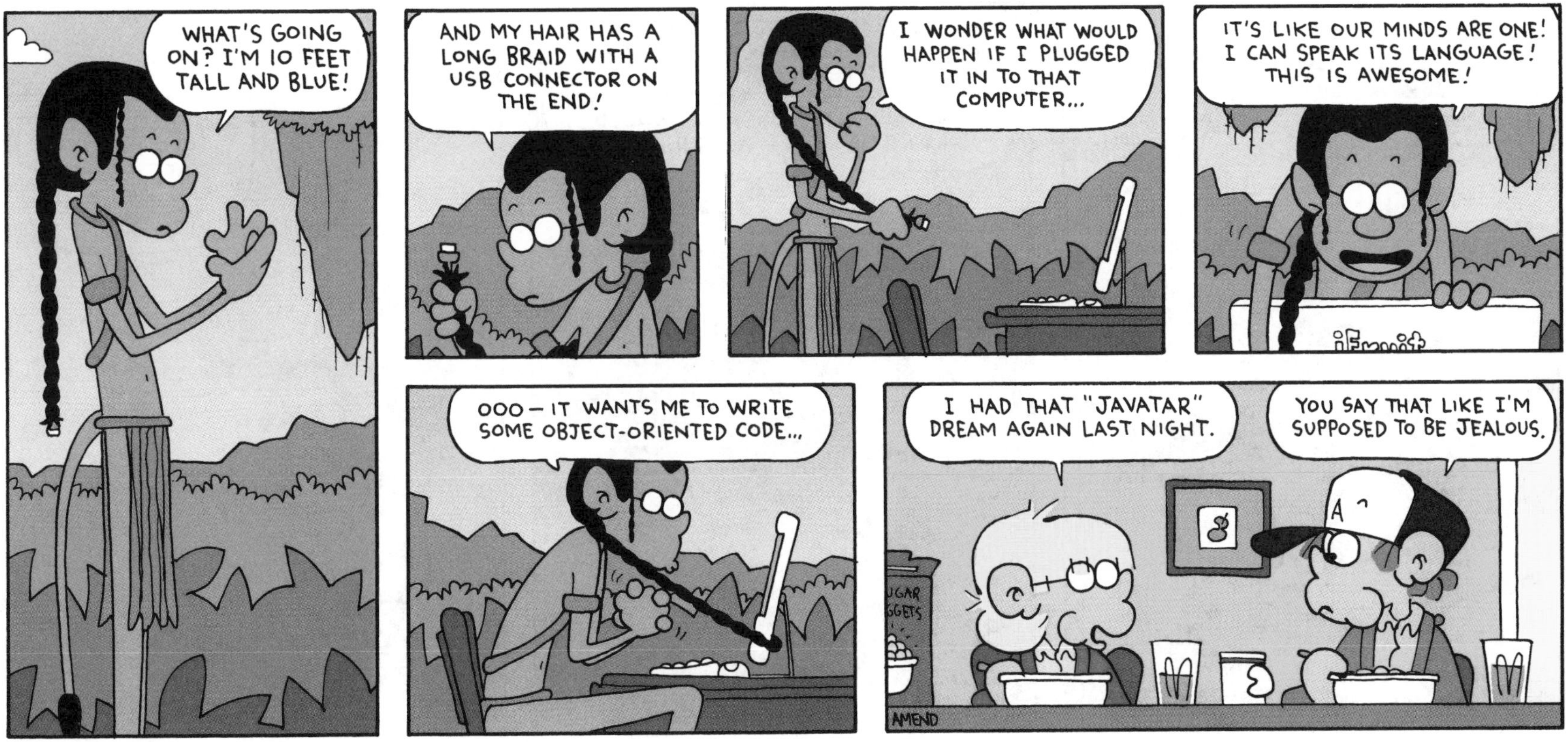
WHAT'S GOING ON? I'M 10 FEET TALL AND BLUE!
AND MY HAIR HAS A LONG BRAID WITH A USB CONNECTOR ON THE END!
I WONDER WHAT WOULD HAPPEN IF I PLUGGED IT IN TO THAT COMPUTER...
IT'S LIKE OUR MINDS ARE ONE! I CAN SPEAK ITS LANGUAGE! THIS IS AWESOME!
OOO— IT WANTS ME TO WRITE SOME OBJECT-ORIENTED CODE...
I HAD THAT "JAVATAR" DREAM AGAIN LAST NIGHT.
YOU SAY THAT LIKE I'M SUPPOSED TO BE JEALOUS.
AMEND

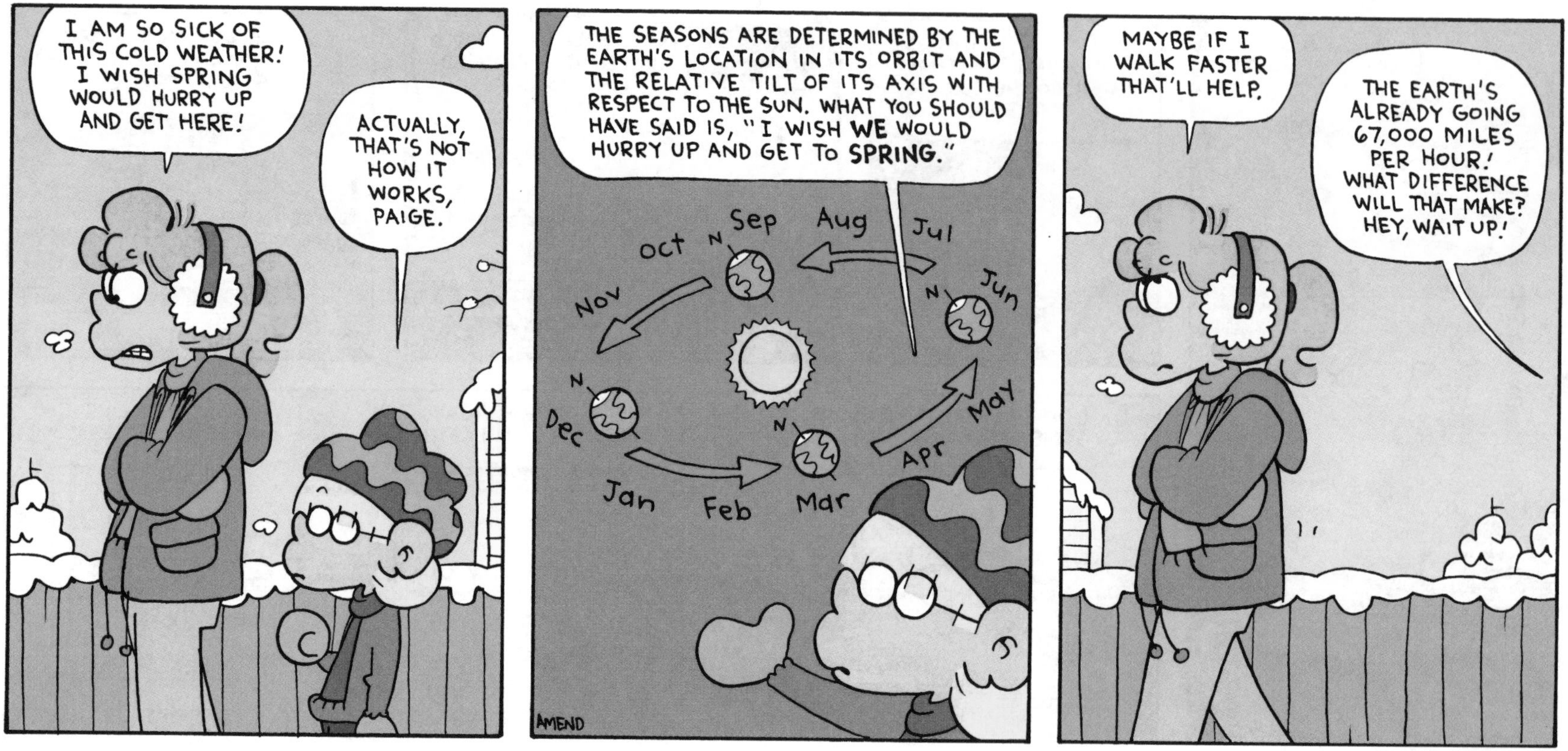
I AM SO SICK OF THIS COLD WEATHER! I WISH SPRING WOULD HURRY UP AND GET HERE!
ACTUALLY, THAT'S NOT HOW IT WORKS, PAIGE.
THE SEASONS ARE DETERMINED BY THE EARTH'S LOCATION IN ITS ORBIT AND THE RELATIVE TILT OF ITS AXIS WITH RESPECT TO THE SUN. WHAT YOU SHOULD HAVE SAID IS, "I WISH **WE** WOULD HURRY UP AND GET TO **SPRING**."
Sep Aug Jul
Oct
Nov
Jun
Dec
May
Apr
Jan Feb Mar
N
AMEND
MAYBE IF I WALK FASTER THAT'LL HELP.
THE EARTH'S ALREADY GOING 67,000 MILES PER HOUR! WHAT DIFFERENCE WILL THAT MAKE? HEY, WAIT UP!

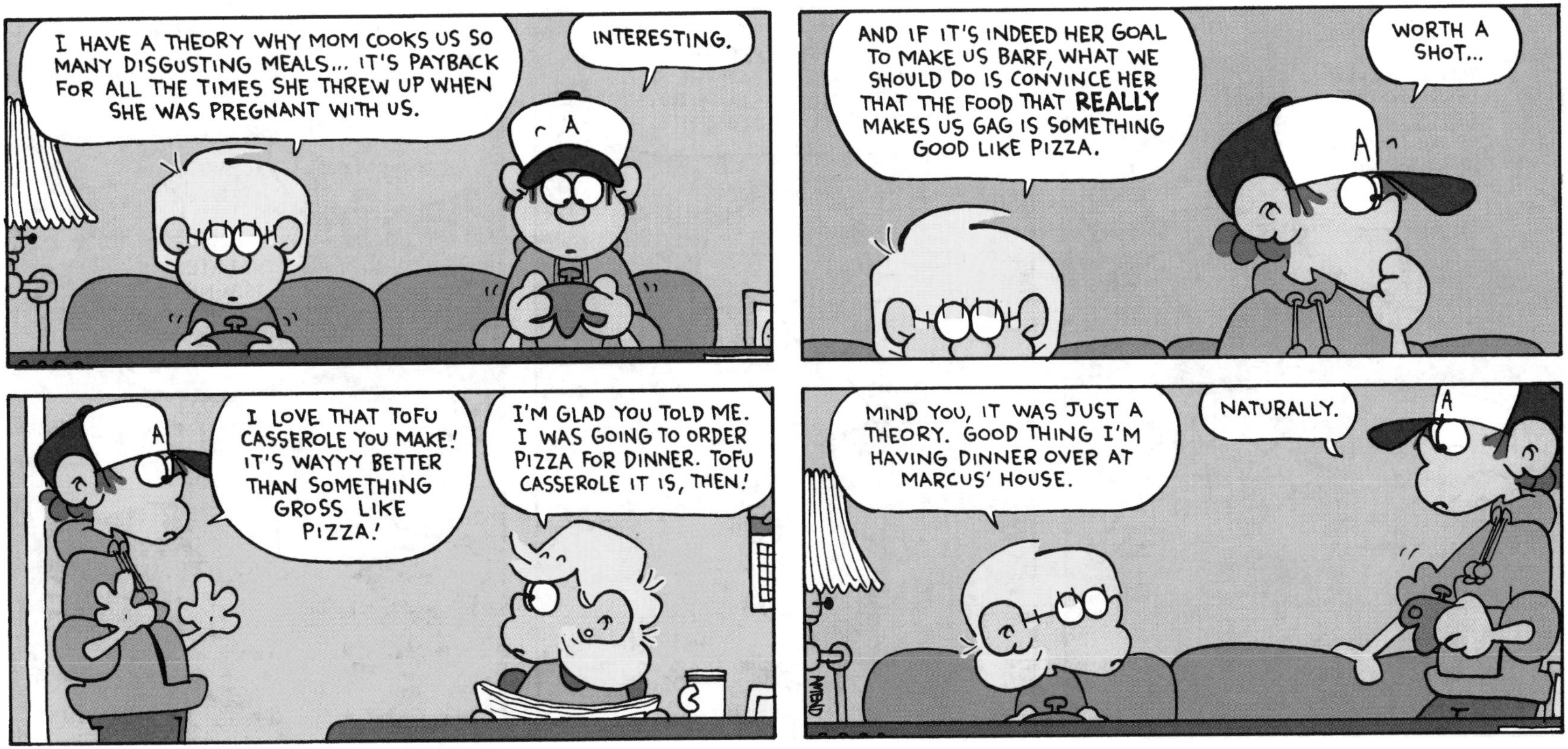
I HAVE A THEORY WHY MOM COOKS US SO MANY DISGUSTING MEALS... IT'S PAYBACK FOR ALL THE TIMES SHE THREW UP WHEN SHE WAS PREGNANT WITH US.
INTERESTING.
AND IF IT'S INDEED HER GOAL TO MAKE US BARF, WHAT WE SHOULD DO IS CONVINCE HER THAT THE FOOD THAT **REALLY** MAKES US GAG IS SOMETHING GOOD LIKE PIZZA.
WORTH A SHOT...
I LOVE THAT TOFU CASSEROLE YOU MAKE! IT'S WAYYY BETTER THAN SOMETHING GROSS LIKE PIZZA!
I'M GLAD YOU TOLD ME. I WAS GOING TO ORDER PIZZA FOR DINNER. TOFU CASSEROLE IT IS, THEN!
MIND YOU, IT WAS JUST A THEORY. GOOD THING I'M HAVING DINNER OVER AT MARCUS' HOUSE.
NATURALLY.

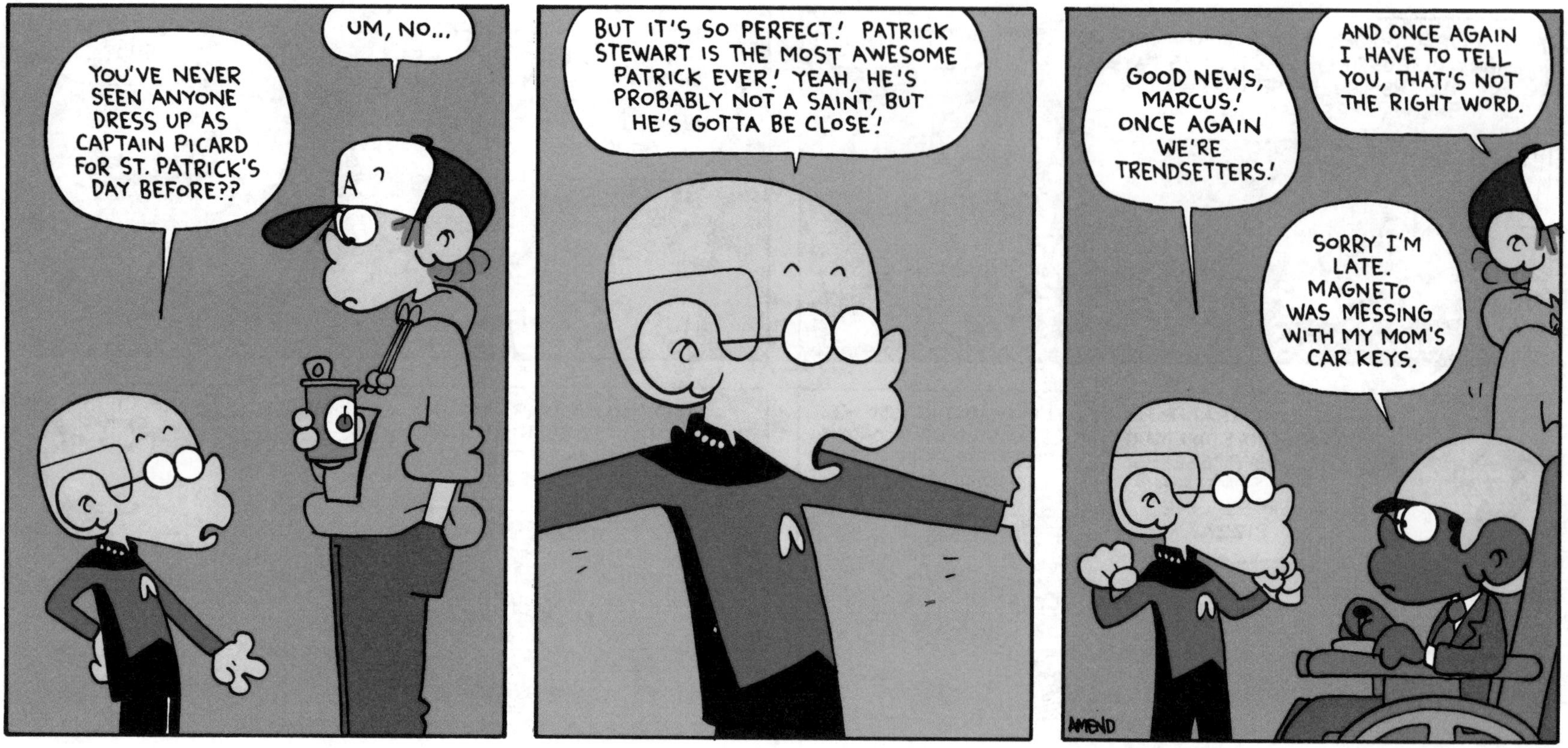
YOU'VE NEVER SEEN ANYONE DRESS UP AS CAPTAIN PICARD FOR ST. PATRICK'S DAY BEFORE??
UM, NO...
BUT IT'S SO PERFECT! PATRICK STEWART IS THE MOST AWESOME PATRICK EVER! YEAH, HE'S PROBABLY NOT A SAINT, BUT HE'S GOTTA BE CLOSE!
GOOD NEWS, MARCUS! ONCE AGAIN WE'RE TRENDSETTERS!
AND ONCE AGAIN I HAVE TO TELL YOU, THAT'S NOT THE RIGHT WORD.
SORRY I'M LATE. MAGNETO WAS MESSING WITH MY MOM'S CAR KEYS.
AMEND

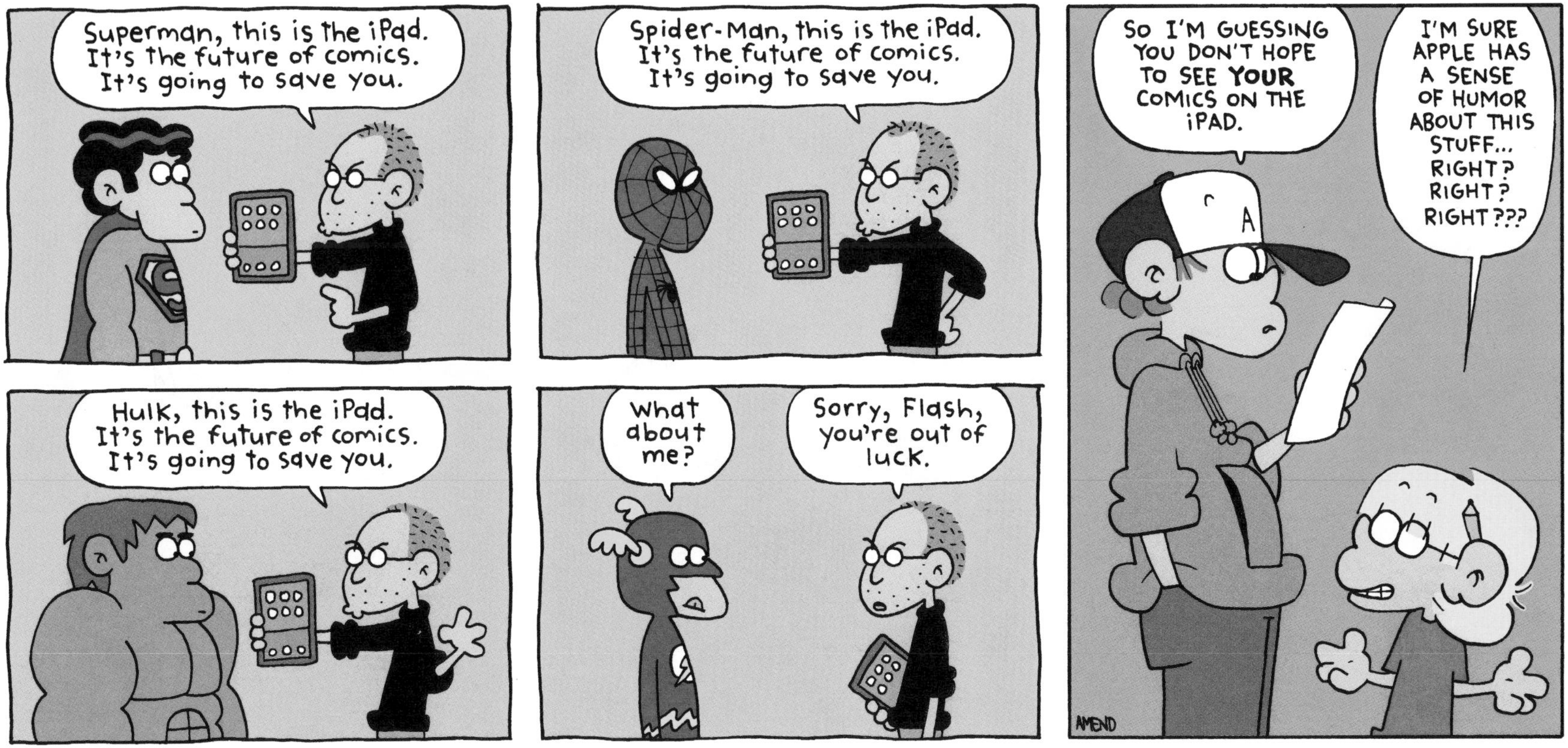
Superman, this is the iPad. It's the future of comics. It's going to save you.
Spider-Man, this is the iPad. It's the future of comics. It's going to save you.
Hulk, this is the iPad. It's the future of comics. It's going to save you.
What about me?
Sorry, Flash, you're out of luck.
So I'M GUESSING YOU DON'T HOPE TO SEE **YOUR** COMICS ON THE iPAD.
I'M SURE APPLE HAS A SENSE OF HUMOR ABOUT THIS STUFF... RIGHT? RIGHT? RIGHT???
AMEND

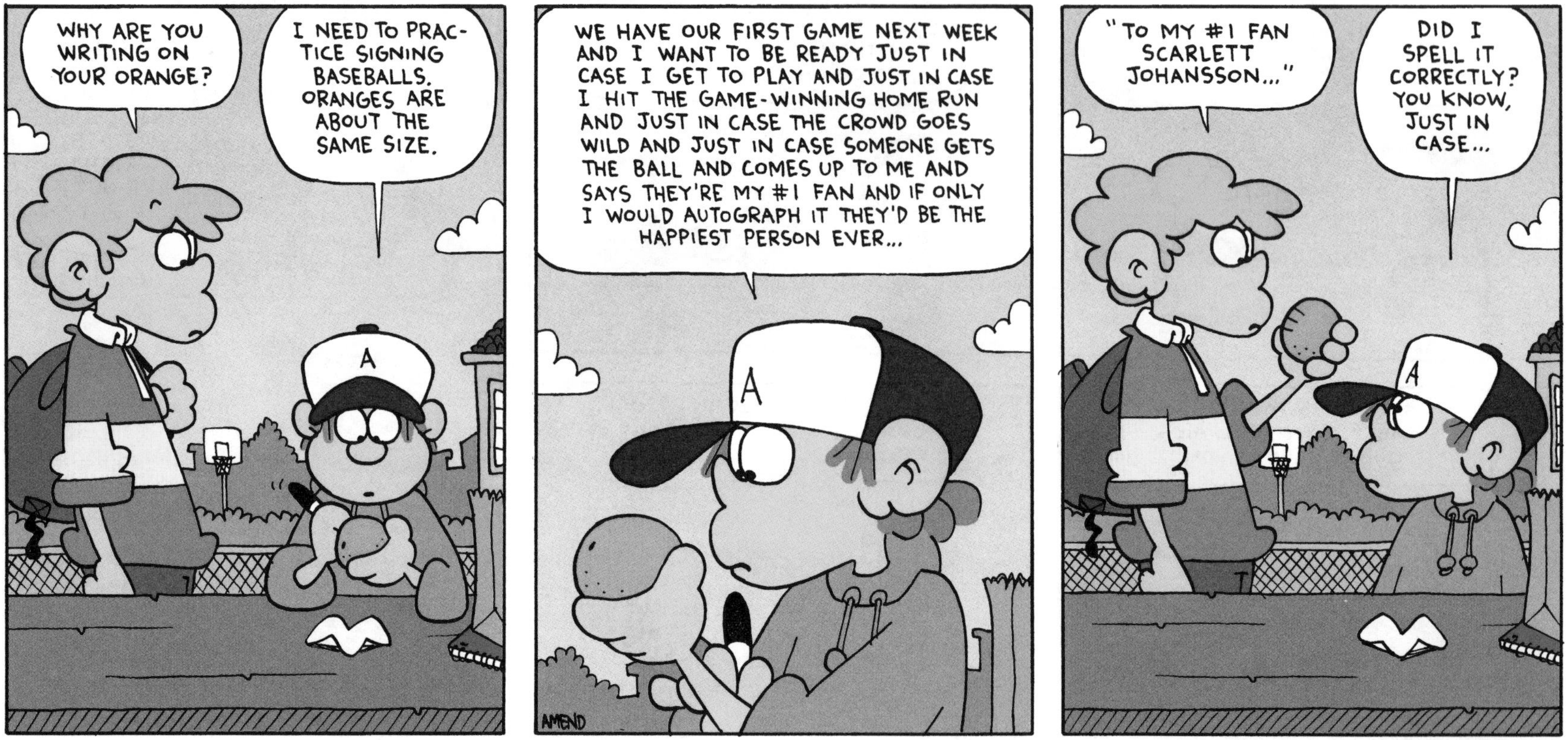
WHY ARE YOU WRITING ON YOUR ORANGE?
I NEED TO PRAC-TICE SIGNING BASEBALLS. ORANGES ARE ABOUT THE SAME SIZE.
WE HAVE OUR FIRST GAME NEXT WEEK AND I WANT TO BE READY JUST IN CASE I GET TO PLAY AND JUST IN CASE I HIT THE GAME-WINNING HOME RUN AND JUST IN CASE THE CROWD GOES WILD AND JUST IN CASE SOMEONE GETS THE BALL AND COMES UP TO ME AND SAYS THEY'RE MY #1 FAN AND IF ONLY I WOULD AUTOGRAPH IT THEY'D BE THE HAPPIEST PERSON EVER...
AMEND
"TO MY #1 FAN SCARLETT JOHANSSON..."
DID I SPELL IT CORRECTLY? YOU KNOW, JUST IN CASE...

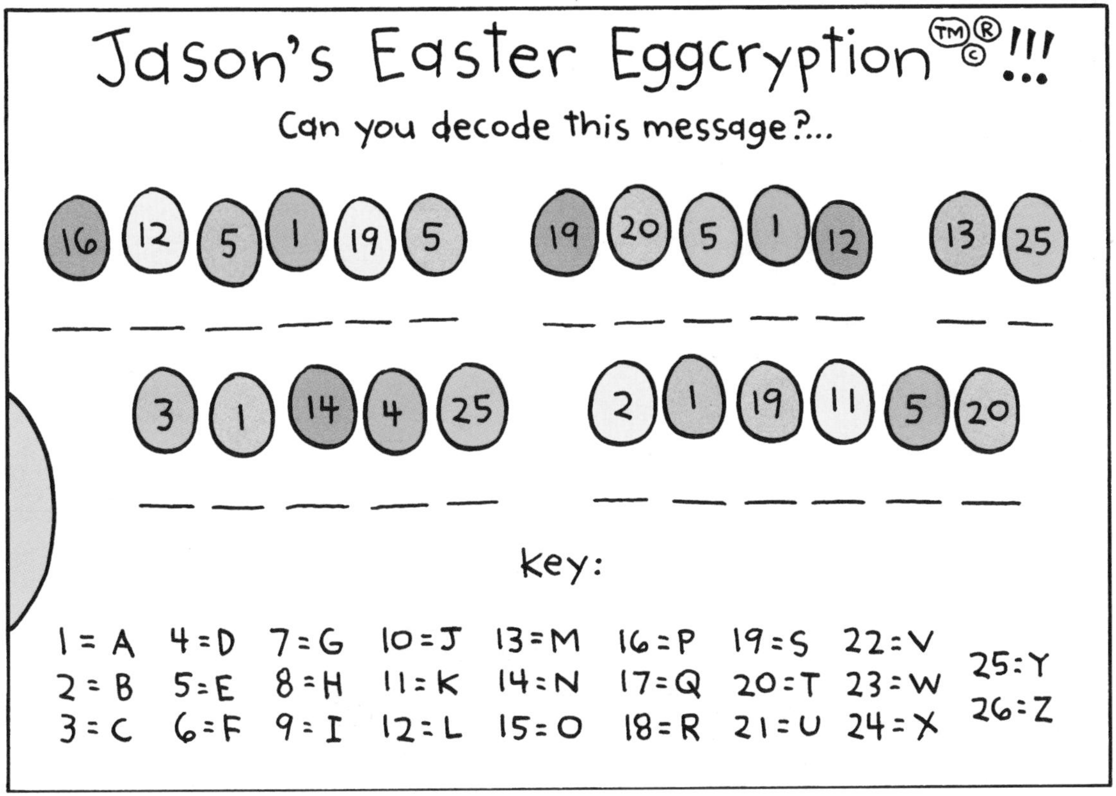

Jason's Easter Eggcryption ™ ® © !!!

Can you decode this message?...

16 12 5 1 19 5   19 20 5 1 12   13 25

_ _ _ _ _ _   _ _ _ _ _   _ _

3 1 14 4 25   2 1 19 11 5 20

_ _ _ _ _   _ _ _ _ _ _

key:

1 = A	4 = D	7 = G	10 = J	13 = M	16 = P	19 = S	22 = V
2 = B	5 = E	8 = H	11 = K	14 = N	17 = Q	20 = T	23 = W
3 = C	6 = F	9 = I	12 = L	15 = O	18 = R	21 = U	24 = X

25 = Y
26 = Z

CALL ME SUSPICIOUS, BUT THIS SEEMS A LOT EASIER THAN YOUR USUAL PUZZLES.

ALSO, BE SURE TO SAY IT OUT LOUD WHEN YOU GET IT.

AMEND

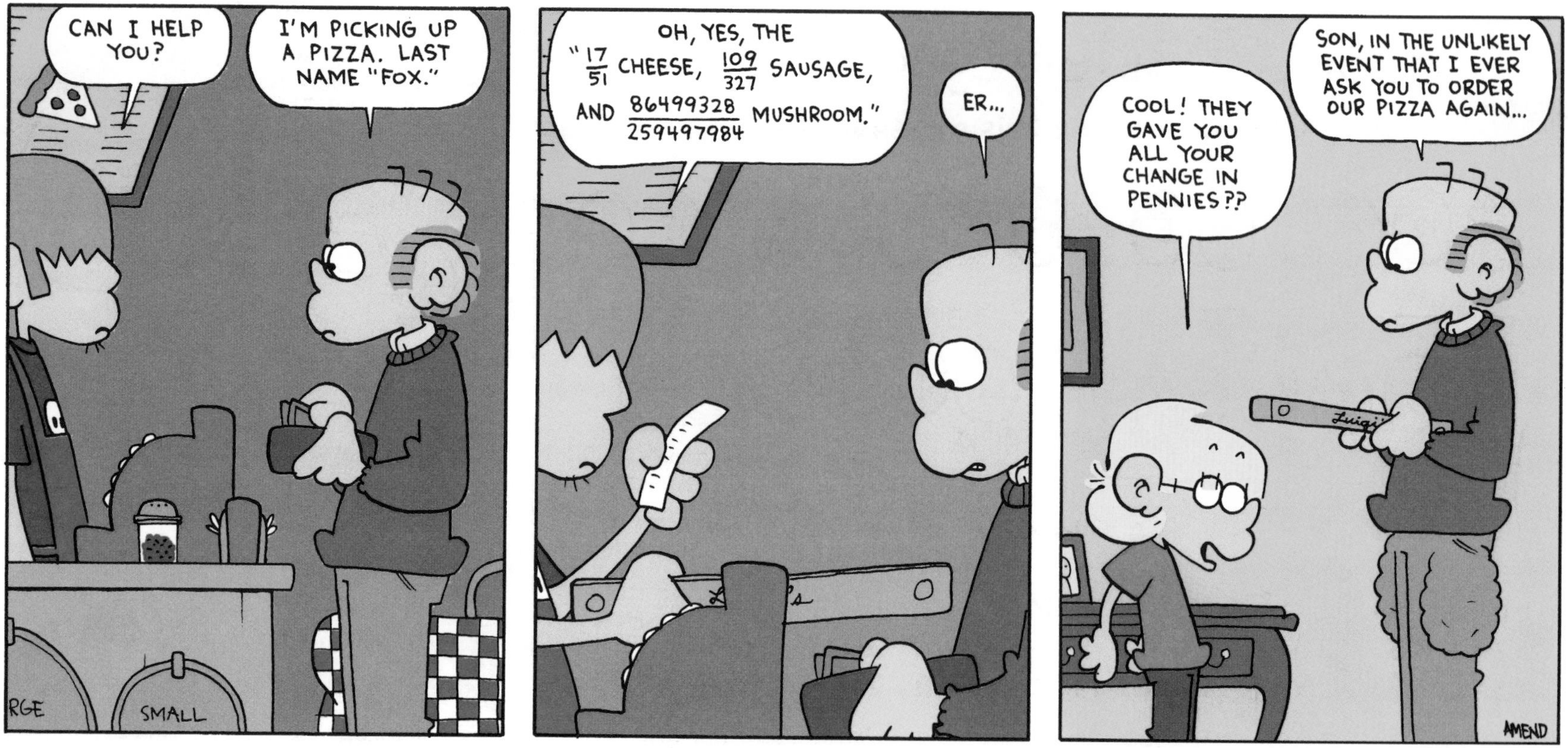
CAN I HELP YOU?
I'M PICKING UP A PIZZA. LAST NAME "FOX."
RGE
SMALL
OH, YES, THE "17/51 CHEESE, 109/327 SAUSAGE, AND 86499328/259497984 MUSHROOM."
ER...
COOL! THEY GAVE YOU ALL YOUR CHANGE IN PENNIES??
SON, IN THE UNLIKELY EVENT THAT I EVER ASK YOU TO ORDER OUR PIZZA AGAIN...
AMEND

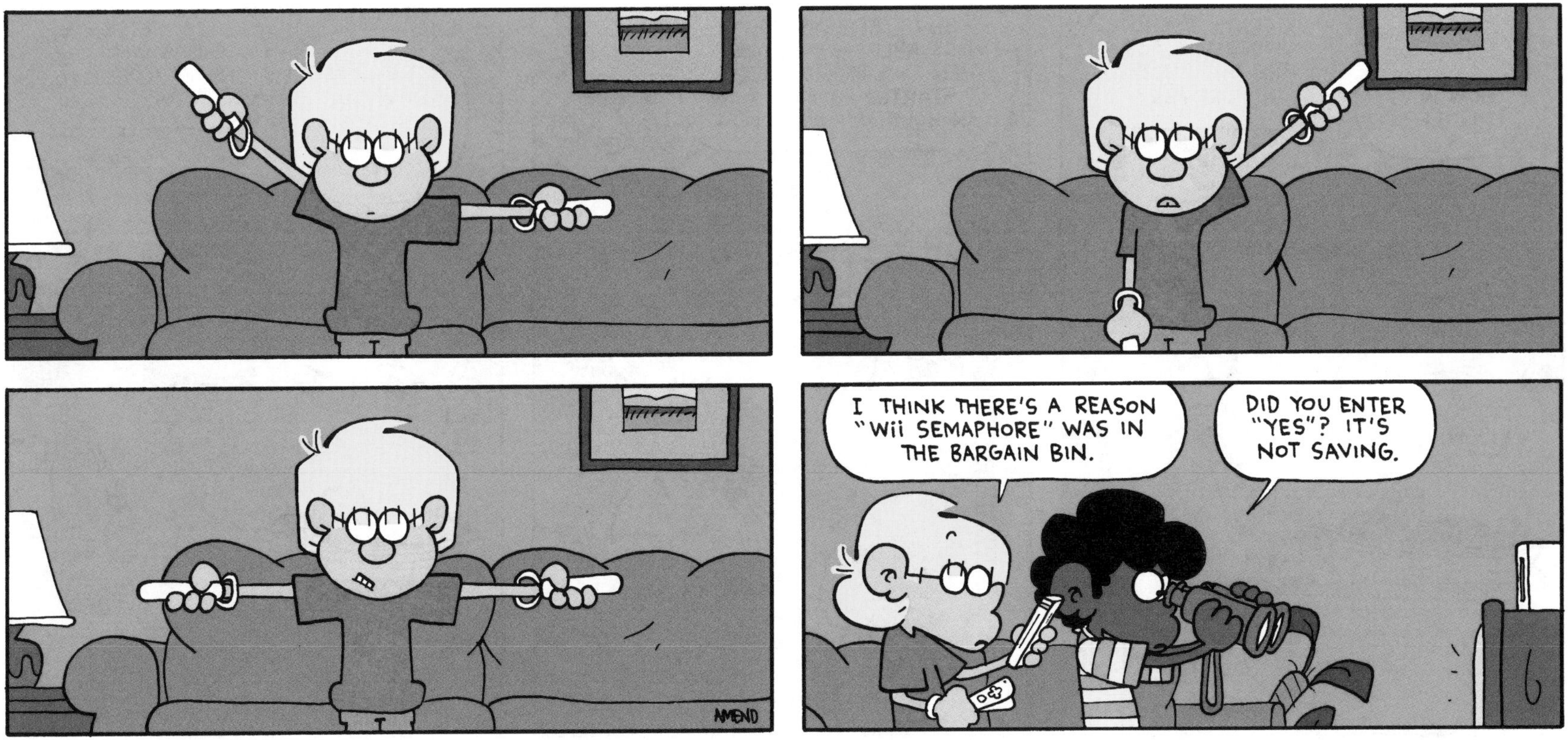
I THINK THERE'S A REASON "Wii SEMAPHORE" WAS IN THE BARGAIN BIN.
DID YOU ENTER "YES"? IT'S NOT SAVING.
AMEND

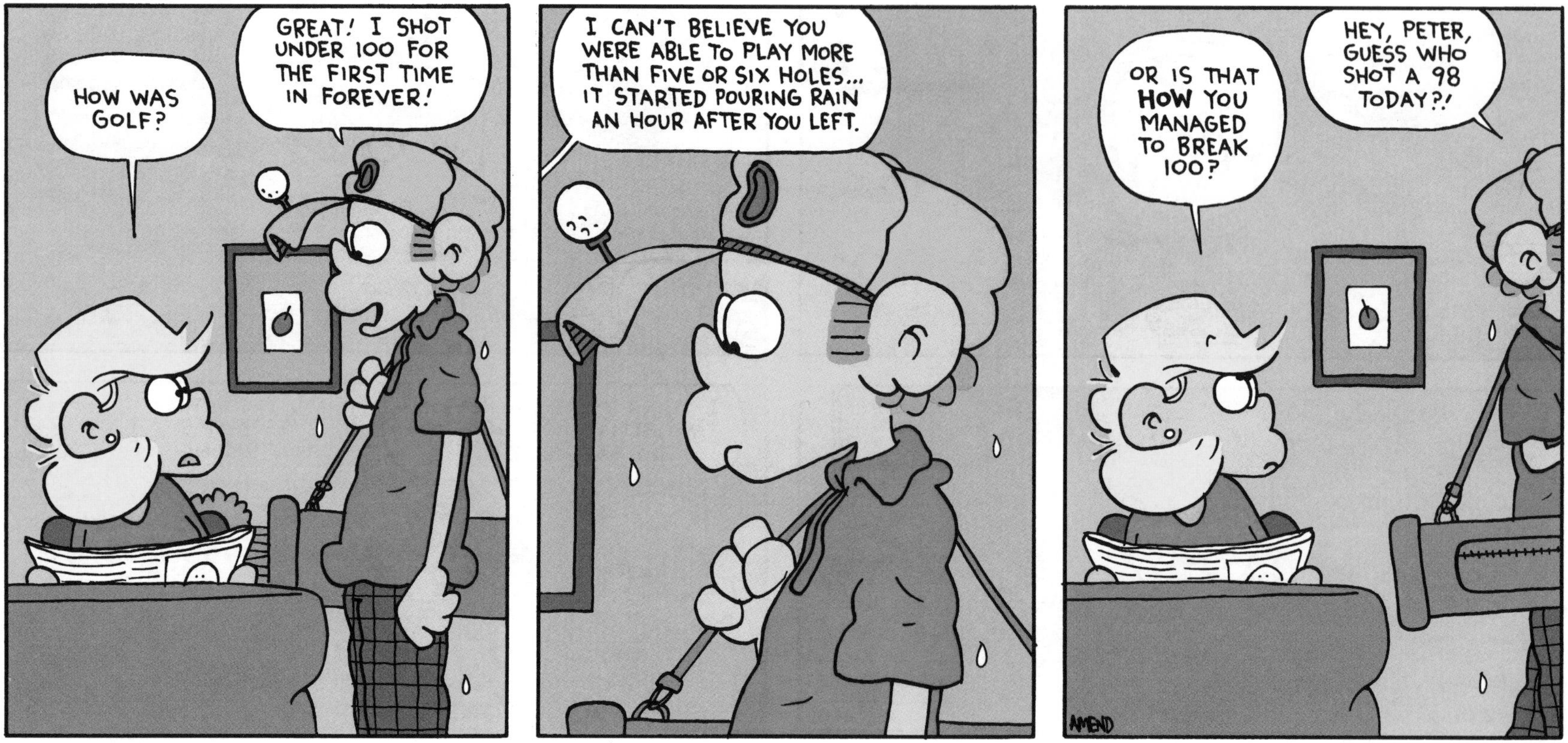
HOW WAS GOLF?
GREAT! I SHOT UNDER 100 FOR THE FIRST TIME IN FOREVER!
I CAN'T BELIEVE YOU WERE ABLE TO PLAY MORE THAN FIVE OR SIX HOLES... IT STARTED POURING RAIN AN HOUR AFTER YOU LEFT.
OR IS THAT **HOW** YOU MANAGED TO BREAK 100?
HEY, PETER, GUESS WHO SHOT A 98 TODAY?!
AMEND

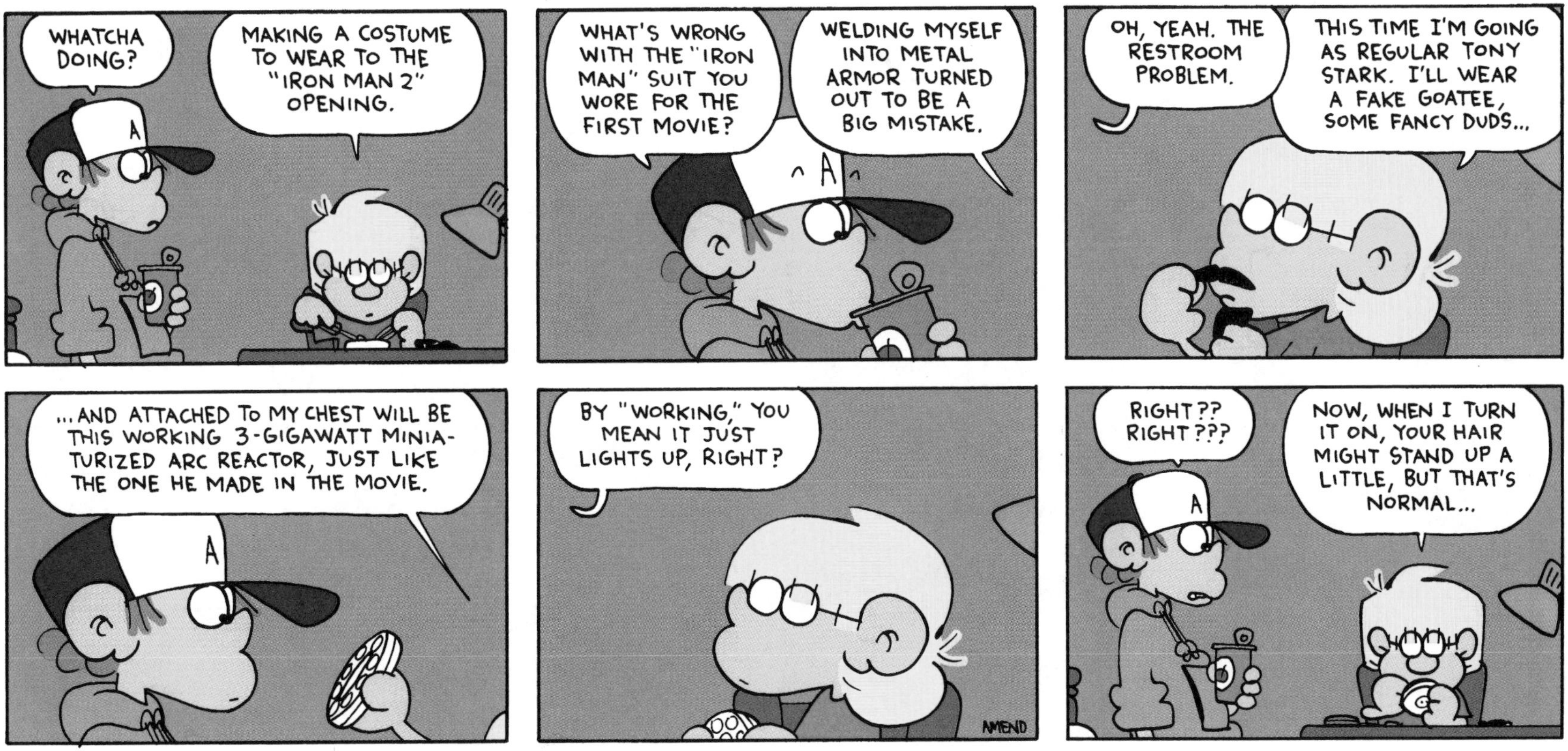
WHATCHA DOING?
MAKING A COSTUME TO WEAR TO THE "IRON MAN 2" OPENING.
WHAT'S WRONG WITH THE "IRON MAN" SUIT YOU WORE FOR THE FIRST MOVIE?
WELDING MYSELF INTO METAL ARMOR TURNED OUT TO BE A BIG MISTAKE.
OH, YEAH. THE RESTROOM PROBLEM.
THIS TIME I'M GOING AS REGULAR TONY STARK. I'LL WEAR A FAKE GOATEE, SOME FANCY DUDS...
...AND ATTACHED TO MY CHEST WILL BE THIS WORKING 3-GIGAWATT MINIATURIZED ARC REACTOR, JUST LIKE THE ONE HE MADE IN THE MOVIE.
BY "WORKING," YOU MEAN IT JUST LIGHTS UP, RIGHT?
AMEND
RIGHT?? RIGHT???
NOW, WHEN I TURN IT ON, YOUR HAIR MIGHT STAND UP A LITTLE, BUT THAT'S NORMAL...

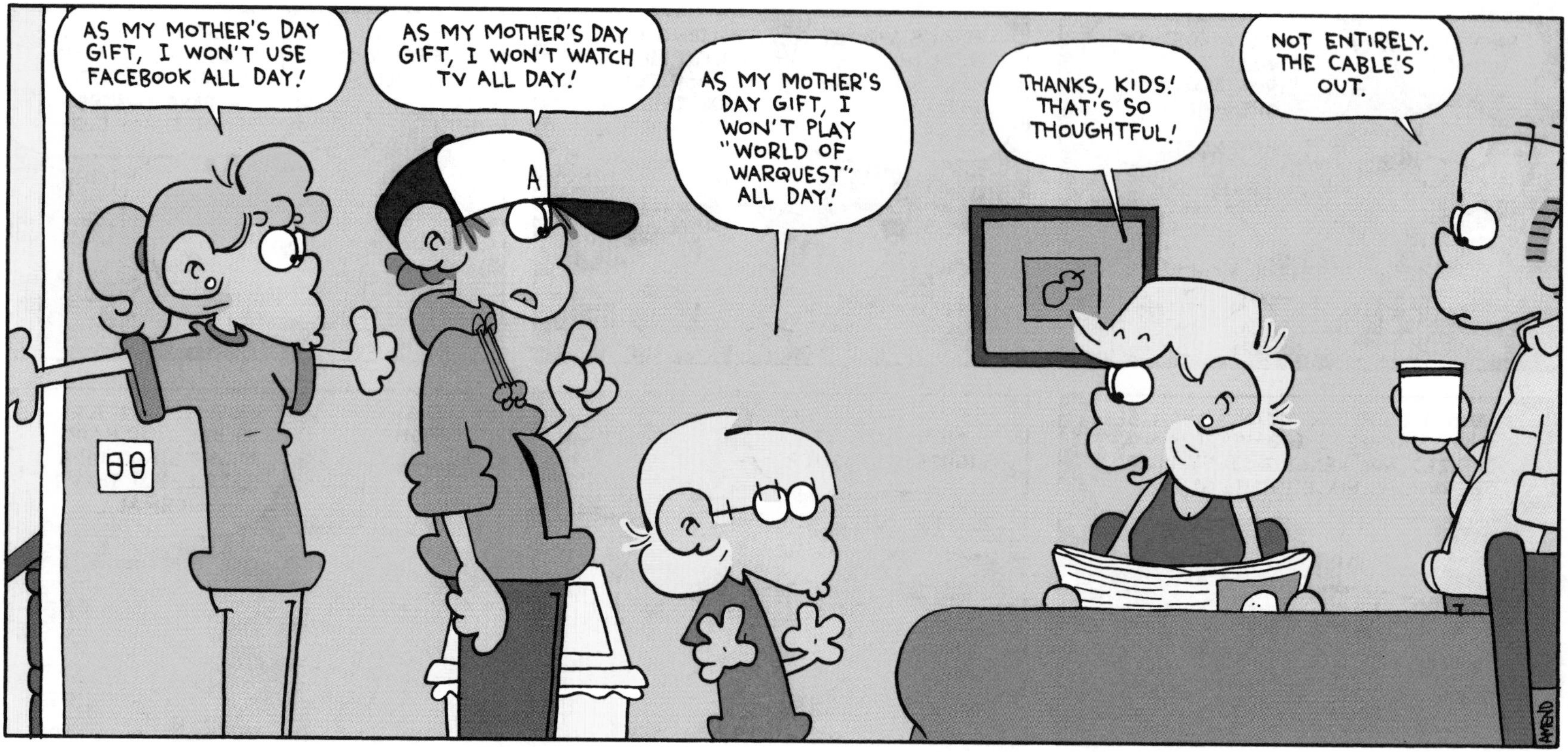
AS MY MOTHER'S DAY GIFT, I WON'T USE FACEBOOK ALL DAY!
AS MY MOTHER'S DAY GIFT, I WON'T WATCH TV ALL DAY!
AS MY MOTHER'S DAY GIFT, I WON'T PLAY "WORLD OF WARQUEST" ALL DAY!
THANKS, KIDS! THAT'S SO THOUGHTFUL!
NOT ENTIRELY. THE CABLE'S OUT.
AMEND

CAN YOU TELL I CHANGED MY BIRTH YEAR ON IT?
IT SAYS YOU'RE 21.
I KNOW. I NEED TO BE 21 TO GET INTO BARS.
DARE I ASK WHY YOU WANT TO GET INTO BARS?
I WANT TO START LEAVING FAKE iPHONE PROTOTYPES ON BAR STOOLS FOR TECH BLOGGERS TO FIND. IF HISTORY IS ANY GUIDE, THIS WILL SEND THE ENTIRE INTERNET INTO A FRENZY OF FOAMING-AT-THE-MOUTH ANALYSIS AND DEBATE.
THE FIRST ONE I'M MAKING WILL USE A CAR BATTERY AND WEIGH 30 POUNDS. IT'LL HAVE THOSE BIG RABBIT EAR ANTENNAS THEY USED TO PUT ON TOP OF TV SETS. NO SANE PERSON WILL WANT THIS PHONE.
iPhone 12gv
WATCHING APPLE FANBOYS DEFEND IT WILL BE THE FUNNIEST THING EVER!
NO, THE FUNNIEST THING EVER WOULD BE YOU FLASHING YOUR ELEMENTARY SCHOOL I.D. CARD TO A BAR BOUNCER.
I COULD TRY MY "HONORARY STAR FLEET CADET" CARD, BUT I'M WEARING SPOCK EARS IN THE PHOTO...
I STAND CORRECTED.
AMEND

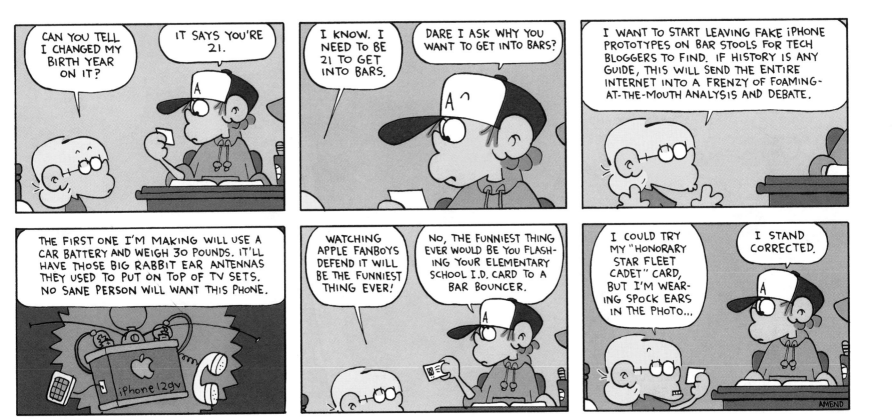

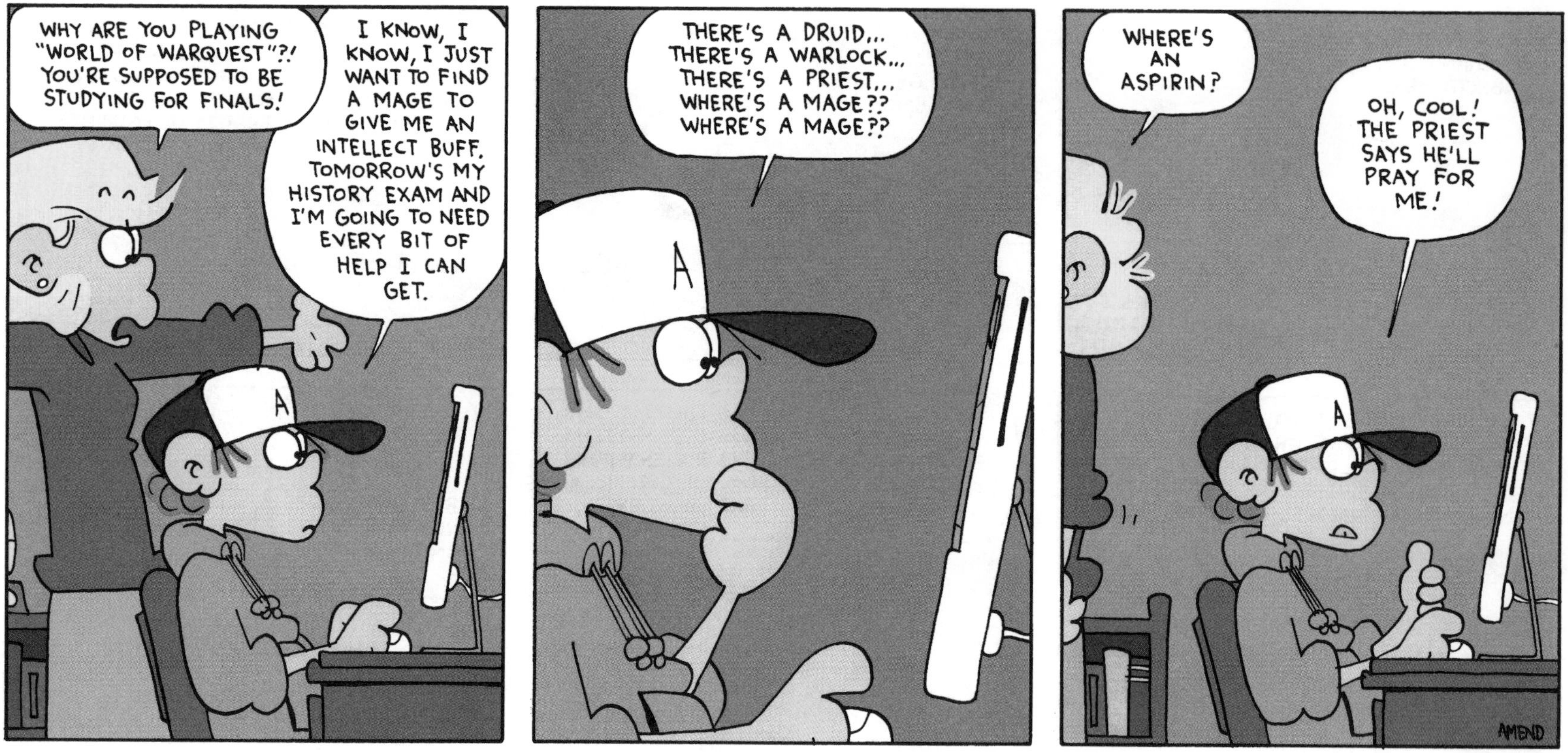
WHY ARE YOU PLAYING "WORLD OF WARQUEST"?! YOU'RE SUPPOSED TO BE STUDYING FOR FINALS!
I KNOW, I KNOW, I JUST WANT TO FIND A MAGE TO GIVE ME AN INTELLECT BUFF. TOMORROW'S MY HISTORY EXAM AND I'M GOING TO NEED EVERY BIT OF HELP I CAN GET.
THERE'S A DRUID... THERE'S A WARLOCK... THERE'S A PRIEST... WHERE'S A MAGE?? WHERE'S A MAGE??
WHERE'S AN ASPIRIN?
OH, COOL! THE PRIEST SAYS HE'LL PRAY FOR ME!
AMEND

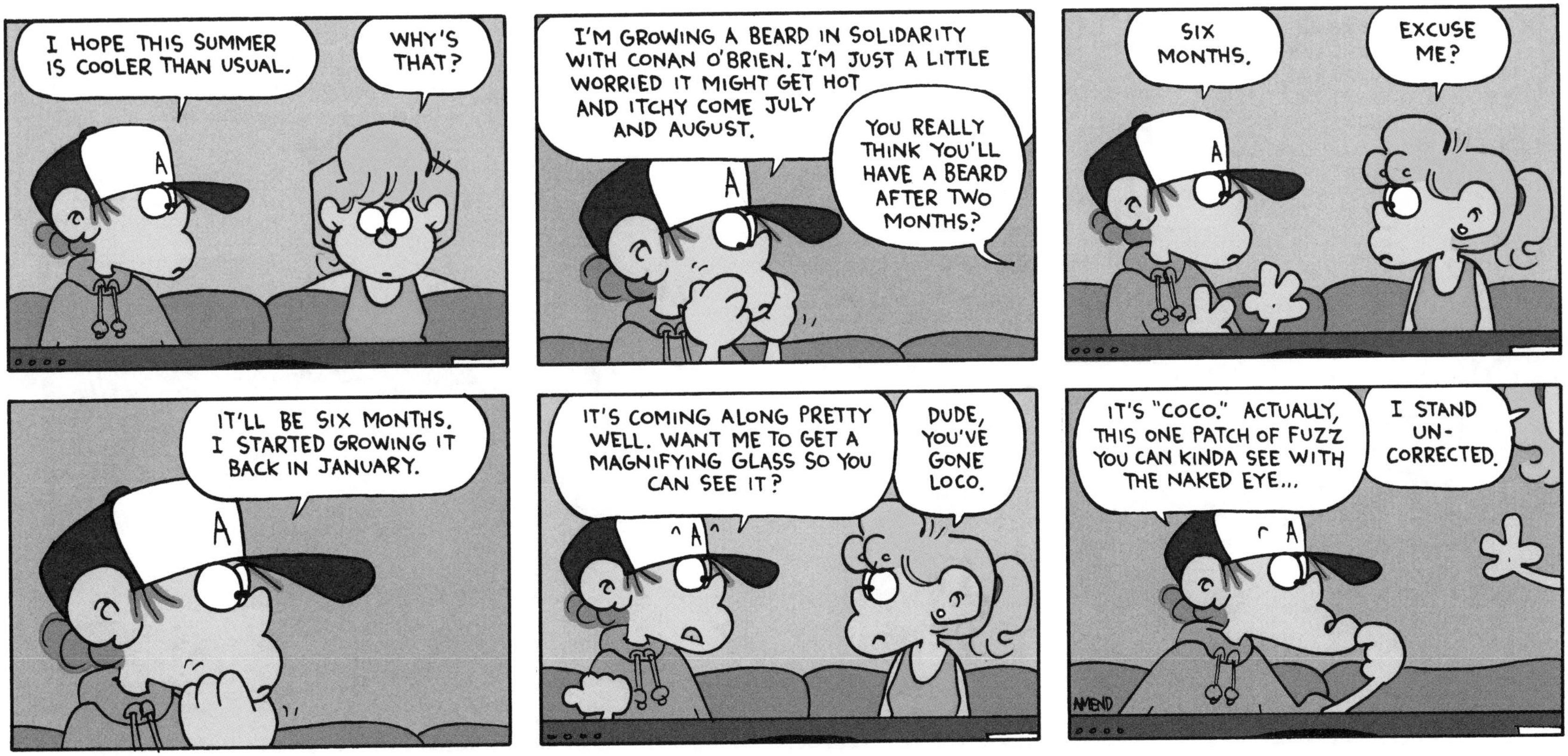
I HOPE THIS SUMMER IS COOLER THAN USUAL.
WHY'S THAT?
I'M GROWING A BEARD IN SOLIDARITY WITH CONAN O'BRIEN. I'M JUST A LITTLE WORRIED IT MIGHT GET HOT AND ITCHY COME JULY AND AUGUST.
YOU REALLY THINK YOU'LL HAVE A BEARD AFTER TWO MONTHS?
SIX MONTHS.
EXCUSE ME?
IT'LL BE SIX MONTHS. I STARTED GROWING IT BACK IN JANUARY.
IT'S COMING ALONG PRETTY WELL. WANT ME TO GET A MAGNIFYING GLASS SO YOU CAN SEE IT?
DUDE, YOU'VE GONE LOCO.
IT'S "COCO." ACTUALLY, THIS ONE PATCH OF FUZZ YOU CAN KINDA SEE WITH THE NAKED EYE...
I STAND UN-CORRECTED.
AMEND

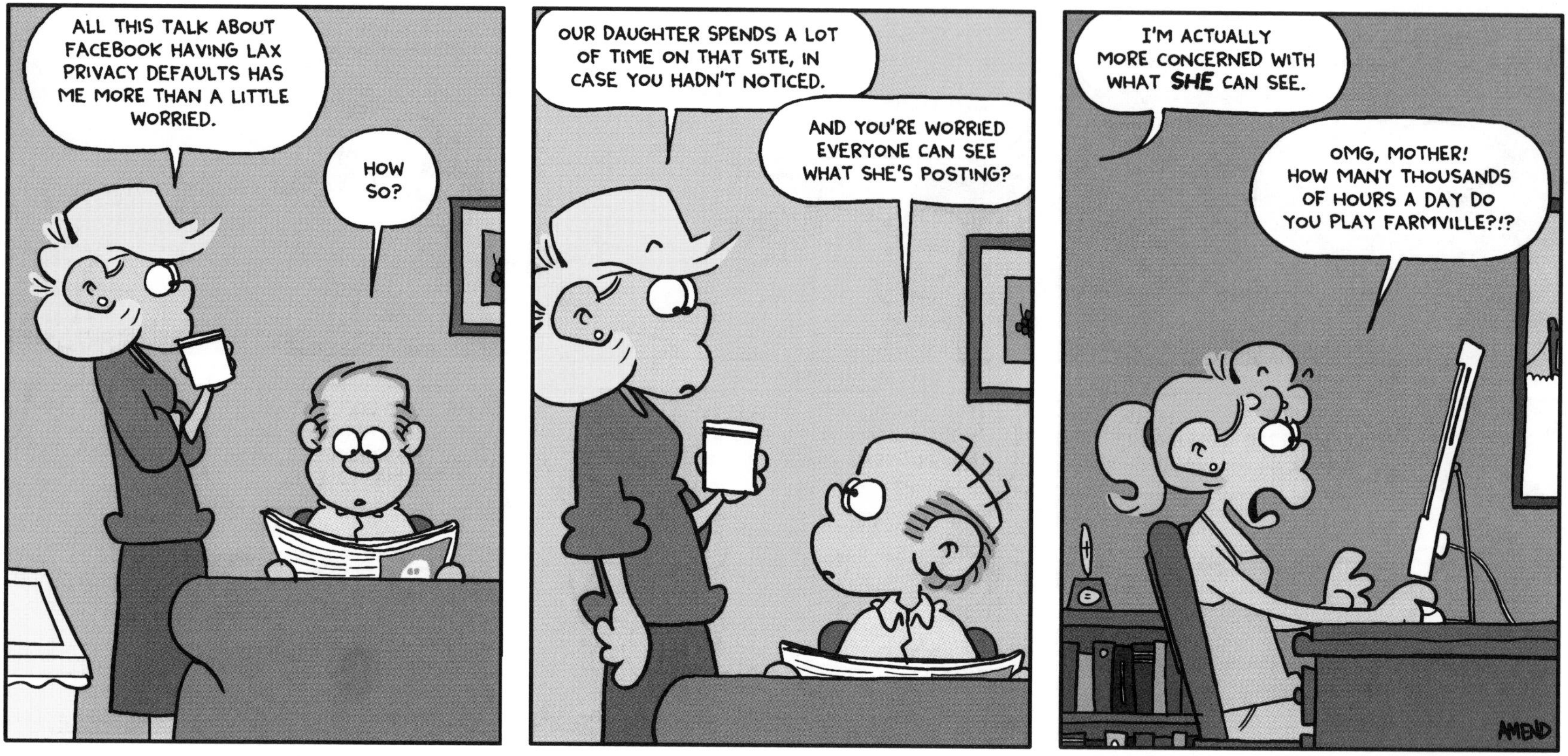
ALL THIS TALK ABOUT FACEBOOK HAVING LAX PRIVACY DEFAULTS HAS ME MORE THAN A LITTLE WORRIED.
HOW SO?
OUR DAUGHTER SPENDS A LOT OF TIME ON THAT SITE, IN CASE YOU HADN'T NOTICED.
AND YOU'RE WORRIED EVERYONE CAN SEE WHAT SHE'S POSTING?
I'M ACTUALLY MORE CONCERNED WITH WHAT **SHE** CAN SEE.
OMG, MOTHER! HOW MANY THOUSANDS OF HOURS A DAY DO YOU PLAY FARMVILLE?!?
AMEND

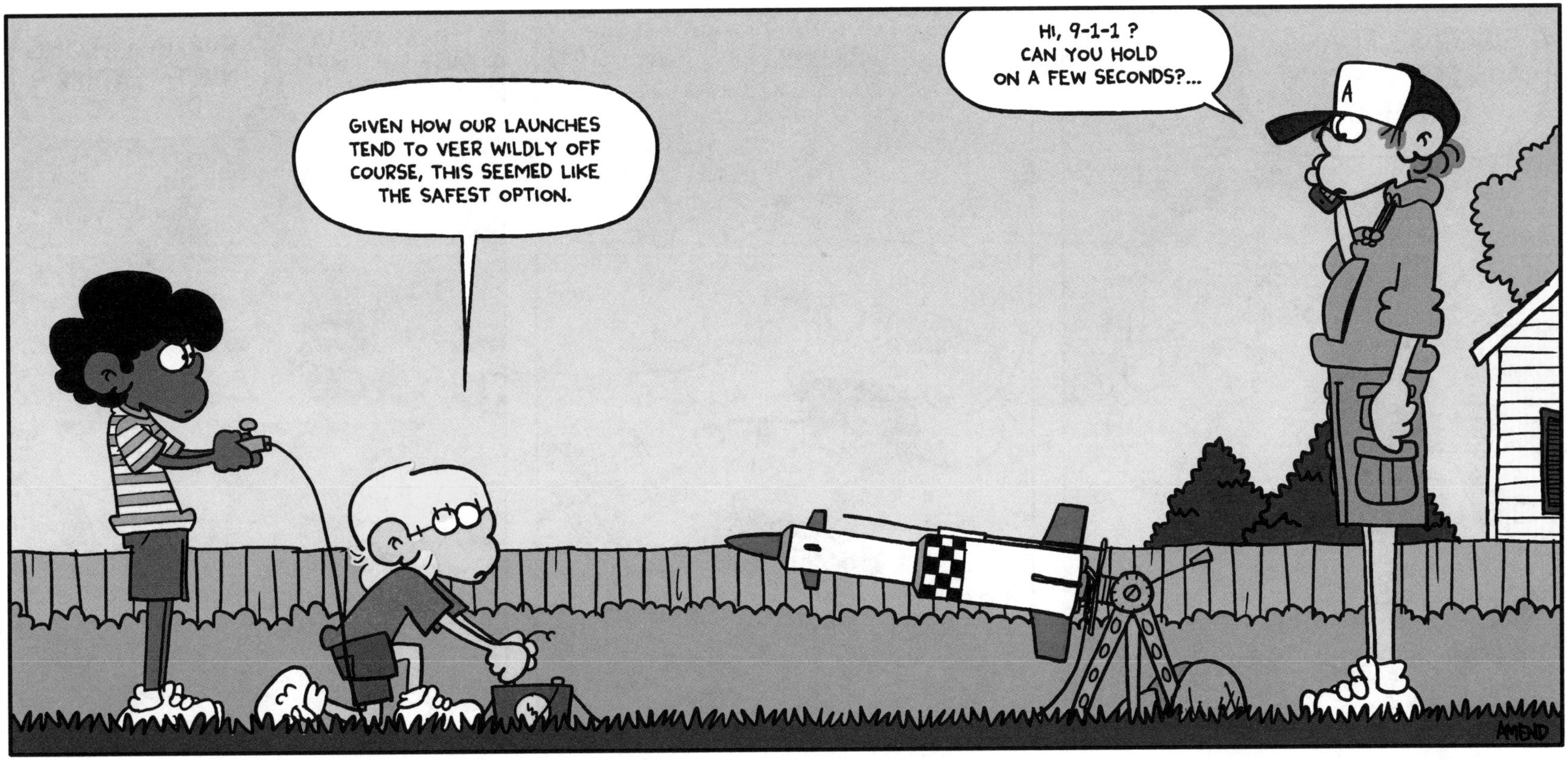
GIVEN HOW OUR LAUNCHES TEND TO VEER WILDLY OFF COURSE, THIS SEEMED LIKE THE SAFEST OPTION.
HI, 9-1-1 ? CAN YOU HOLD ON A FEW SECONDS?...
A
AMEND

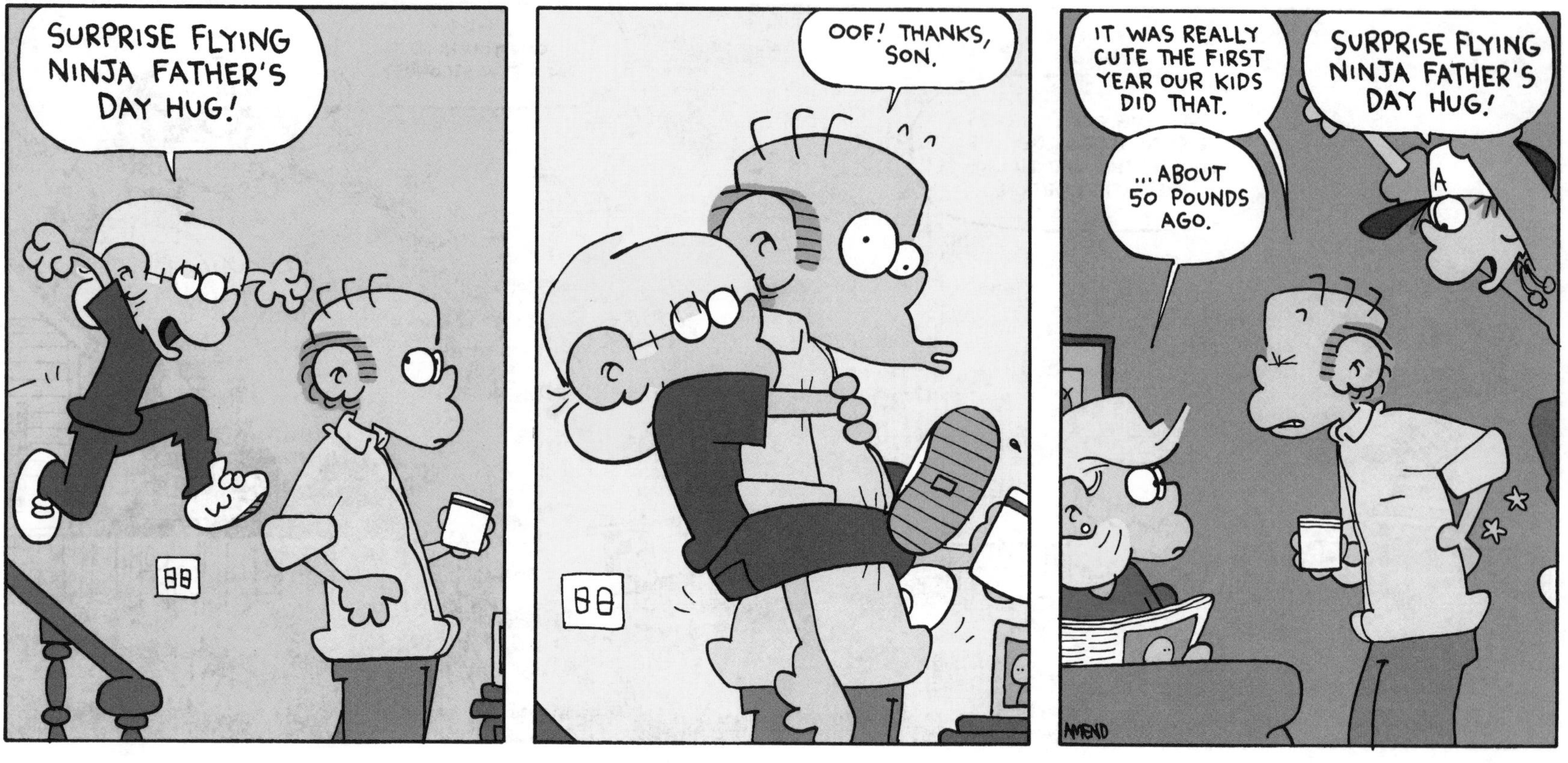
SURPRISE FLYING NINJA FATHER'S DAY HUG!
OOF! THANKS, SON.
IT WAS REALLY CUTE THE FIRST YEAR OUR KIDS DID THAT.
SURPRISE FLYING NINJA FATHER'S DAY HUG!
...ABOUT 50 POUNDS AGO.
AMEND

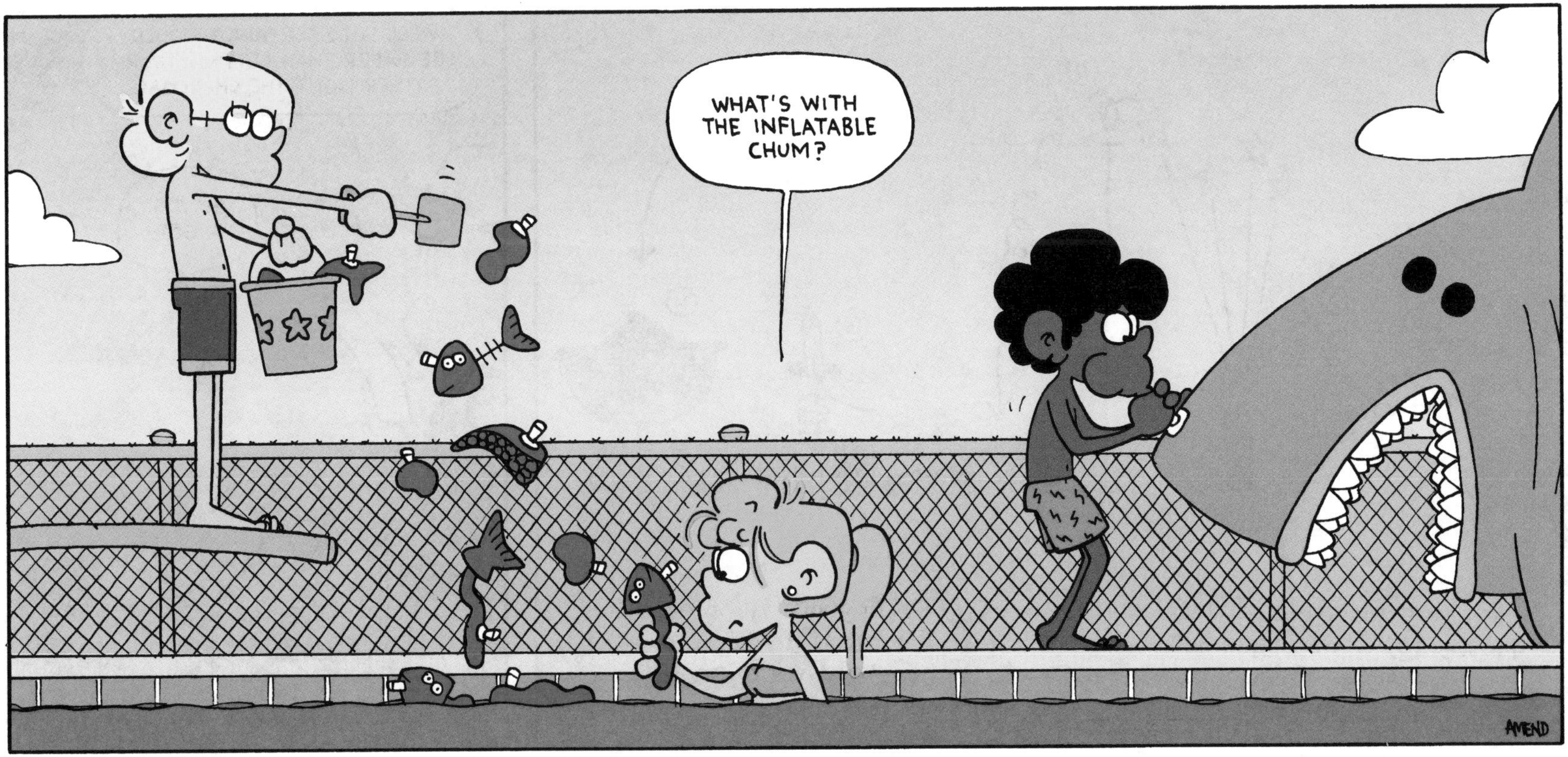
WHAT'S WITH THE INFLATABLE CHUM?
AMEND

Sparkler Ⓐ ignites fuse Ⓑ of fireworks Ⓒ setting off spinning Bloom Flower Ⓓ which falls onto lever Ⓔ striking match Ⓕ which launches weighted fireworks rocket Ⓖ into grill Ⓗ lighting charcoal.
WELL, THIS CERTAINLY WOULD BE SAFER THAN LETTING YOUR FATHER LIGHT THE CHARCOAL.
SO IT'S A GO?
AMEND

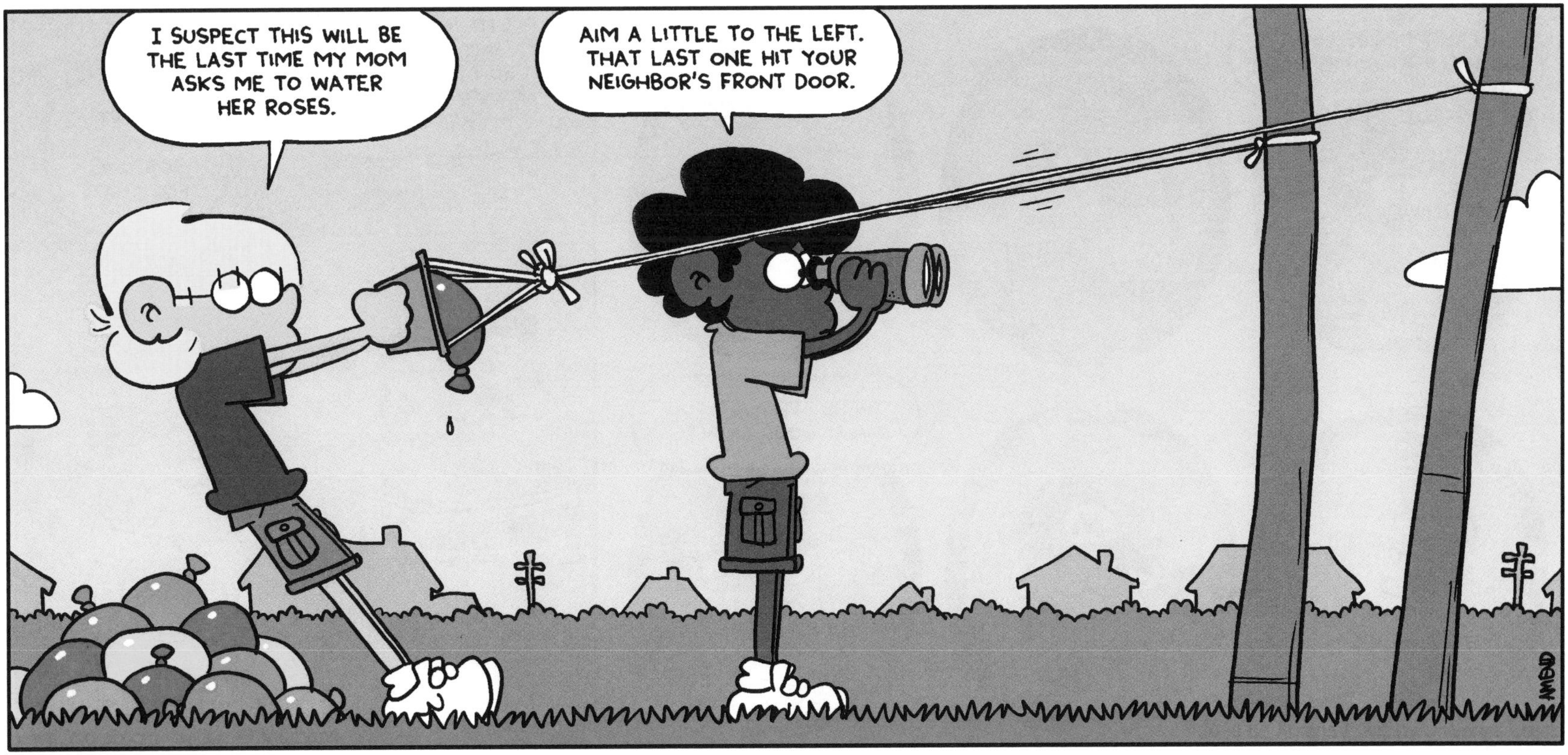
I SUSPECT THIS WILL BE THE LAST TIME MY MOM ASKS ME TO WATER HER ROSES.
AIM A LITTLE TO THE LEFT. THAT LAST ONE HIT YOUR NEIGHBOR'S FRONT DOOR.

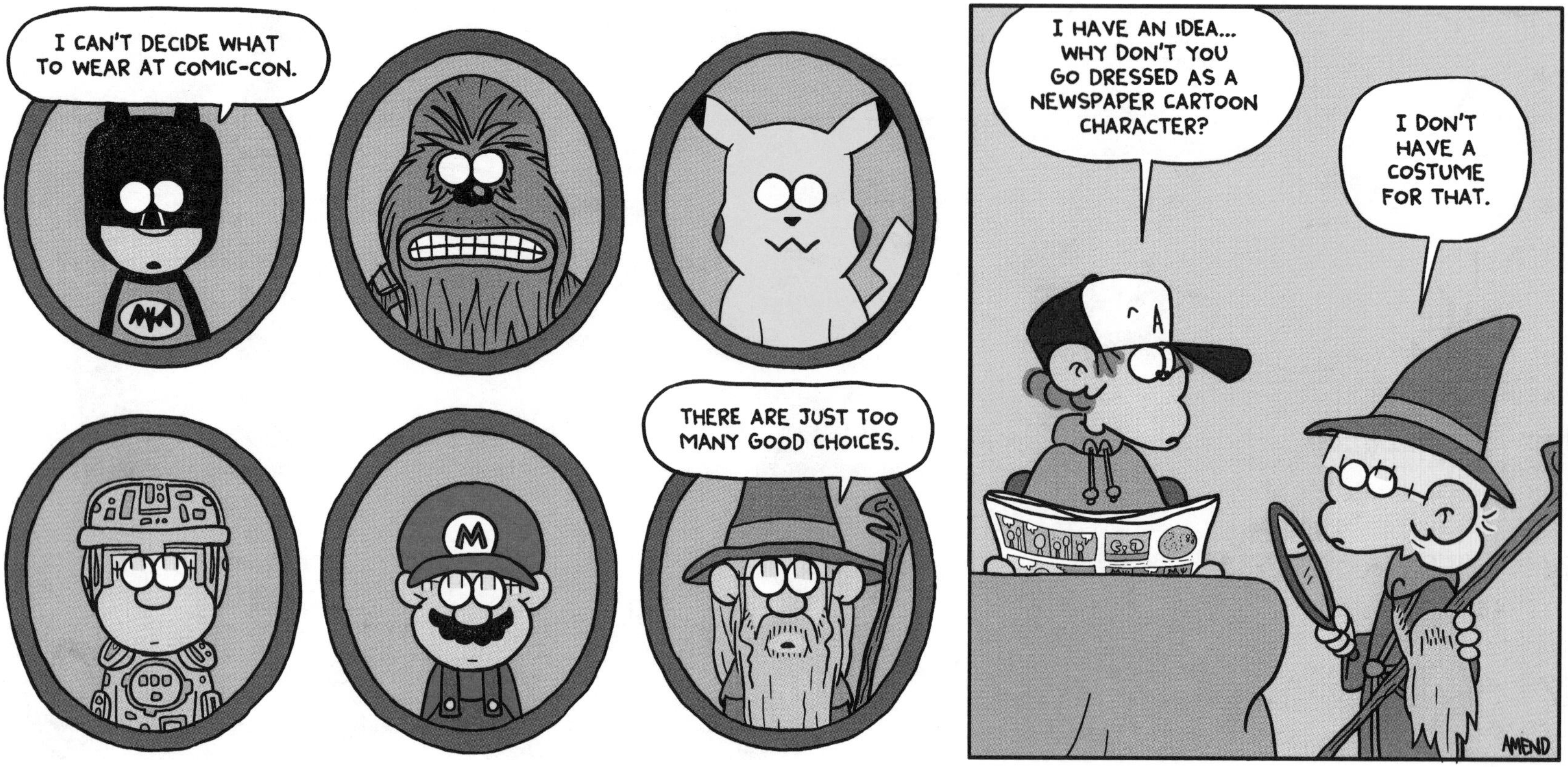
I CAN'T DECIDE WHAT TO WEAR AT COMIC-CON.
THERE ARE JUST TOO MANY GOOD CHOICES.
M
I HAVE AN IDEA... WHY DON'T YOU GO DRESSED AS A NEWSPAPER CARTOON CHARACTER?
I DON'T HAVE A COSTUME FOR THAT.
AMEND

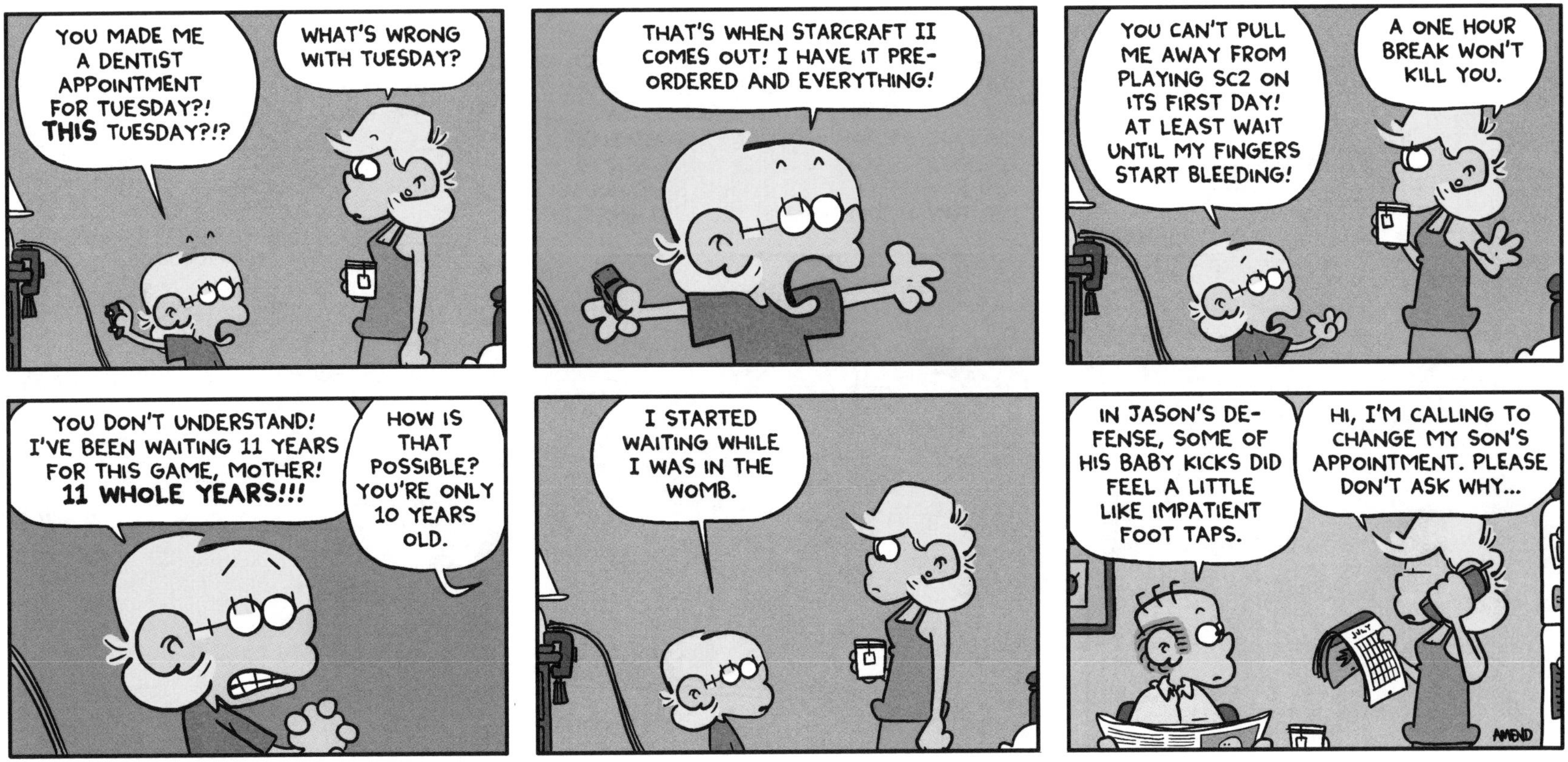
YOU MADE ME A DENTIST APPOINTMENT FOR TUESDAY?! **THIS** TUESDAY?!?
WHAT'S WRONG WITH TUESDAY?
THAT'S WHEN STARCRAFT II COMES OUT! I HAVE IT PRE-ORDERED AND EVERYTHING!
YOU CAN'T PULL ME AWAY FROM PLAYING SC2 ON ITS FIRST DAY! AT LEAST WAIT UNTIL MY FINGERS START BLEEDING!
A ONE HOUR BREAK WON'T KILL YOU.
YOU DON'T UNDERSTAND! I'VE BEEN WAITING 11 YEARS FOR THIS GAME, MOTHER! **11 WHOLE YEARS!!!**
HOW IS THAT POSSIBLE? YOU'RE ONLY 10 YEARS OLD.
I STARTED WAITING WHILE I WAS IN THE WOMB.
IN JASON'S DE-FENSE, SOME OF HIS BABY KICKS DID FEEL A LITTLE LIKE IMPATIENT FOOT TAPS.
HI, I'M CALLING TO CHANGE MY SON'S APPOINTMENT. PLEASE DON'T ASK WHY...
JULY
AMEND

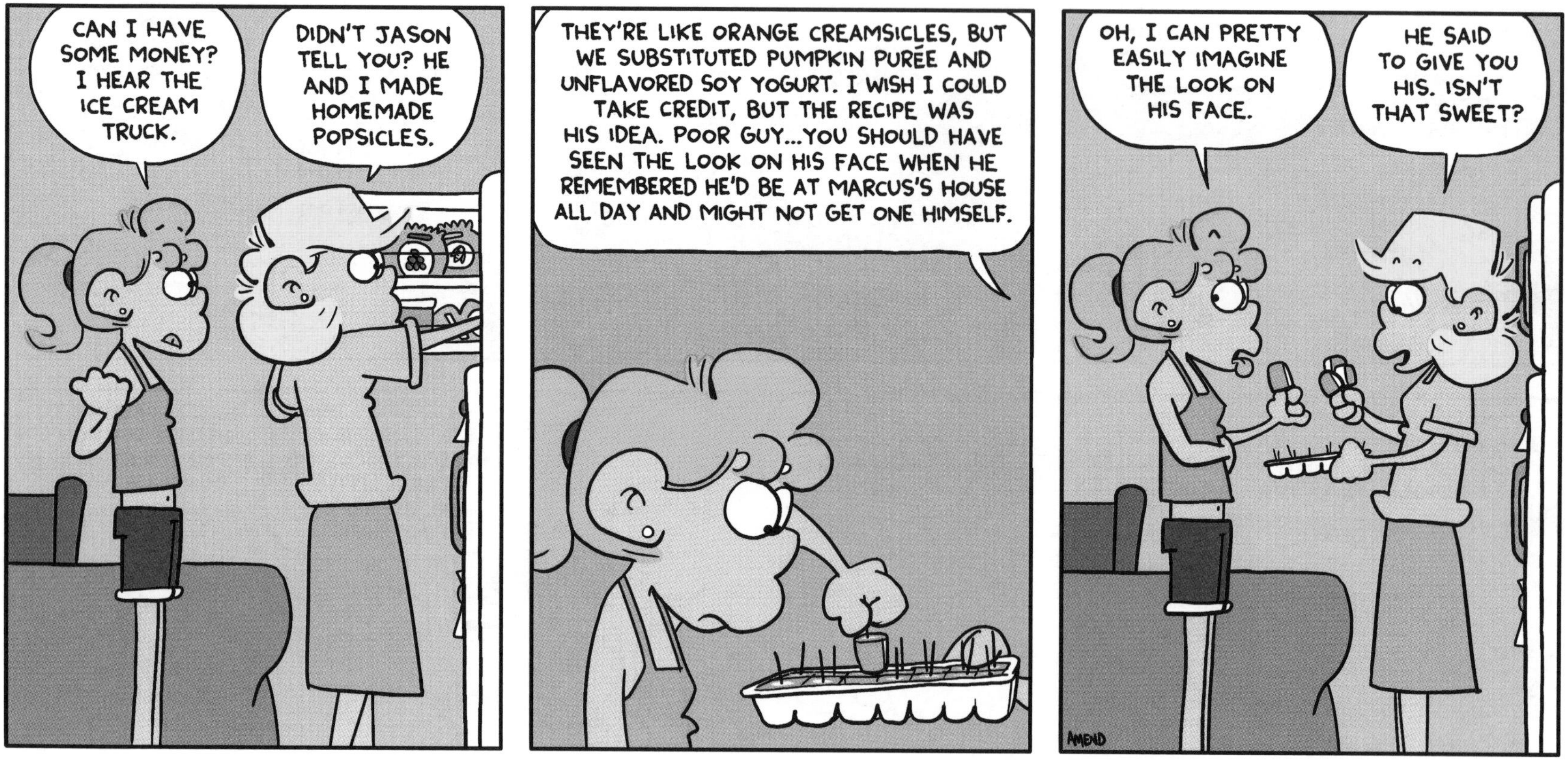
CAN I HAVE SOME MONEY? I HEAR THE ICE CREAM TRUCK.
DIDN'T JASON TELL YOU? HE AND I MADE HOMEMADE POPSICLES.
THEY'RE LIKE ORANGE CREAMSICLES, BUT WE SUBSTITUTED PUMPKIN PURÉE AND UNFLAVORED SOY YOGURT. I WISH I COULD TAKE CREDIT, BUT THE RECIPE WAS HIS IDEA. POOR GUY...YOU SHOULD HAVE SEEN THE LOOK ON HIS FACE WHEN HE REMEMBERED HE'D BE AT MARCUS'S HOUSE ALL DAY AND MIGHT NOT GET ONE HIMSELF.
OH, I CAN PRETTY EASILY IMAGINE THE LOOK ON HIS FACE.
HE SAID TO GIVE YOU HIS. ISN'T THAT SWEET?
AMEND

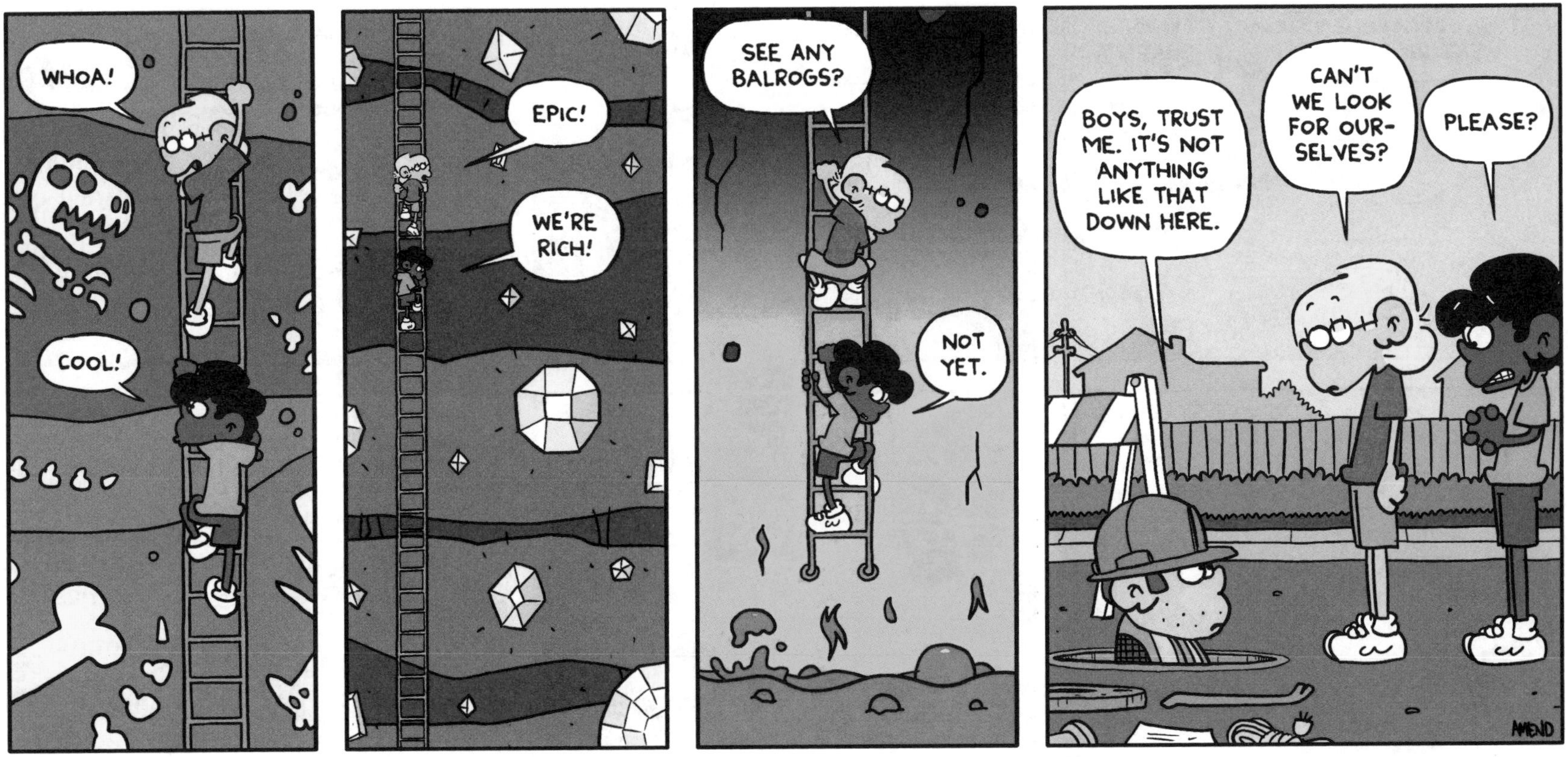
WHOA!
COOL!
EPIC!
WE'RE RICH!
SEE ANY BALROGS?
NOT YET.
BOYS, TRUST ME. IT'S NOT ANYTHING LIKE THAT DOWN HERE.
CAN'T WE LOOK FOR OUR-SELVES?
PLEASE?
AMEND

I'D SAY MY TROUT FISHING WENT RATHER WELL.
WHOA... THAT'S A FULL RAINBOW!
WAIT...THERE'S MORE!
DOUBLE RAINBOWS! OMG!
WHOA... MAN... WHOA-HO-HO... OMG! OMG! OMG! WOOOOOO!
THEY'RE STARTING TO LOOK LIKE TRIPLE RAINBOWS!
OMG! IT'S FULL-ON DOUBLE RAINBOWS ALL THE WAY ACROSS THE SKY! WHAT DOES THIS MEAN?! THEY'RE SO BRIGHT! THEY'RE SO BRIGHT AND VIVID! OMG! OMG!
I THINK WE GOT JASON AWAY FROM THE INTERNET NOT A MOMENT TOO SOON.
WE'RE TOO LATE, IF YOU ASK ME.
(SOB SOB) THEY'RE SO BEAUTIFUL...

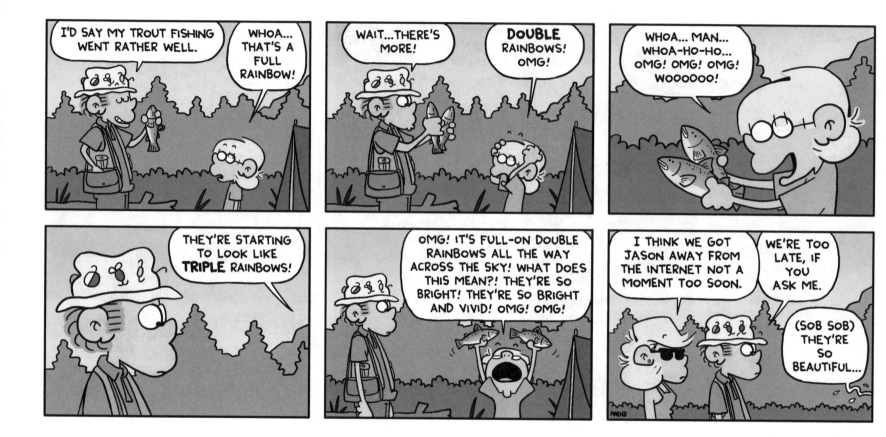

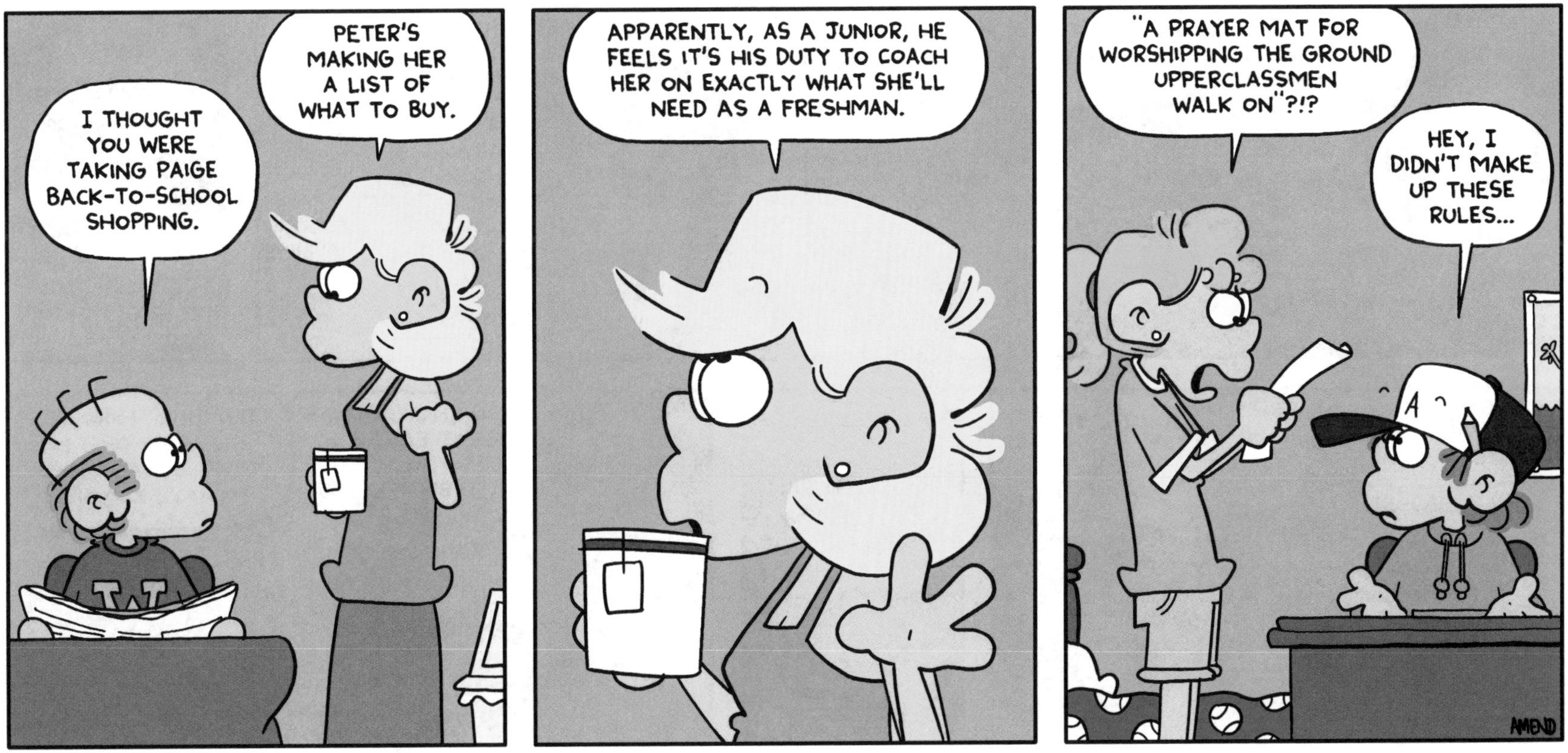
I THOUGHT YOU WERE TAKING PAIGE BACK-TO-SCHOOL SHOPPING.
PETER'S MAKING HER A LIST OF WHAT TO BUY.
APPARENTLY, AS A JUNIOR, HE FEELS IT'S HIS DUTY TO COACH HER ON EXACTLY WHAT SHE'LL NEED AS A FRESHMAN.
"A PRAYER MAT FOR WORSHIPPING THE GROUND UPPERCLASSMEN WALK ON"?!?
HEY, I DIDN'T MAKE UP THESE RULES...
AMEND

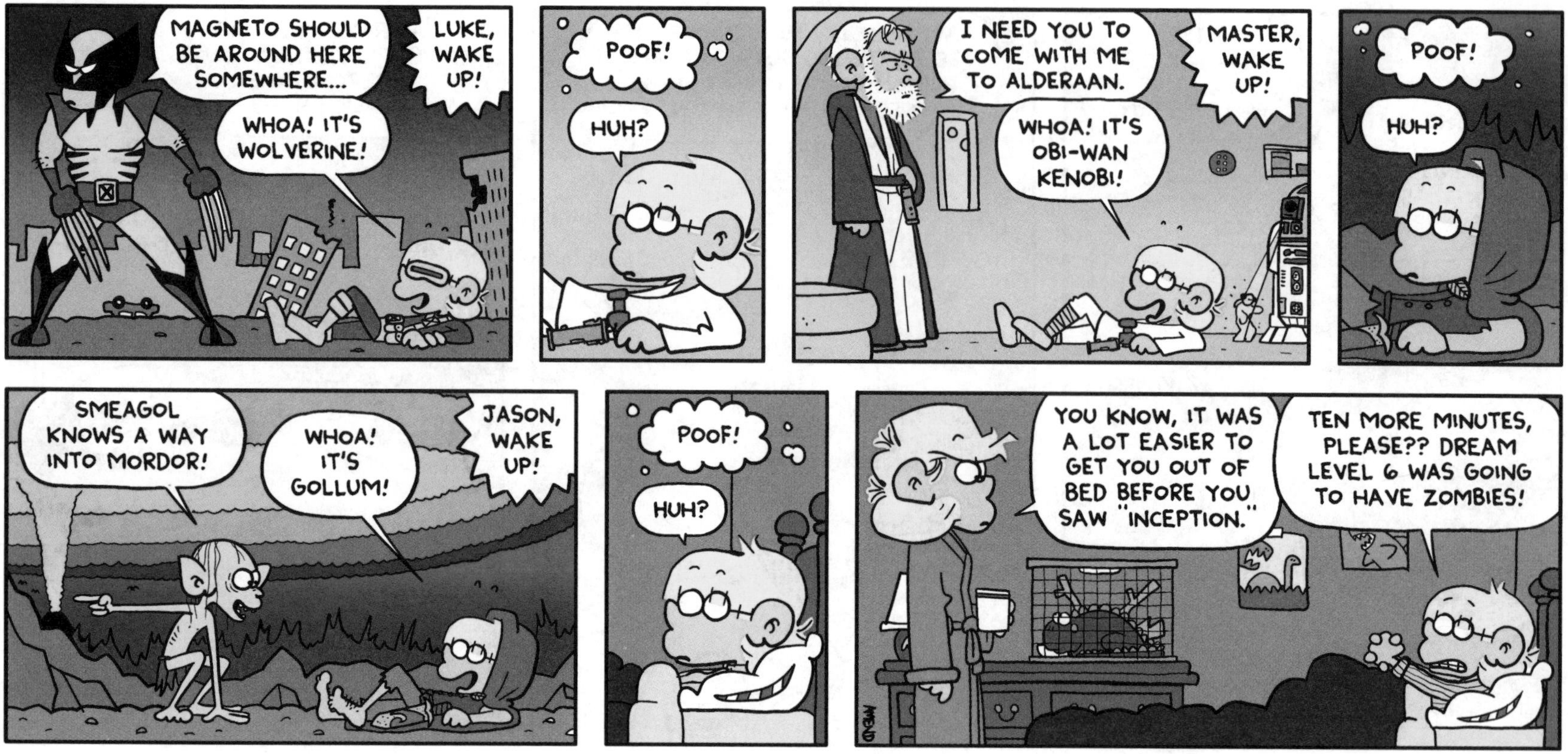
MAGNETO SHOULD BE AROUND HERE SOMEWHERE...
LUKE, WAKE UP!
WHOA! IT'S WOLVERINE!
POOF!
HUH?
I NEED YOU TO COME WITH ME TO ALDERAAN.
MASTER, WAKE UP!
WHOA! IT'S OBI-WAN KENOBI!
POOF!
HUH?
SMEAGOL KNOWS A WAY INTO MORDOR!
JASON, WAKE UP!
WHOA! IT'S GOLLUM!
POOF!
HUH?
YOU KNOW, IT WAS A LOT EASIER TO GET YOU OUT OF BED BEFORE YOU SAW "INCEPTION."
TEN MORE MINUTES, PLEASE?? DREAM LEVEL 6 WAS GOING TO HAVE ZOMBIES!

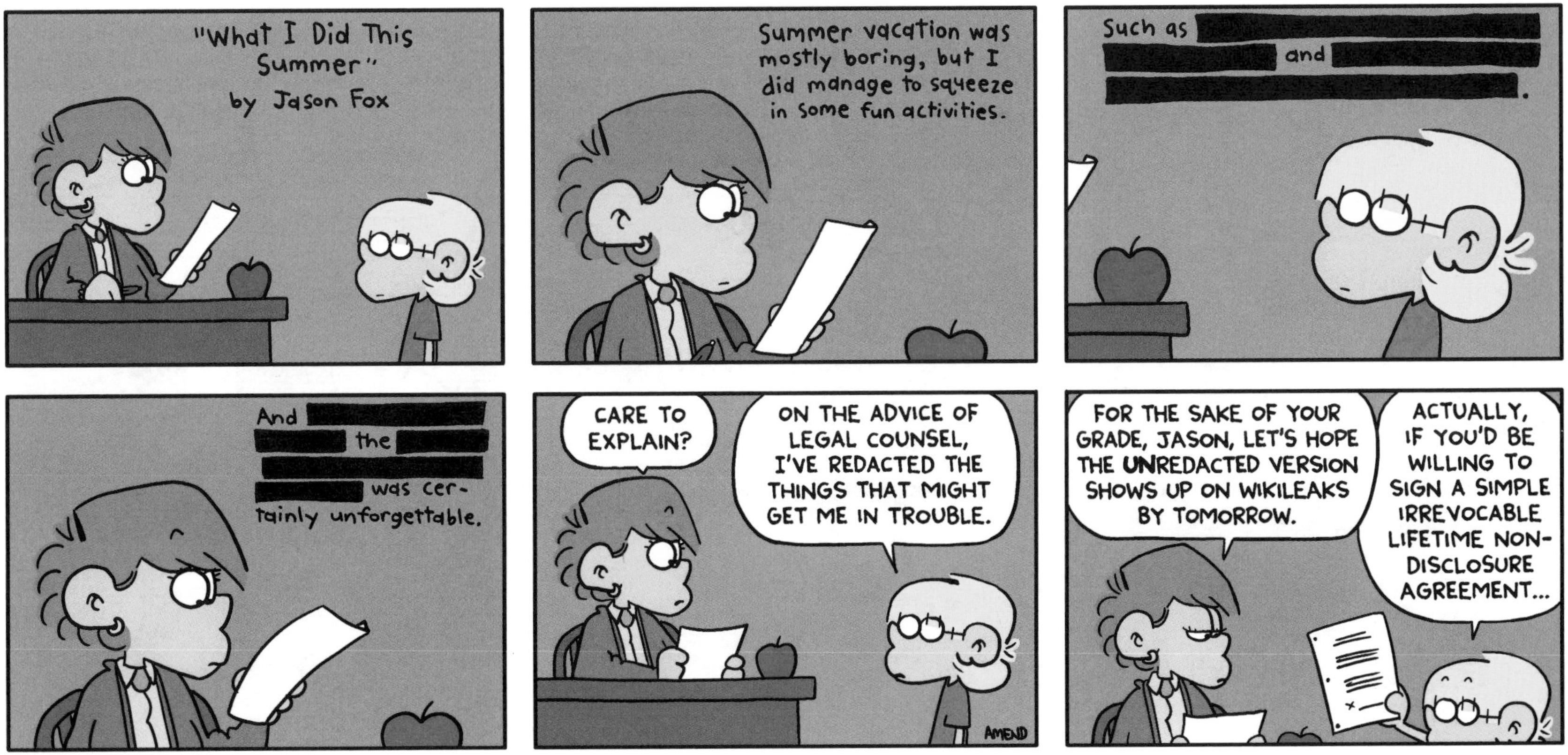
"What I Did This Summer" by Jason Fox
Summer vacation was mostly boring, but I did manage to squeeze in some fun activities.
Such as [redacted] and [redacted].
And [redacted] the [redacted] was certainly unforgettable.
CARE TO EXPLAIN?
ON THE ADVICE OF LEGAL COUNSEL, I'VE REDACTED THE THINGS THAT MIGHT GET ME IN TROUBLE.
AMEND
FOR THE SAKE OF YOUR GRADE, JASON, LET'S HOPE THE UNREDACTED VERSION SHOWS UP ON WIKILEAKS BY TOMORROW.
ACTUALLY, IF YOU'D BE WILLING TO SIGN A SIMPLE IRREVOCABLE LIFETIME NON-DISCLOSURE AGREEMENT...

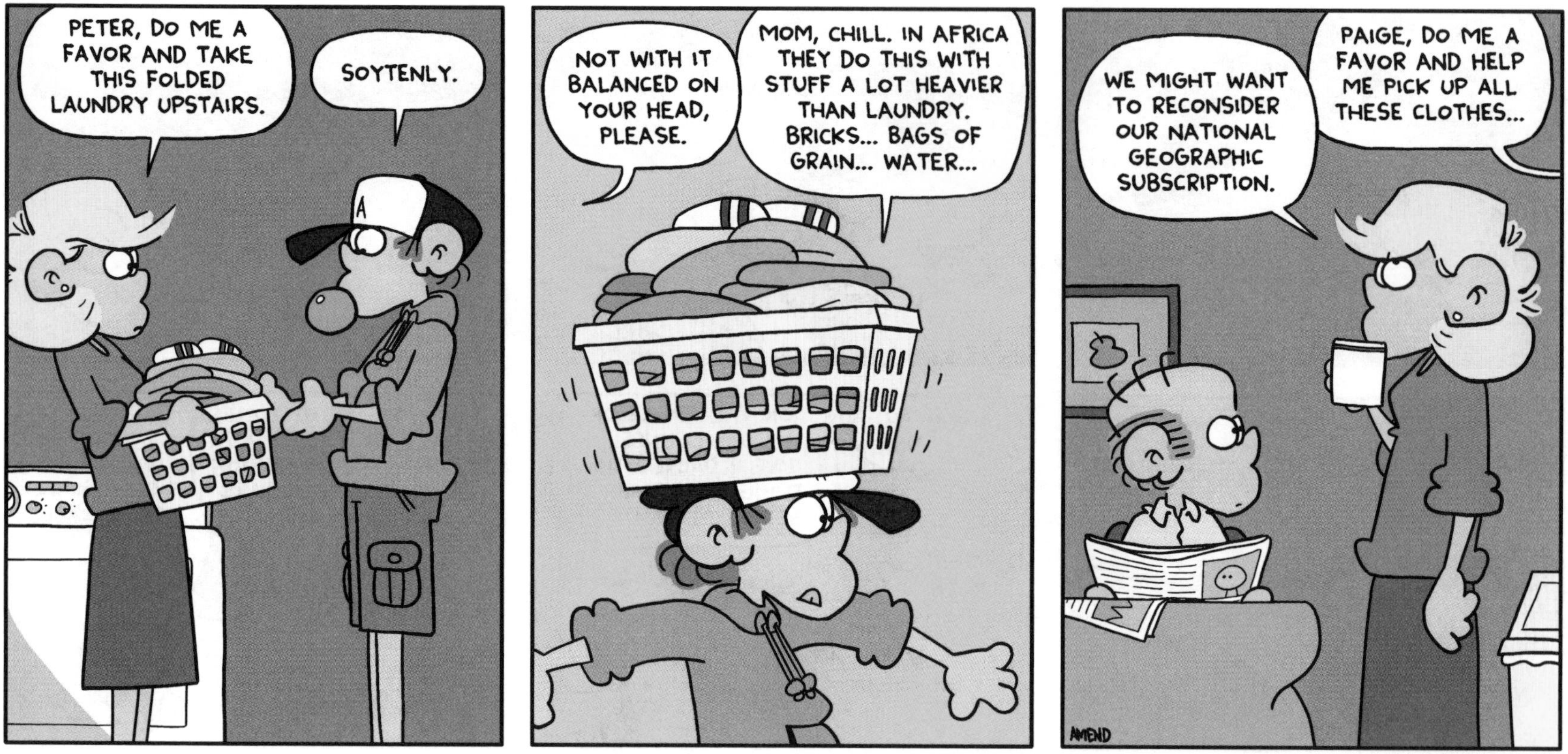
PETER, DO ME A FAVOR AND TAKE THIS FOLDED LAUNDRY UPSTAIRS.
SOYTENLY.
NOT WITH IT BALANCED ON YOUR HEAD, PLEASE.
MOM, CHILL. IN AFRICA THEY DO THIS WITH STUFF A LOT HEAVIER THAN LAUNDRY. BRICKS... BAGS OF GRAIN... WATER...
WE MIGHT WANT TO RECONSIDER OUR NATIONAL GEOGRAPHIC SUBSCRIPTION.
PAIGE, DO ME A FAVOR AND HELP ME PICK UP ALL THESE CLOTHES...
AMEND

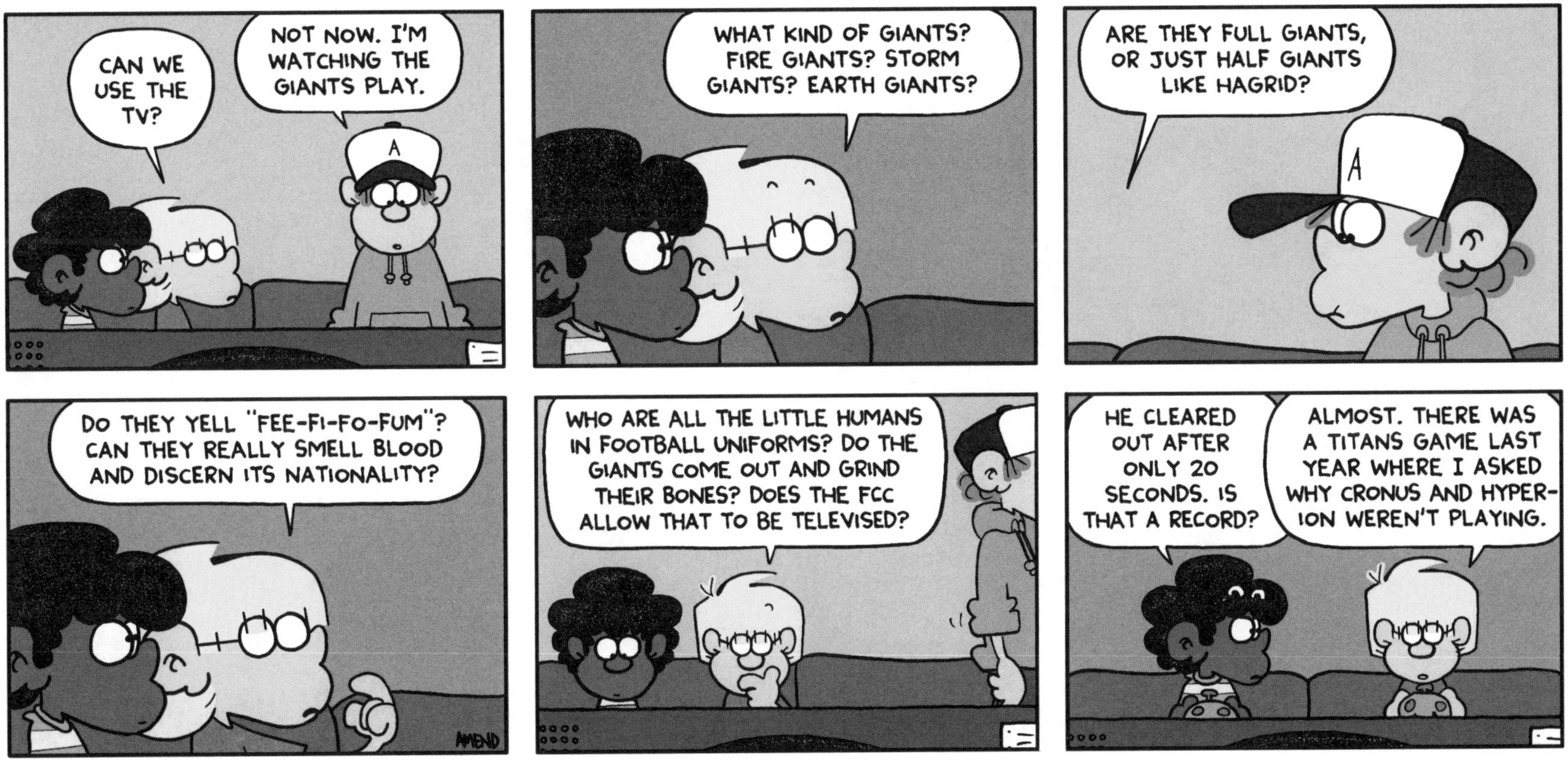

CAN WE USE THE TV?
NOT NOW. I'M WATCHING THE GIANTS PLAY.
WHAT KIND OF GIANTS? FIRE GIANTS? STORM GIANTS? EARTH GIANTS?
ARE THEY FULL GIANTS, OR JUST HALF GIANTS LIKE HAGRID?
DO THEY YELL "FEE-FI-FO-FUM"? CAN THEY REALLY SMELL BLOOD AND DISCERN ITS NATIONALITY?
AMEND
WHO ARE ALL THE LITTLE HUMANS IN FOOTBALL UNIFORMS? DO THE GIANTS COME OUT AND GRIND THEIR BONES? DOES THE FCC ALLOW THAT TO BE TELEVISED?
HE CLEARED OUT AFTER ONLY 20 SECONDS. IS THAT A RECORD?
ALMOST. THERE WAS A TITANS GAME LAST YEAR WHERE I ASKED WHY CRONUS AND HYPER-ION WEREN'T PLAYING.

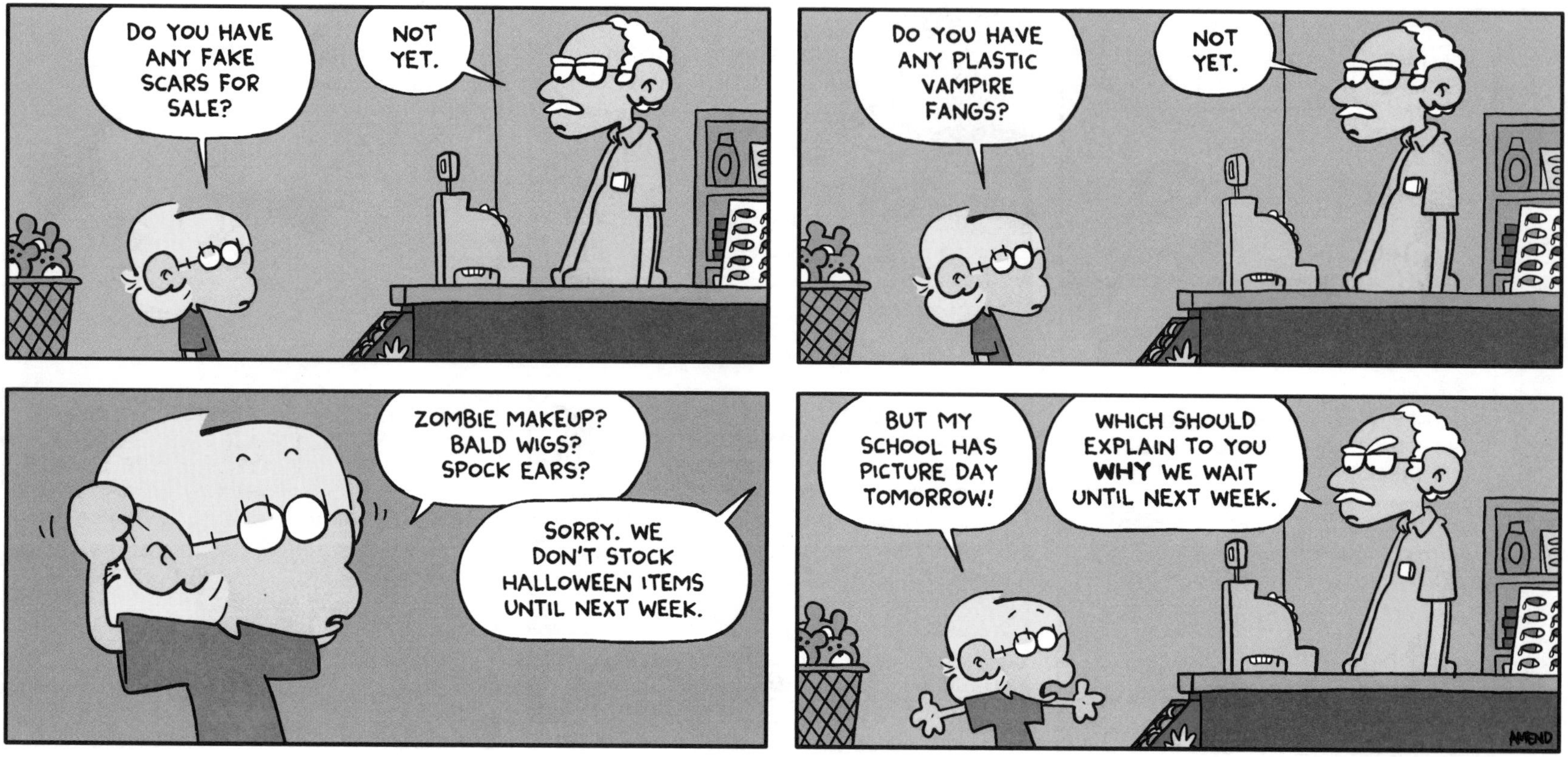
DO YOU HAVE ANY FAKE SCARS FOR SALE?
NOT YET.
DO YOU HAVE ANY PLASTIC VAMPIRE FANGS?
NOT YET.
ZOMBIE MAKEUP? BALD WIGS? SPOCK EARS?
SORRY. WE DON'T STOCK HALLOWEEN ITEMS UNTIL NEXT WEEK.
BUT MY SCHOOL HAS PICTURE DAY TOMORROW!
WHICH SHOULD EXPLAIN TO YOU **WHY** WE WAIT UNTIL NEXT WEEK.
AMEND

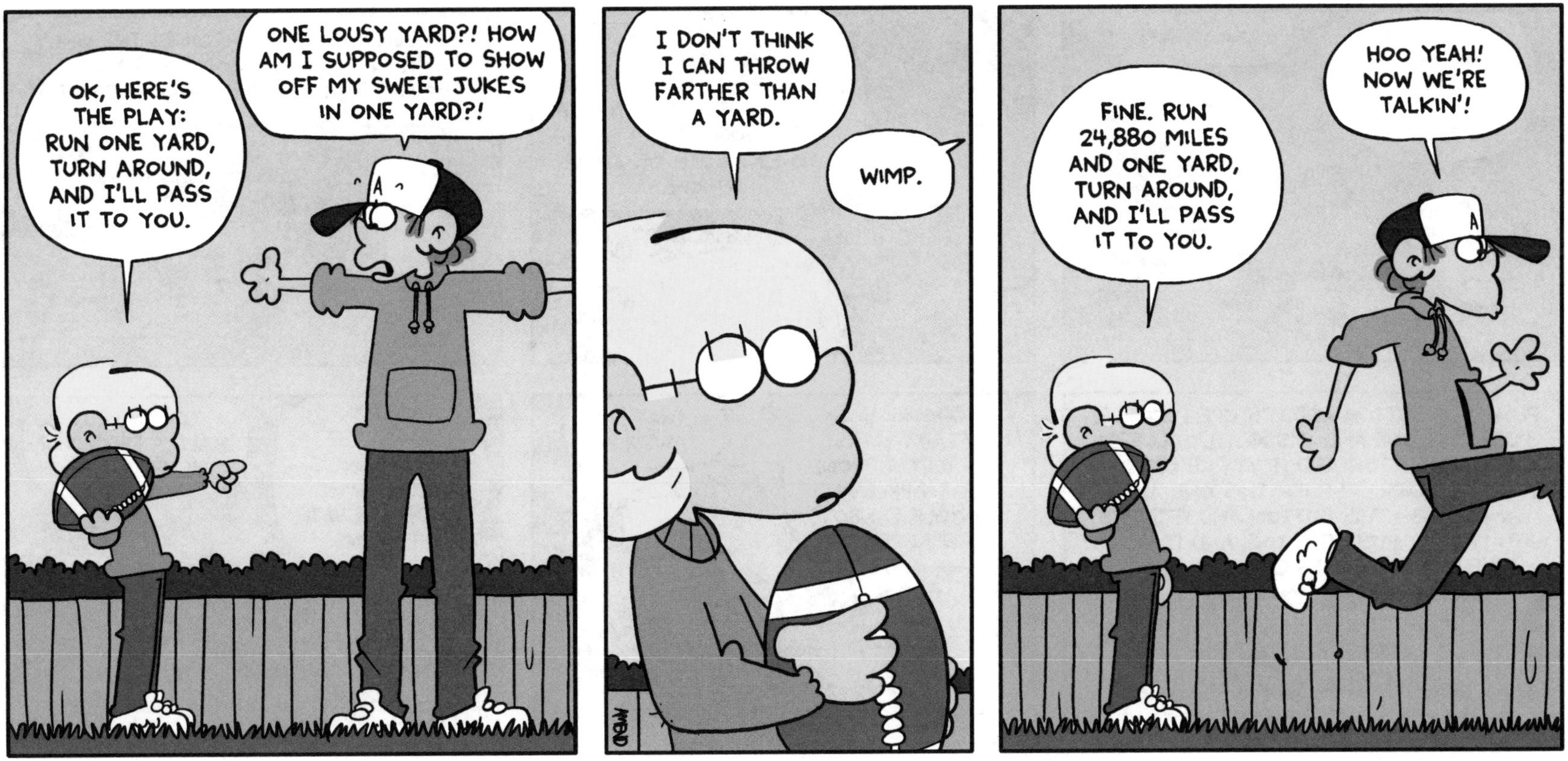
OK, HERE'S THE PLAY: RUN ONE YARD, TURN AROUND, AND I'LL PASS IT TO YOU.
ONE LOUSY YARD?! HOW AM I SUPPOSED TO SHOW OFF MY SWEET JUKES IN ONE YARD?!
I DON'T THINK I CAN THROW FARTHER THAN A YARD.
WIMP.
FINE. RUN 24,880 MILES AND ONE YARD, TURN AROUND, AND I'LL PASS IT TO YOU.
HOO YEAH! NOW WE'RE TALKIN'!

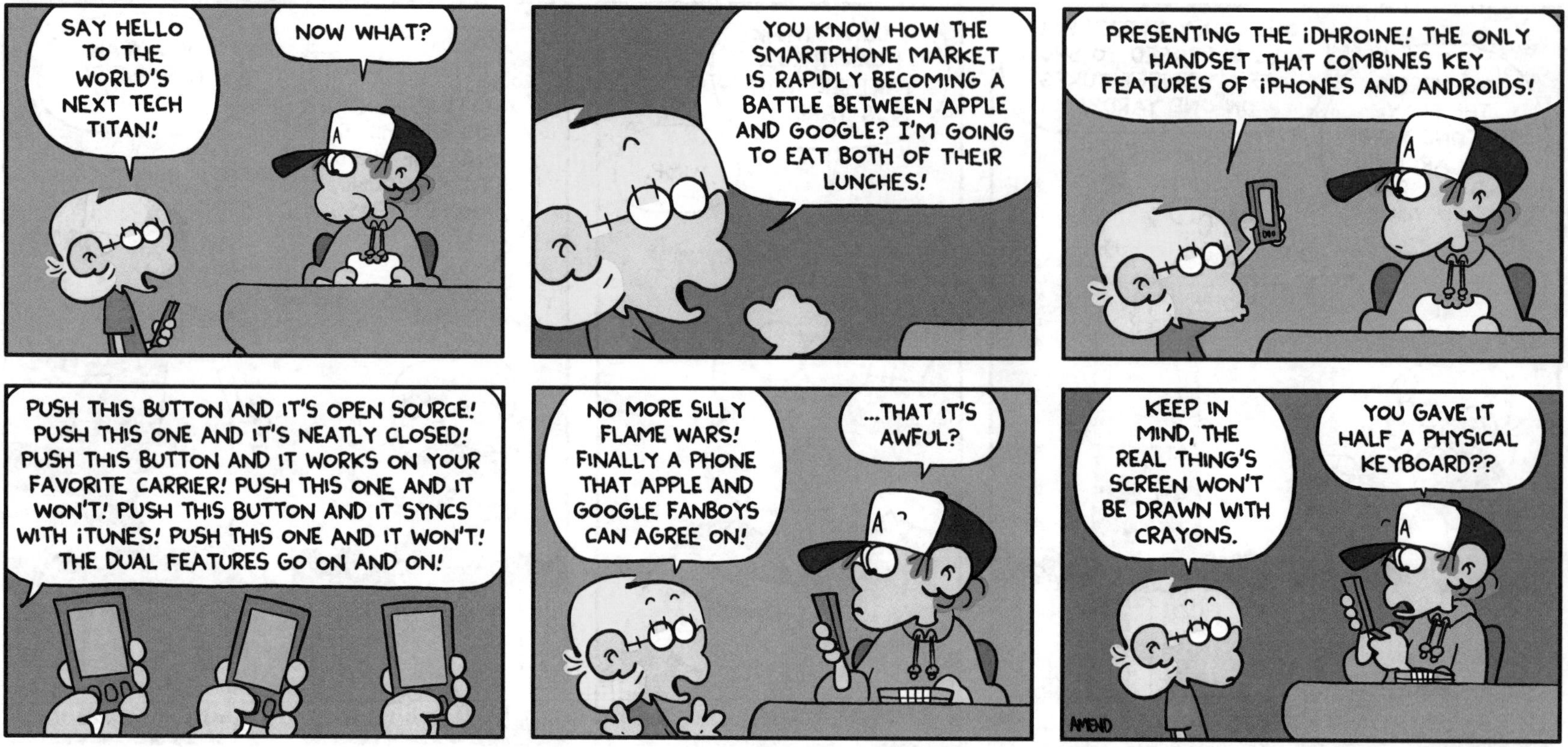
SAY HELLO TO THE WORLD'S NEXT TECH TITAN!
NOW WHAT?
YOU KNOW HOW THE SMARTPHONE MARKET IS RAPIDLY BECOMING A BATTLE BETWEEN APPLE AND GOOGLE? I'M GOING TO EAT BOTH OF THEIR LUNCHES!
PRESENTING THE iDHROiNE! THE ONLY HANDSET THAT COMBINES KEY FEATURES OF iPHONES AND ANDROiDS!
PUSH THIS BUTTON AND IT'S OPEN SOURCE! PUSH THIS ONE AND IT'S NEATLY CLOSED! PUSH THIS BUTTON AND IT WORKS ON YOUR FAVORITE CARRIER! PUSH THIS ONE AND IT WON'T! PUSH THIS BUTTON AND IT SYNCS WITH iTUNES! PUSH THIS ONE AND IT WON'T! THE DUAL FEATURES GO ON AND ON!
NO MORE SILLY FLAME WARS! FINALLY A PHONE THAT APPLE AND GOOGLE FANBOYS CAN AGREE ON!
...THAT IT'S AWFUL?
KEEP IN MIND, THE REAL THING'S SCREEN WON'T BE DRAWN WITH CRAYONS.
YOU GAVE IT HALF A PHYSICAL KEYBOARD??
AMEND

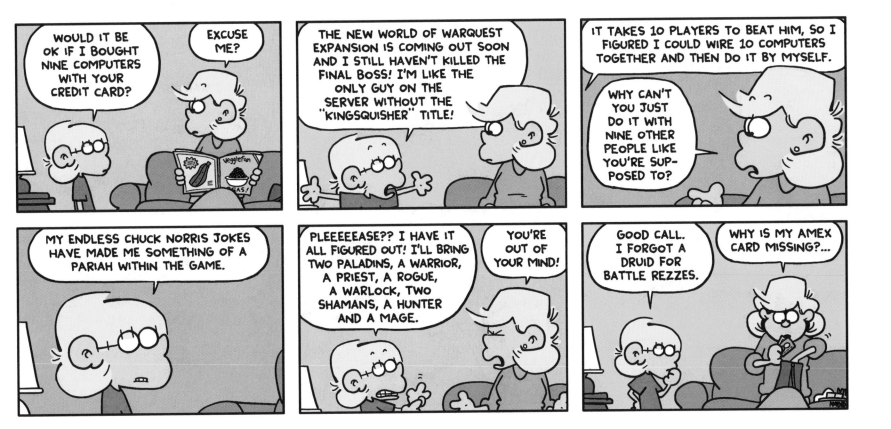

Panel 1:
WOULD IT BE OK IF I BOUGHT NINE COMPUTERS WITH YOUR CREDIT CARD?

EXCUSE ME?

Panel 2:
THE NEW WORLD OF WARQUEST EXPANSION IS COMING OUT SOON AND I STILL HAVEN'T KILLED THE FINAL BOSS! I'M LIKE THE ONLY GUY ON THE SERVER WITHOUT THE "KINGSQUISHER" TITLE!

Panel 3:
IT TAKES 10 PLAYERS TO BEAT HIM, SO I FIGURED I COULD WIRE 10 COMPUTERS TOGETHER AND THEN DO IT BY MYSELF.

WHY CAN'T YOU JUST DO IT WITH NINE OTHER PEOPLE LIKE YOU'RE SUPPOSED TO?

Panel 4:
MY ENDLESS CHUCK NORRIS JOKES HAVE MADE ME SOMETHING OF A PARIAH WITHIN THE GAME.

Panel 5:
PLEEEEEASE?? I HAVE IT ALL FIGURED OUT! I'LL BRING TWO PALADINS, A WARRIOR, A PRIEST, A ROGUE, A WARLOCK, TWO SHAMANS, A HUNTER AND A MAGE.

YOU'RE OUT OF YOUR MIND!

Panel 6:
GOOD CALL. I FORGOT A DRUID FOR BATTLE REZZES.

WHY IS MY AMEX CARD MISSING?...

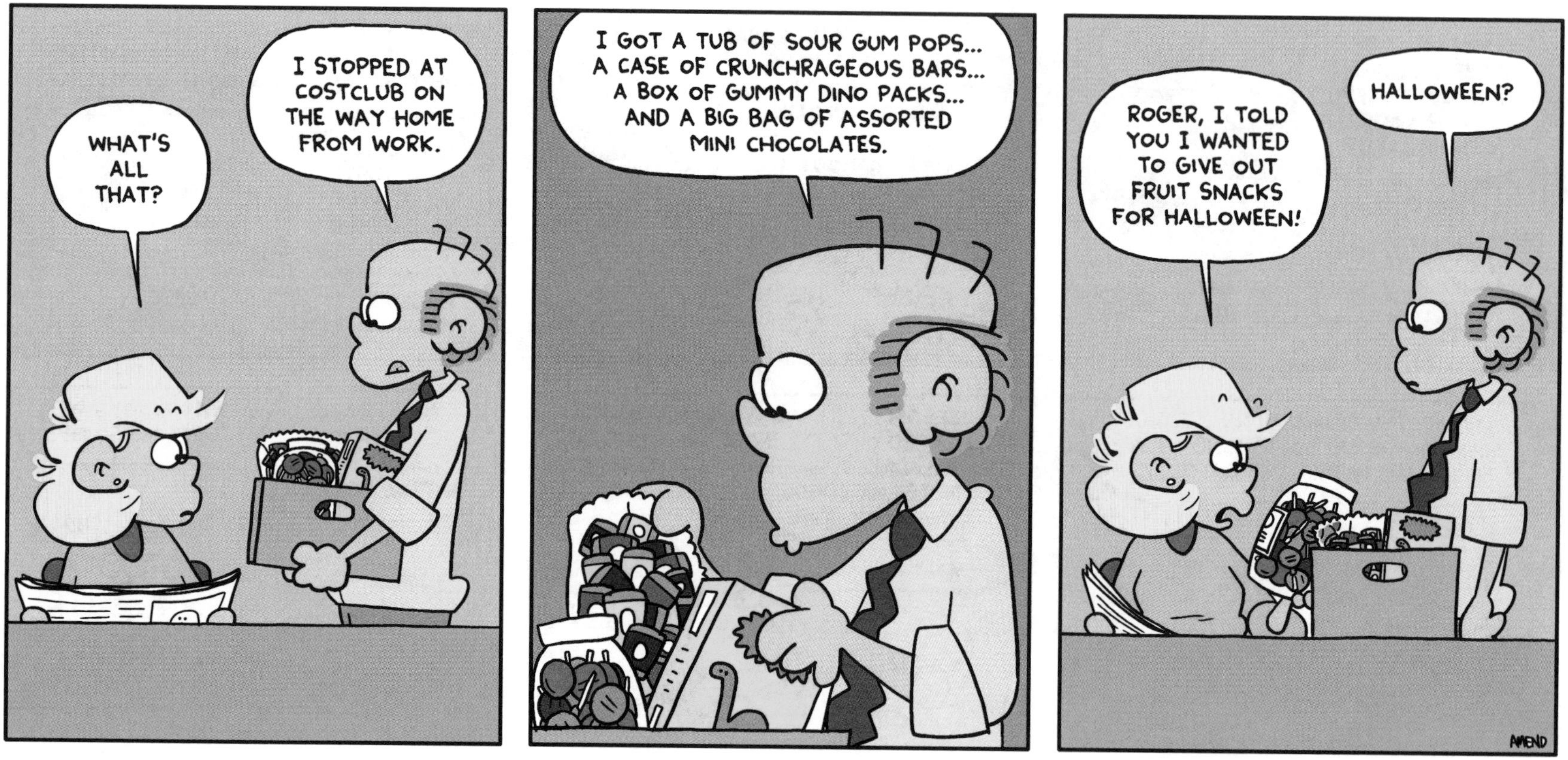
WHAT'S ALL THAT?
I STOPPED AT COSTCLUB ON THE WAY HOME FROM WORK.
I GOT A TUB OF SOUR GUM POPS... A CASE OF CRUNCHRAGEOUS BARS... A BOX OF GUMMY DINO PACKS... AND A BIG BAG OF ASSORTED MINI CHOCOLATES.
ROGER, I TOLD YOU I WANTED TO GIVE OUT FRUIT SNACKS FOR HALLOWEEN!
HALLOWEEN?
AMEND

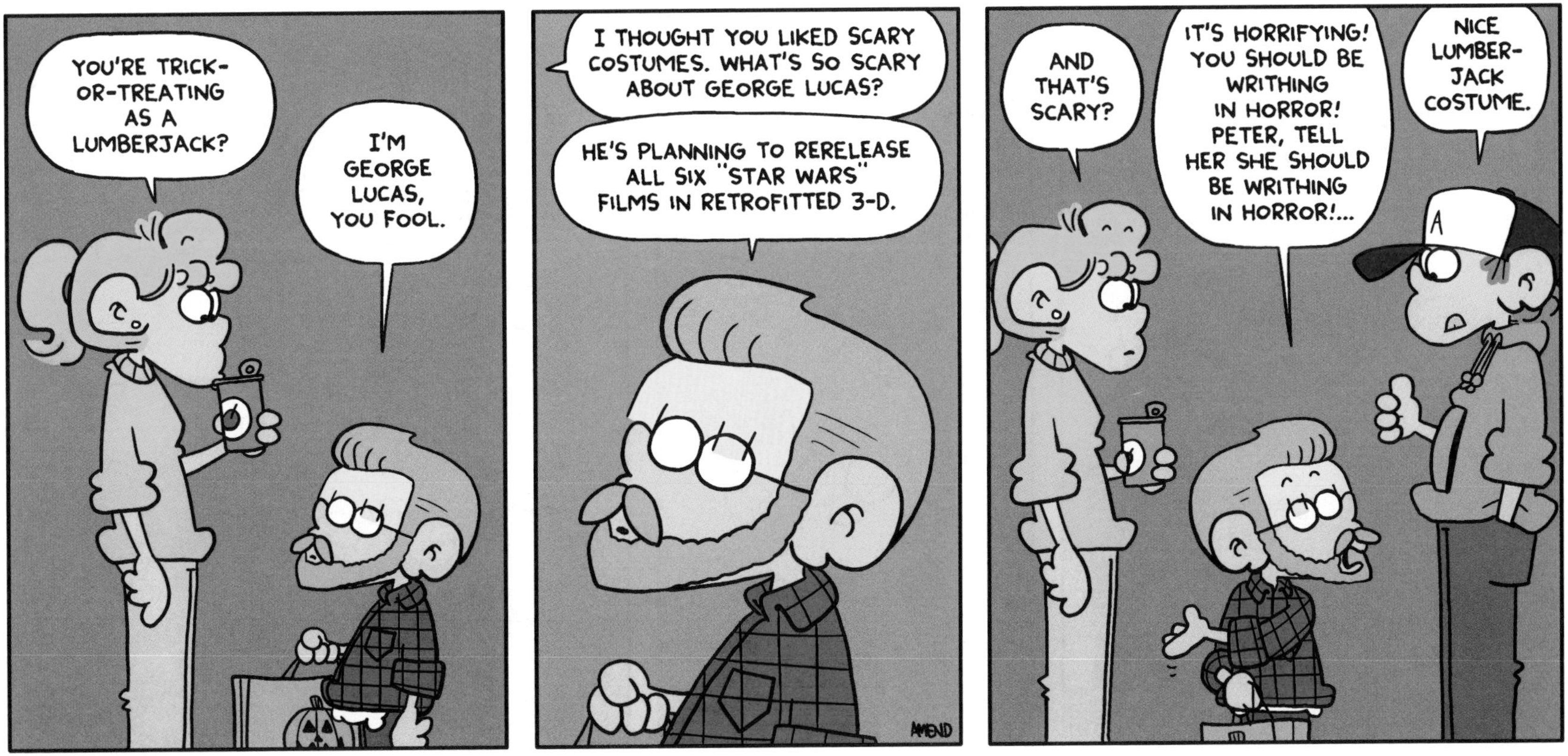
YOU'RE TRICK-OR-TREATING AS A LUMBERJACK?
I'M GEORGE LUCAS, YOU FOOL.
I THOUGHT YOU LIKED SCARY COSTUMES. WHAT'S SO SCARY ABOUT GEORGE LUCAS?
HE'S PLANNING TO RERELEASE ALL SIX "STAR WARS" FILMS IN RETROFITTED 3-D.
AMEND
AND THAT'S SCARY?
IT'S HORRIFYING! YOU SHOULD BE WRITHING IN HORROR! PETER, TELL HER SHE SHOULD BE WRITHING IN HORROR!...
NICE LUMBER-JACK COSTUME.

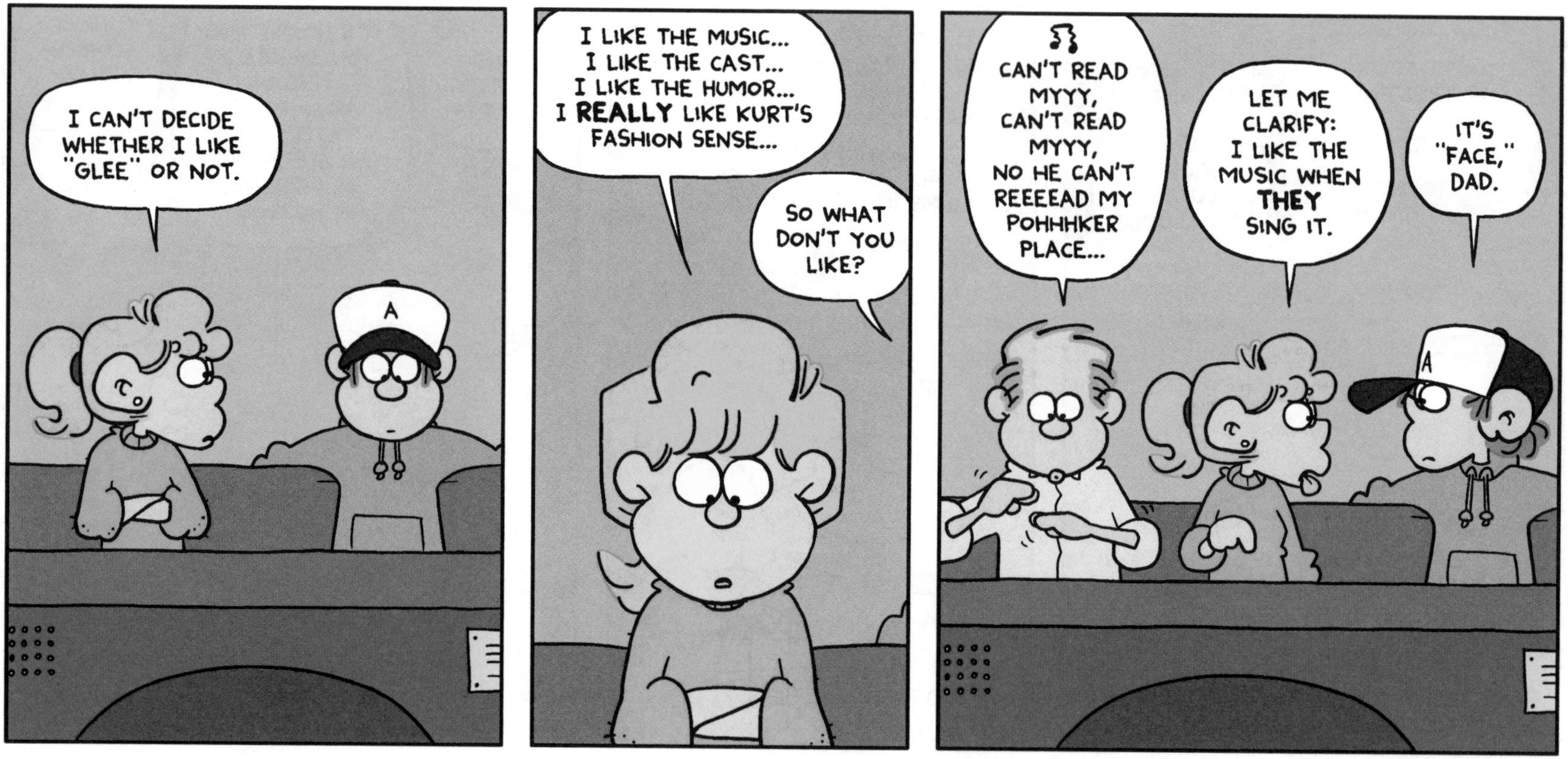
I CAN'T DECIDE WHETHER I LIKE "GLEE" OR NOT.
I LIKE THE MUSIC... I LIKE THE CAST... I LIKE THE HUMOR... I **REALLY** LIKE KURT'S FASHION SENSE...
SO WHAT DON'T YOU LIKE?
CAN'T READ MYYY, CAN'T READ MYYY, NO HE CAN'T REEEEAD MY POHHHKER PLACE...
LET ME CLARIFY: I LIKE THE MUSIC WHEN **THEY** SING IT.
IT'S "FACE," DAD.

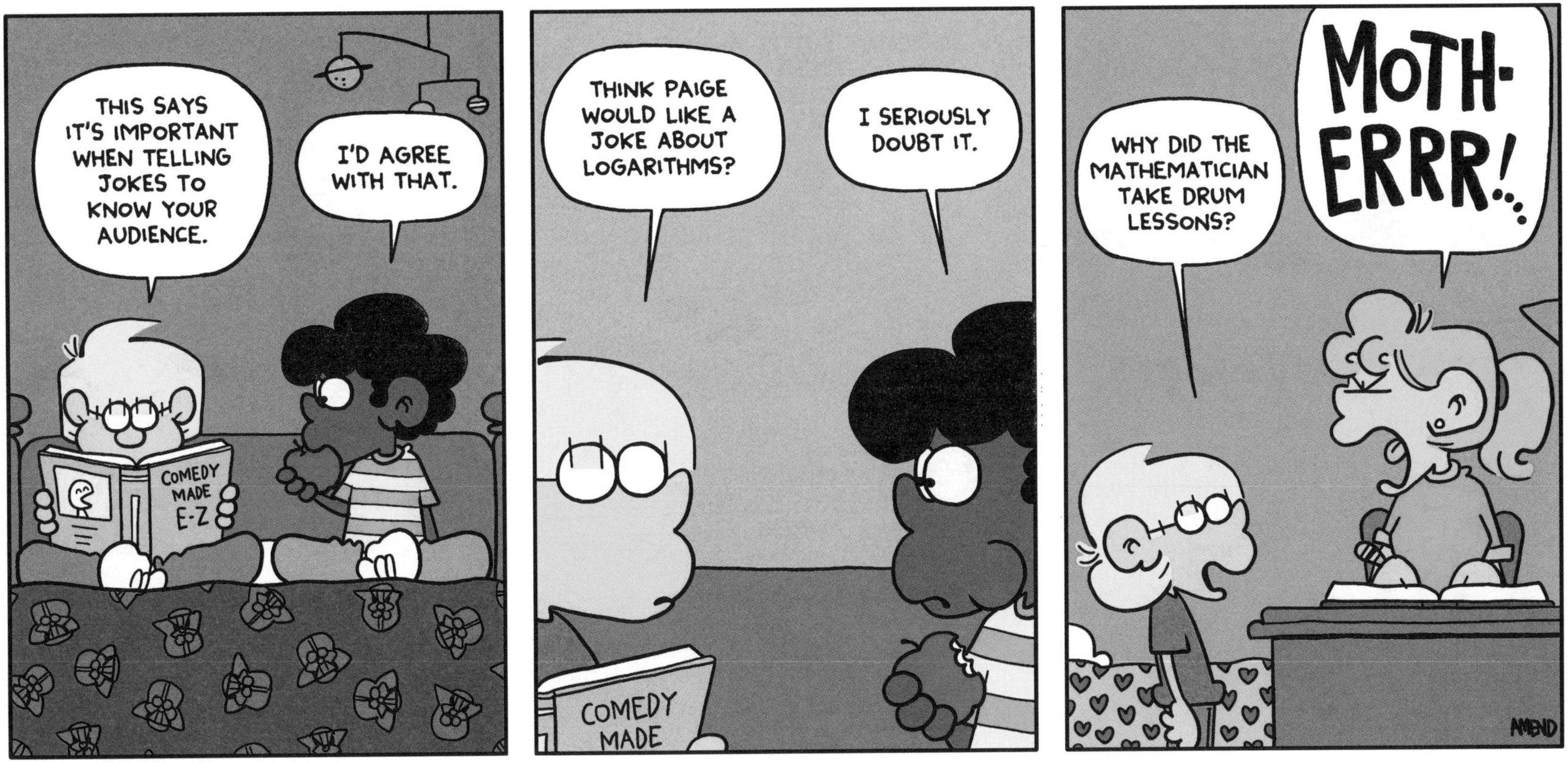
THIS SAYS IT'S IMPORTANT WHEN TELLING JOKES TO KNOW YOUR AUDIENCE.
I'D AGREE WITH THAT.
COMEDY MADE E-Z
THINK PAIGE WOULD LIKE A JOKE ABOUT LOGARITHMS?
I SERIOUSLY DOUBT IT.
COMEDY MADE
WHY DID THE MATHEMATICIAN TAKE DRUM LESSONS?
MOTH-ERRR!...
AMEND

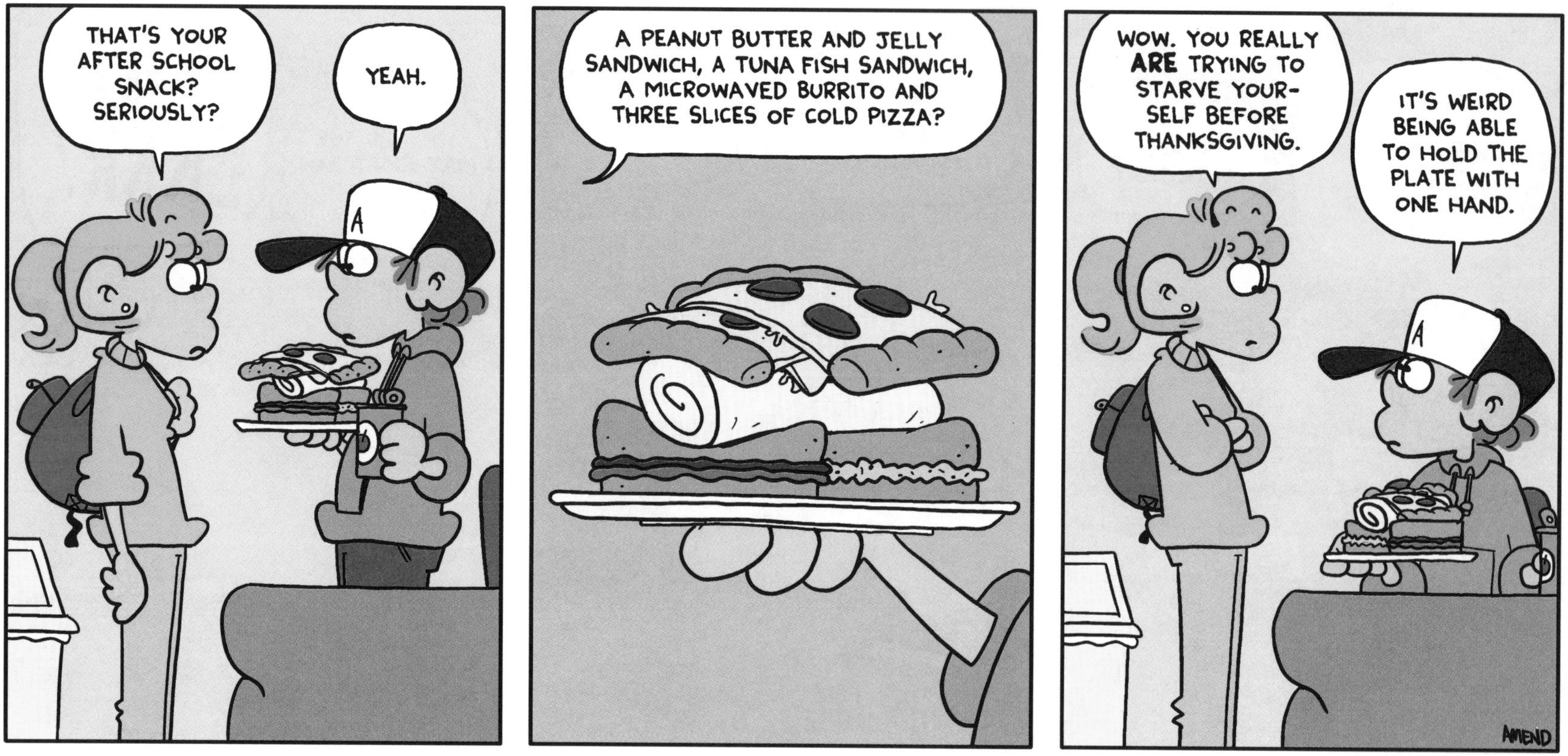
THAT'S YOUR AFTER SCHOOL SNACK? SERIOUSLY?
YEAH.
A PEANUT BUTTER AND JELLY SANDWICH, A TUNA FISH SANDWICH, A MICROWAVED BURRITO AND THREE SLICES OF COLD PIZZA?
WOW. YOU REALLY **ARE** TRYING TO STARVE YOUR-SELF BEFORE THANKSGIVING.
IT'S WEIRD BEING ABLE TO HOLD THE PLATE WITH ONE HAND.
AMEND

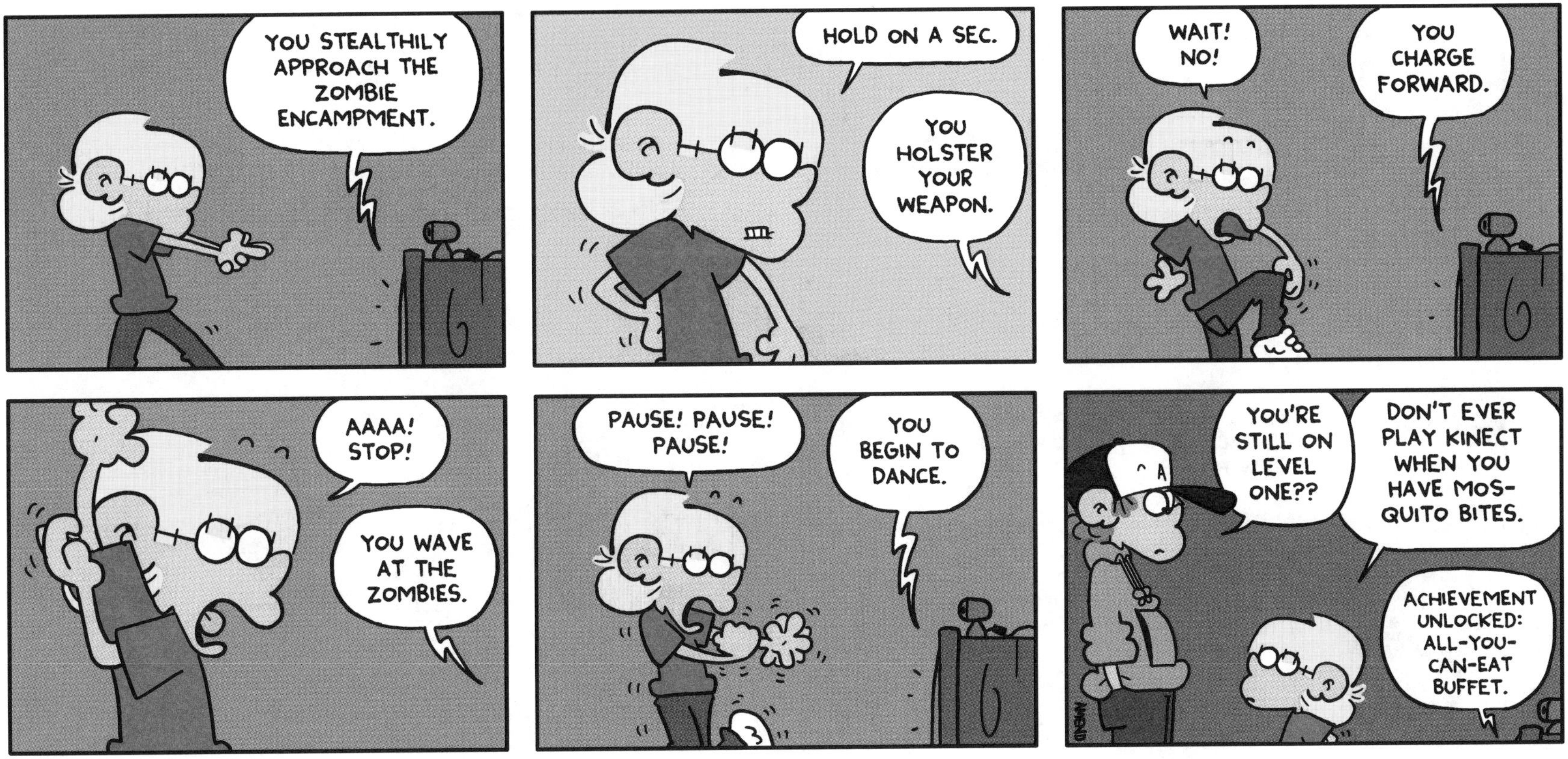
YOU STEALTHILY APPROACH THE ZOMBIE ENCAMPMENT.
HOLD ON A SEC.
YOU HOLSTER YOUR WEAPON.
WAIT! NO!
YOU CHARGE FORWARD.
AAAA! STOP!
YOU WAVE AT THE ZOMBIES.
PAUSE! PAUSE! PAUSE!
YOU BEGIN TO DANCE.
YOU'RE STILL ON LEVEL ONE??
DON'T EVER PLAY KINECT WHEN YOU HAVE MOS-QUITO BITES.
ACHIEVEMENT UNLOCKED: ALL-YOU-CAN-EAT BUFFET.

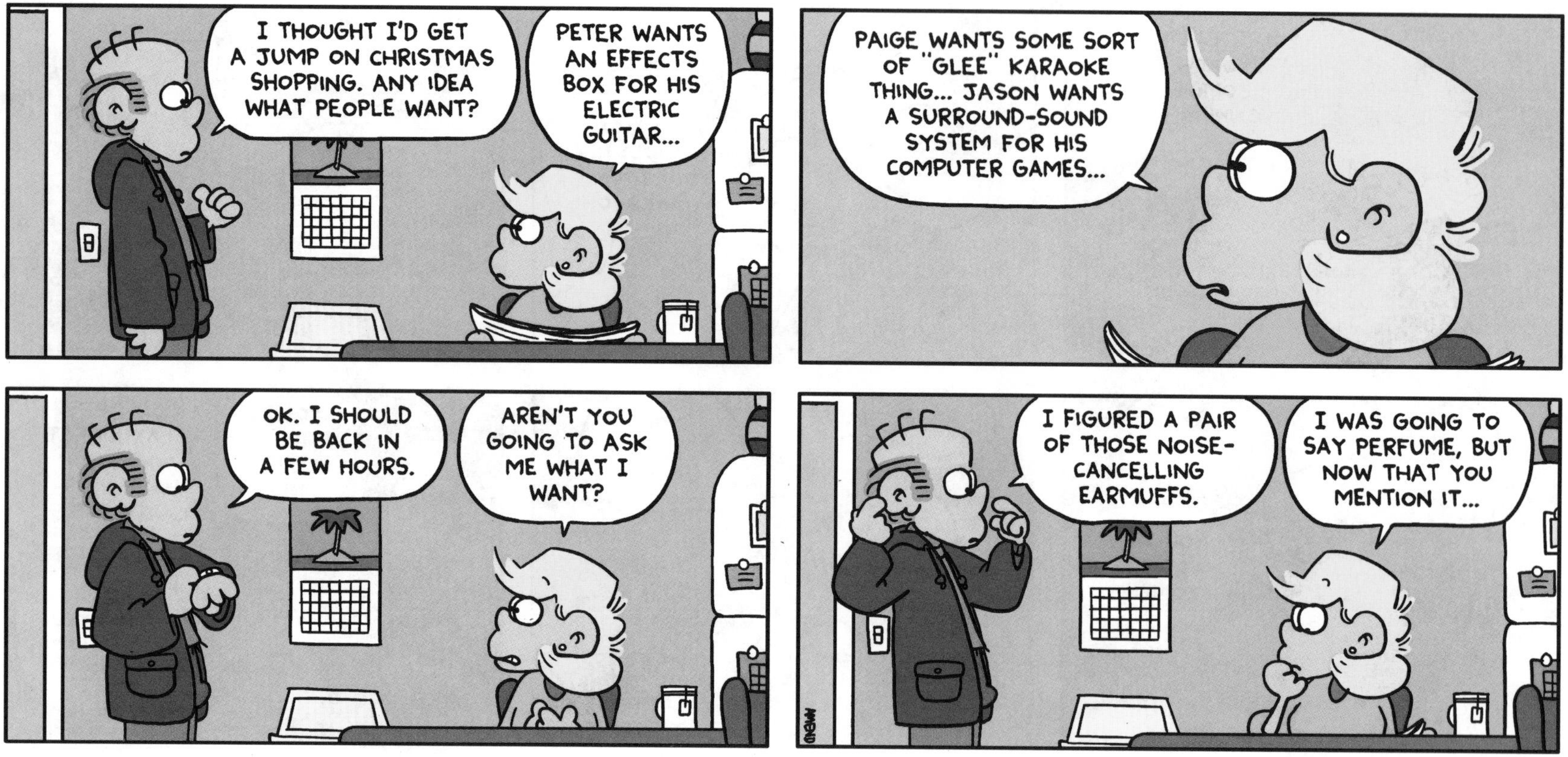
I THOUGHT I'D GET A JUMP ON CHRISTMAS SHOPPING. ANY IDEA WHAT PEOPLE WANT?
PETER WANTS AN EFFECTS BOX FOR HIS ELECTRIC GUITAR...
PAIGE WANTS SOME SORT OF "GLEE" KARAOKE THING... JASON WANTS A SURROUND-SOUND SYSTEM FOR HIS COMPUTER GAMES...
OK. I SHOULD BE BACK IN A FEW HOURS.
AREN'T YOU GOING TO ASK ME WHAT I WANT?
I FIGURED A PAIR OF THOSE NOISE-CANCELLING EARMUFFS.
I WAS GOING TO SAY PERFUME, BUT NOW THAT YOU MENTION IT...

DON'T YOU HAVE A BIG BOOK REPORT TO DO?
I'M WRITING IT AS WE SPEAK.
NO YOU AREN'T! YOU'RE PLAYING WORLD OF WARQUEST!
UNLIKE SOME PEOPLE, I CAN MULTITASK.
iFruit
SEE ALL THESE MONSTERS I'M KILLING? I'M DOING IT IN SUCH A WAY THAT THEIR CORPSES ARE ARRANGED TO FORM LETTERS AND WORDS ON THE GROUND.
THEN IT'S A SIMPLE MATTER OF PRINTING OUT SCREENSHOTS FOR MY TEACHER.
iFruit
MY INTRODUCTORY PARAGRAPH ALONE GOT ME 240,000 EXPERIENCE POINTS AND A SWEET BLUE DAGGER.
AND MOM WONDERS WHY I GO PSYCHO THAT YOUR GRADES ARE BETTER THAN MINE.
OH, SHOOT. THOSE OGRES SHOULD'VE BEEN CAPITALIZED.
AMEND

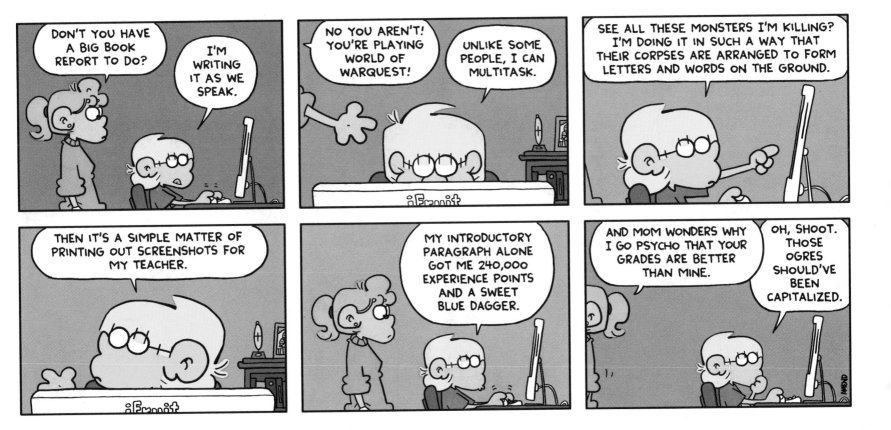

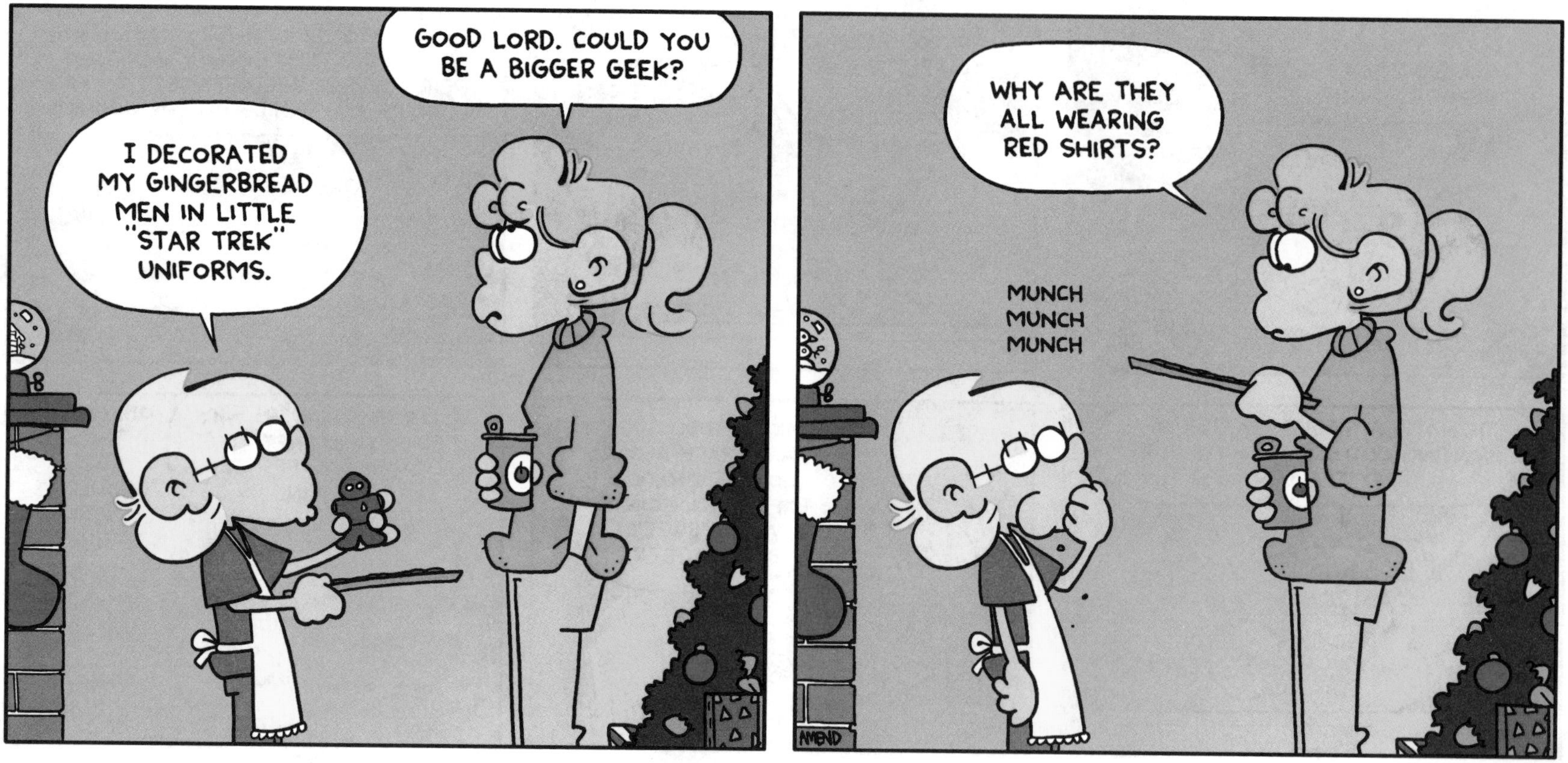
I DECORATED MY GINGERBREAD MEN IN LITTLE "STAR TREK" UNIFORMS.
GOOD LORD. COULD YOU BE A BIGGER GEEK?
MUNCH MUNCH MUNCH
WHY ARE THEY ALL WEARING RED SHIRTS?
AMEND

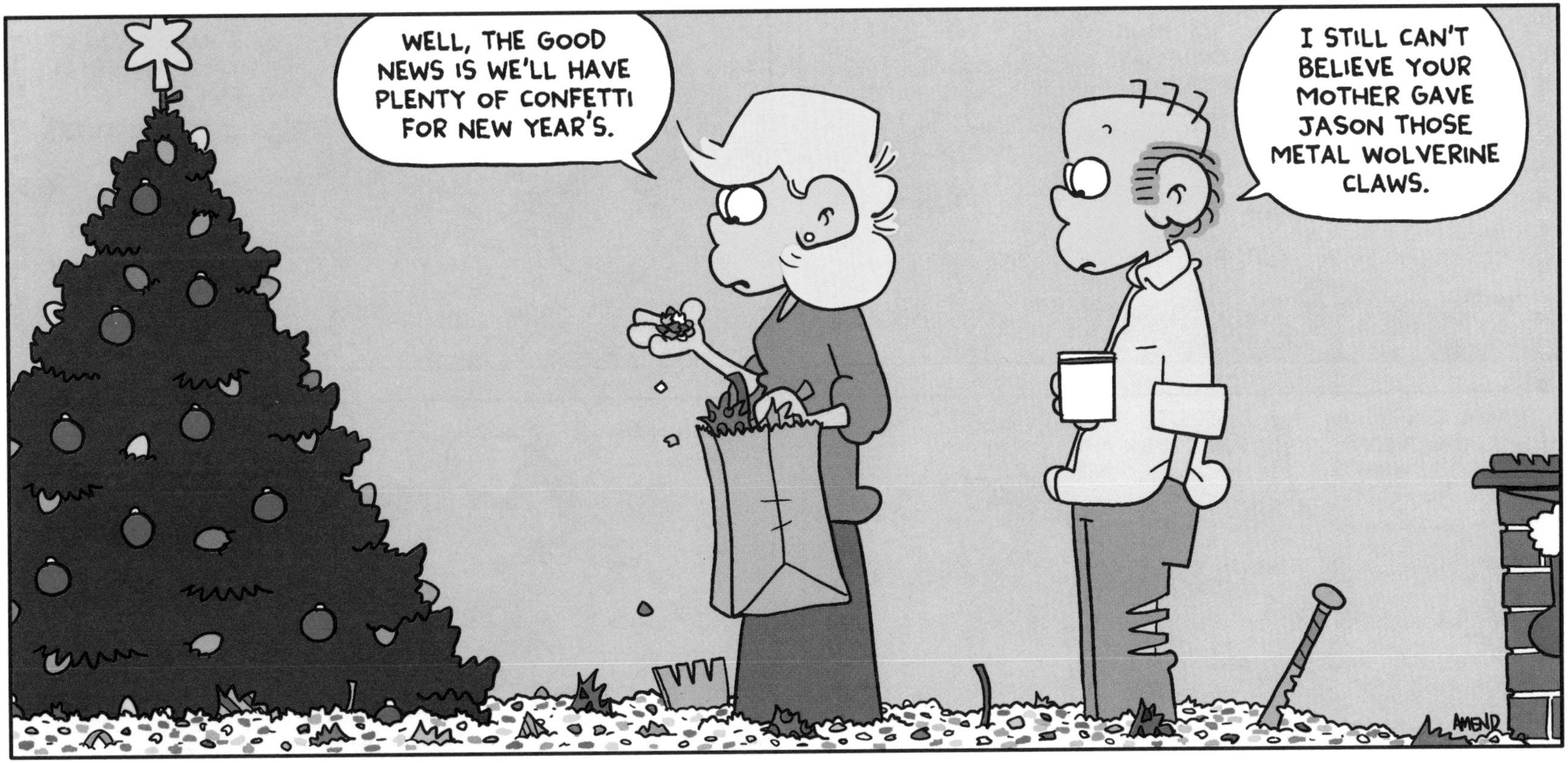
WELL, THE GOOD NEWS IS WE'LL HAVE PLENTY OF CONFETTI FOR NEW YEAR'S.
I STILL CAN'T BELIEVE YOUR MOTHER GAVE JASON THOSE METAL WOLVERINE CLAWS.
AMEND

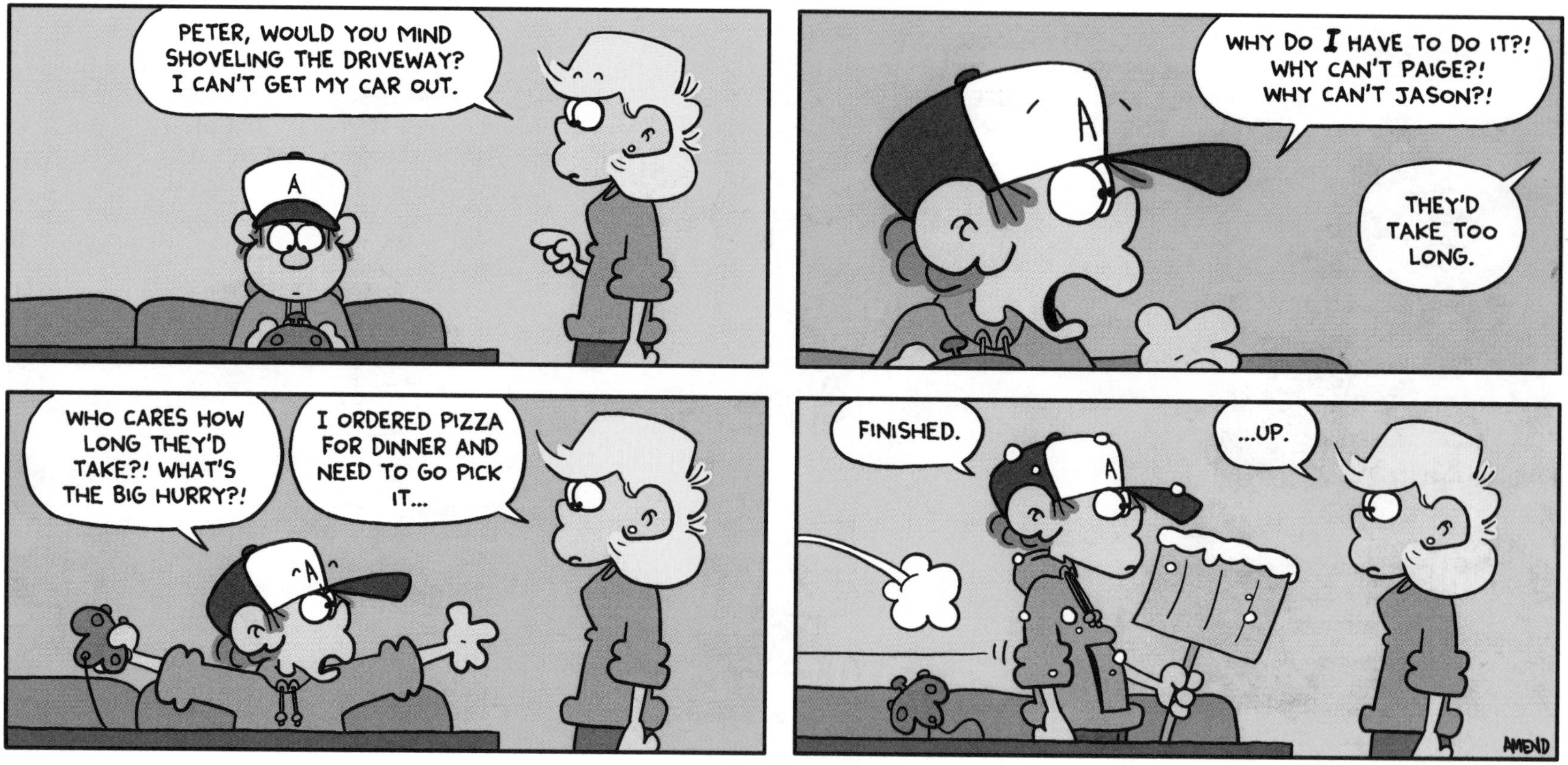
PETER, WOULD YOU MIND SHOVELING THE DRIVEWAY? I CAN'T GET MY CAR OUT.
WHY DO I HAVE TO DO IT?! WHY CAN'T PAIGE?! WHY CAN'T JASON?!
THEY'D TAKE TOO LONG.
WHO CARES HOW LONG THEY'D TAKE?! WHAT'S THE BIG HURRY?!
I ORDERED PIZZA FOR DINNER AND NEED TO GO PICK IT...
FINISHED.
...UP.
AMEND

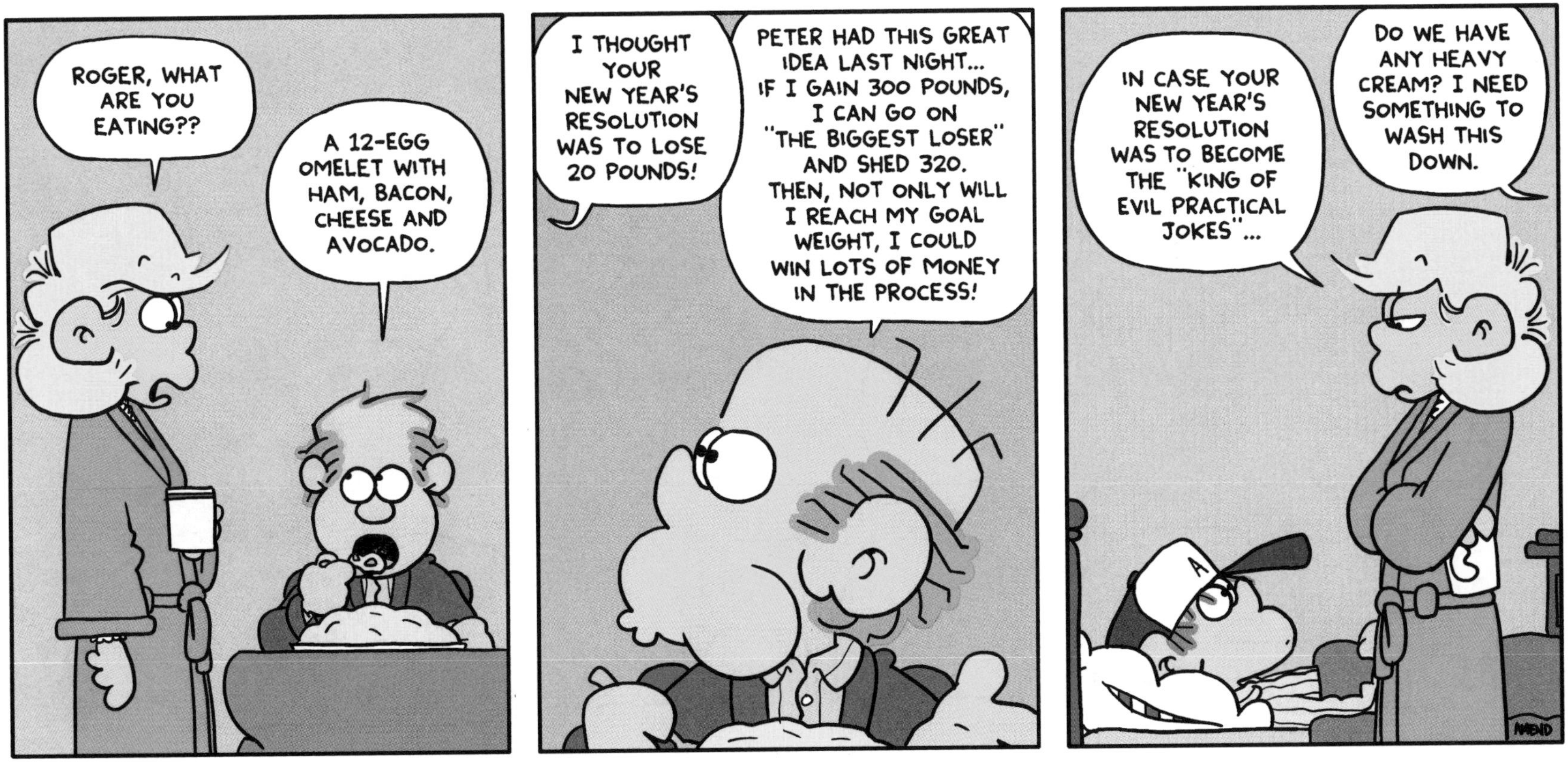
ROGER, WHAT ARE YOU EATING??
A 12-EGG OMELET WITH HAM, BACON, CHEESE AND AVOCADO.
I THOUGHT YOUR NEW YEAR'S RESOLUTION WAS TO LOSE 20 POUNDS!
PETER HAD THIS GREAT IDEA LAST NIGHT... IF I GAIN 300 POUNDS, I CAN GO ON "THE BIGGEST LOSER" AND SHED 320. THEN, NOT ONLY WILL I REACH MY GOAL WEIGHT, I COULD WIN LOTS OF MONEY IN THE PROCESS!
IN CASE YOUR NEW YEAR'S RESOLUTION WAS TO BECOME THE "KING OF EVIL PRACTICAL JOKES"...
DO WE HAVE ANY HEAVY CREAM? I NEED SOMETHING TO WASH THIS DOWN.
A
AMEND

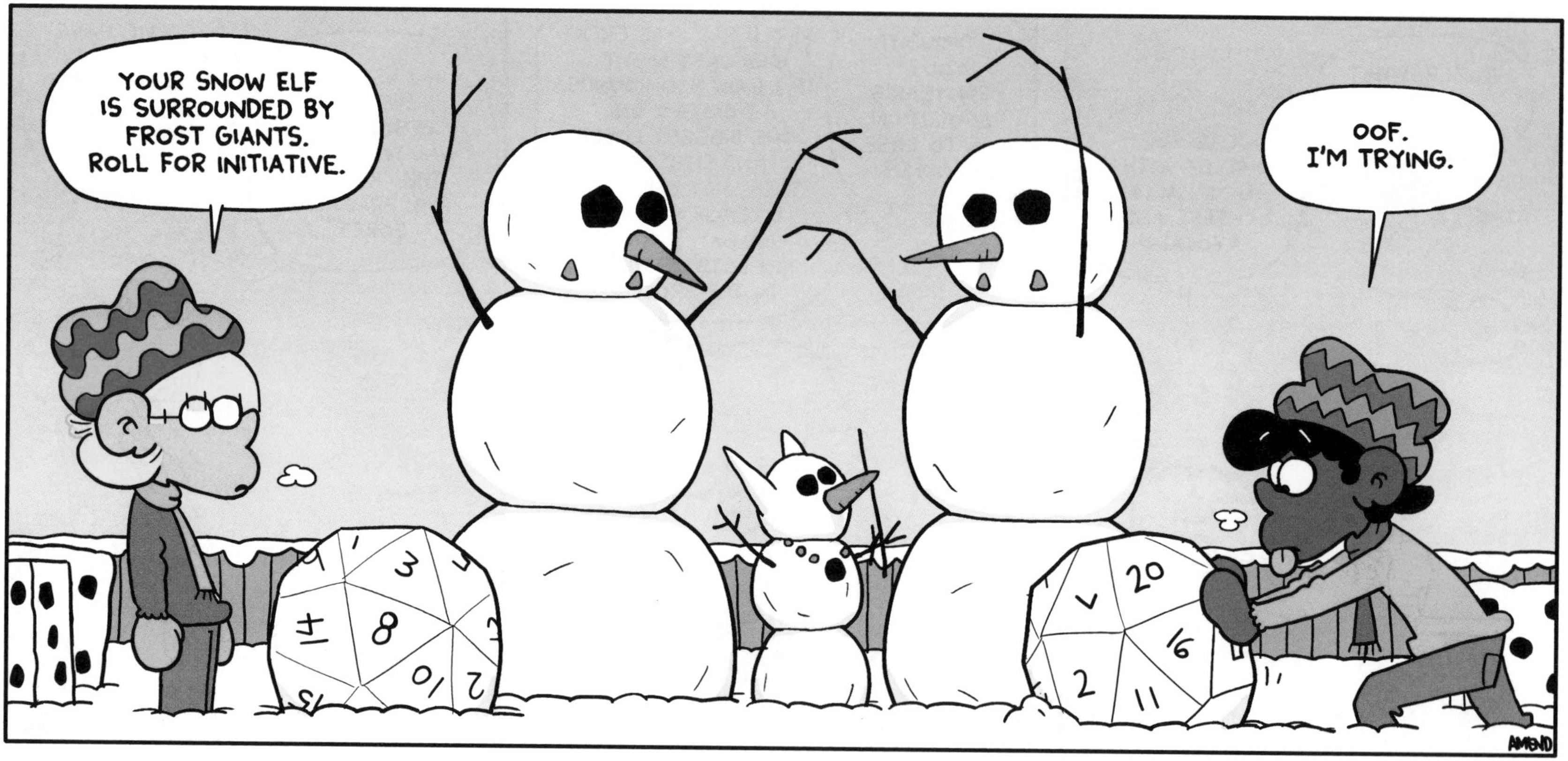
YOUR SNOW ELF IS SURROUNDED BY FROST GIANTS. ROLL FOR INITIATIVE.
OOF. I'M TRYING.
AMEND

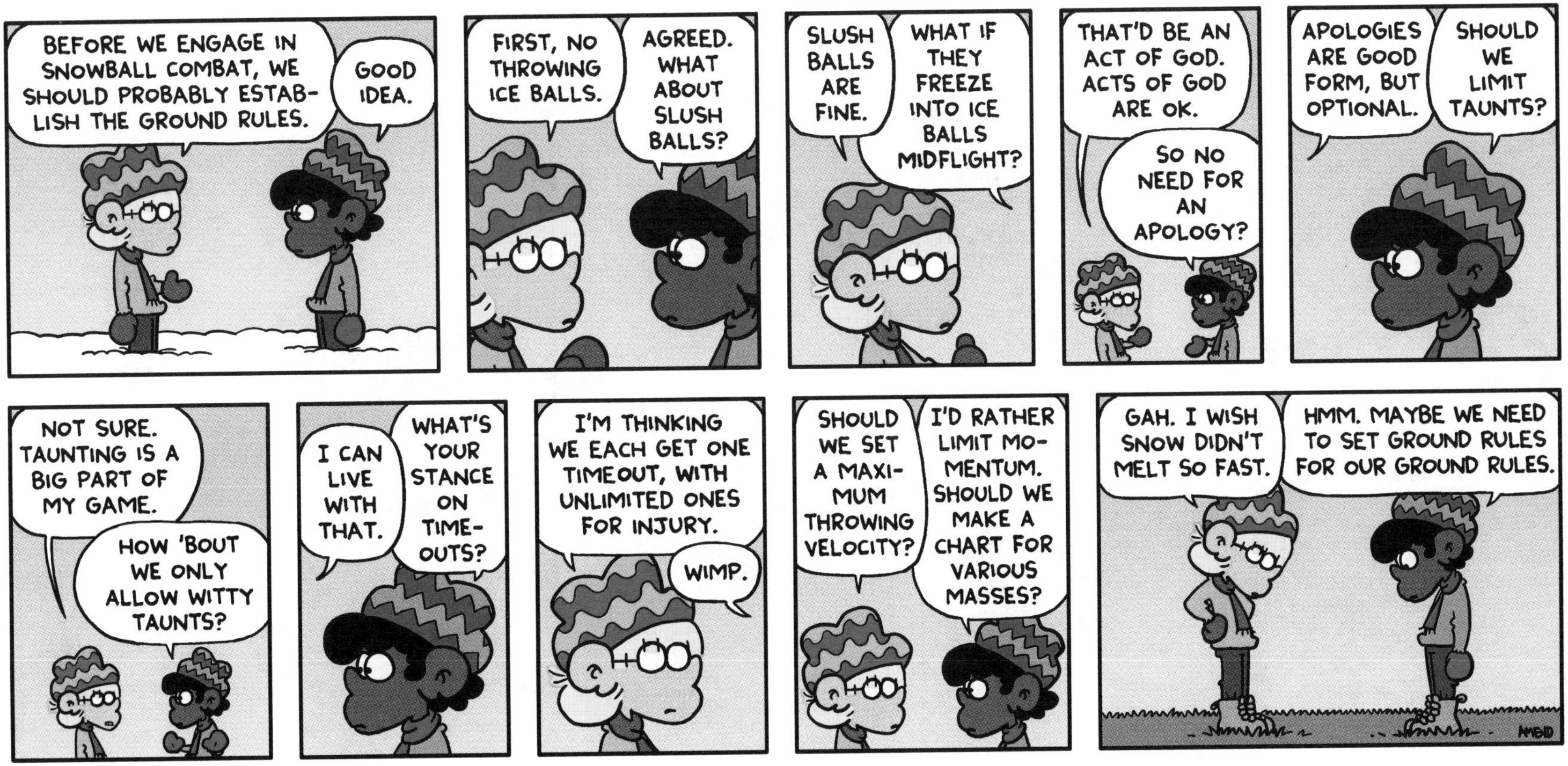
BEFORE WE ENGAGE IN SNOWBALL COMBAT, WE SHOULD PROBABLY ESTABLISH THE GROUND RULES.
GOOD IDEA.
FIRST, NO THROWING ICE BALLS.
AGREED. WHAT ABOUT SLUSH BALLS?
SLUSH BALLS ARE FINE.
WHAT IF THEY FREEZE INTO ICE BALLS MIDFLIGHT?
THAT'D BE AN ACT OF GOD. ACTS OF GOD ARE OK.
SO NO NEED FOR AN APOLOGY?
APOLOGIES ARE GOOD FORM, BUT OPTIONAL.
SHOULD WE LIMIT TAUNTS?
NOT SURE. TAUNTING IS A BIG PART OF MY GAME.
HOW 'BOUT WE ONLY ALLOW WITTY TAUNTS?
I CAN LIVE WITH THAT.
WHAT'S YOUR STANCE ON TIME-OUTS?
I'M THINKING WE EACH GET ONE TIMEOUT, WITH UNLIMITED ONES FOR INJURY.
WIMP.
SHOULD WE SET A MAXIMUM THROWING VELOCITY?
I'D RATHER LIMIT MOMENTUM. SHOULD WE MAKE A CHART FOR VARIOUS MASSES?
GAH. I WISH SNOW DIDN'T MELT SO FAST.
HMM. MAYBE WE NEED TO SET GROUND RULES FOR OUR GROUND RULES.
AMBID

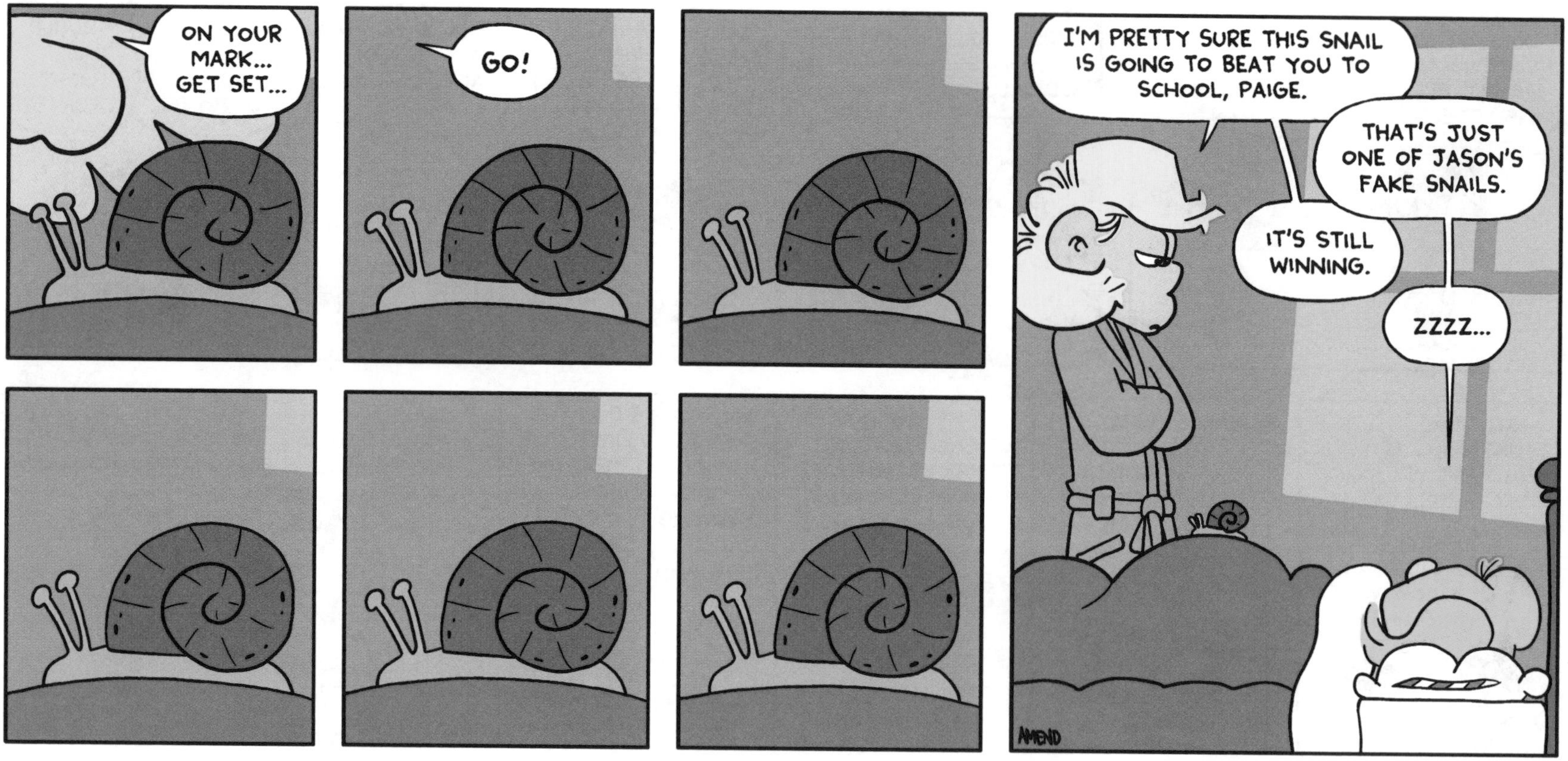
ON YOUR MARK... GET SET...
GO!
I'M PRETTY SURE THIS SNAIL IS GOING TO BEAT YOU TO SCHOOL, PAIGE.
THAT'S JUST ONE OF JASON'S FAKE SNAILS.
IT'S STILL WINNING.
ZZZZ...
AMEND

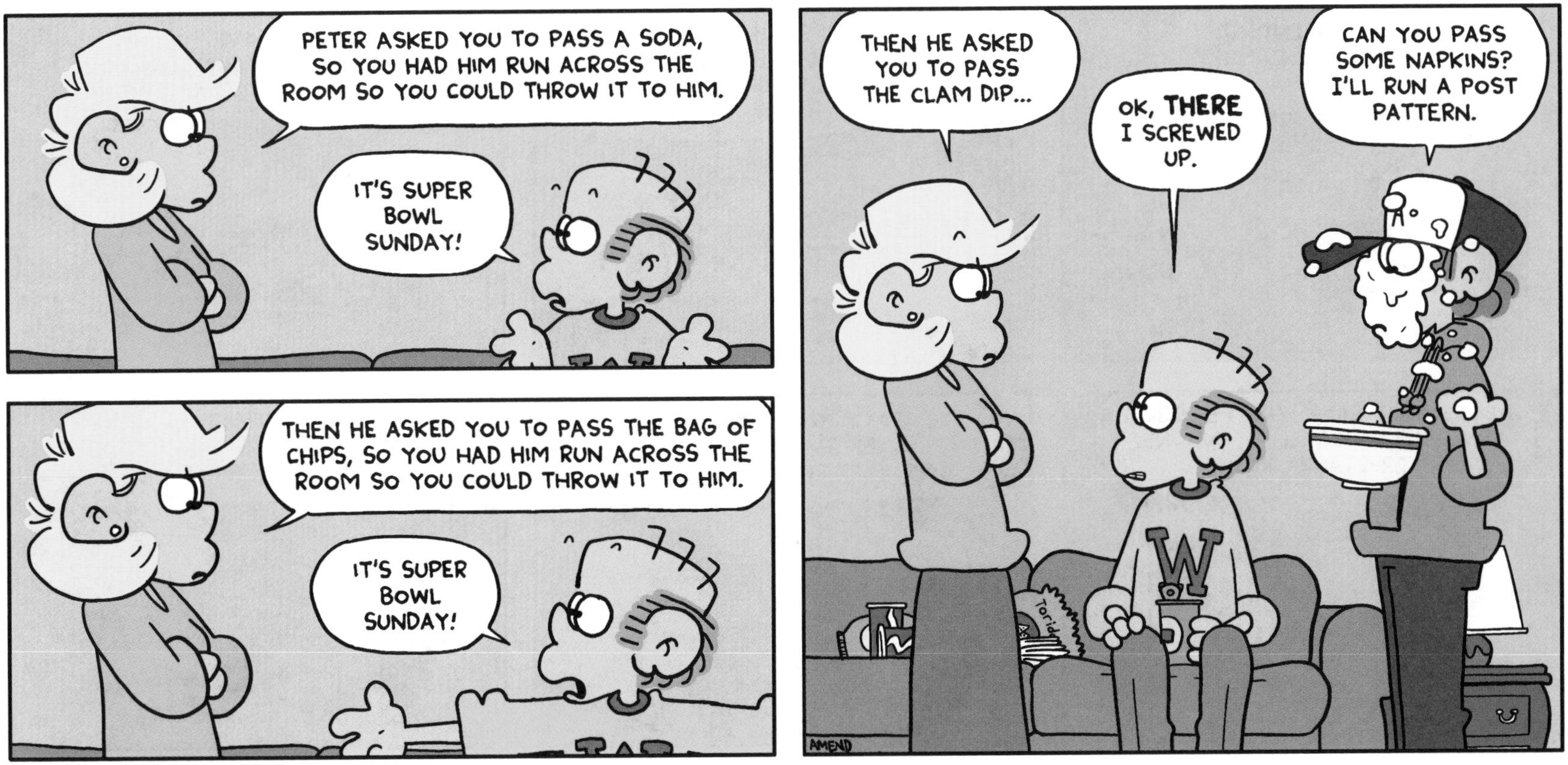
PETER ASKED YOU TO PASS A SODA, SO YOU HAD HIM RUN ACROSS THE ROOM SO YOU COULD THROW IT TO HIM.
IT'S SUPER BOWL SUNDAY!
THEN HE ASKED YOU TO PASS THE BAG OF CHIPS, SO YOU HAD HIM RUN ACROSS THE ROOM SO YOU COULD THROW IT TO HIM.
IT'S SUPER BOWL SUNDAY!
THEN HE ASKED YOU TO PASS THE CLAM DIP...
OK, **THERE** I SCREWED UP.
CAN YOU PASS SOME NAPKINS? I'LL RUN A POST PATTERN.
W
AMEND

THIS IS THE VALENTINE'S CARD YOU'RE GIVING ME?? THIS??
IT'S JUST A GENERIC STORE-BOUGHT CARD! THERE'S NOTHING PERSONAL ABOUT IT AT ALL!
THE CARD I GAVE YOU WAS HANDMADE! IT TOOK THOUGHT! IT TOOK TIME!
YOURS JUST SAYS "FROM EILEEN"! MINE HAD COLOR ILLUSTRATIONS! A 12-STANZA POEM!
I'LL ADMIT "YOUR NOXIOUS FACE" AND "GREEN TOXIC WASTE" WAS AN IMPERFECT RHYME, BUT STILL...
DID I REALLY DESERVE THIS?!? WHY ARE YOU ROLLING YOUR EYES?!?
AMEND

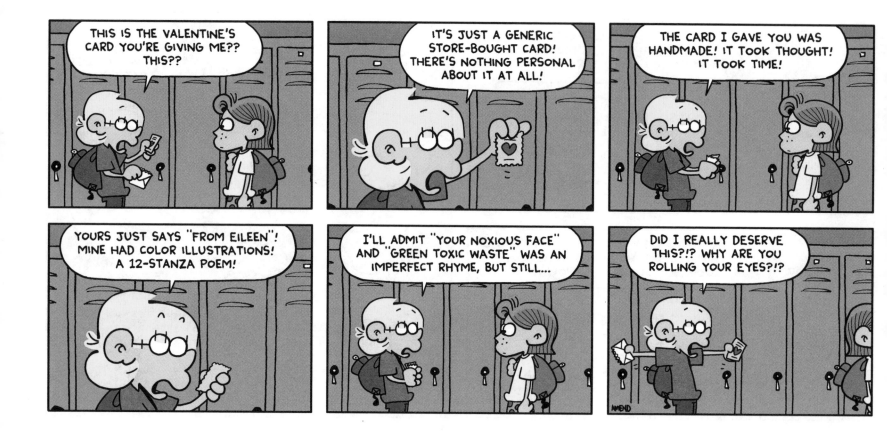

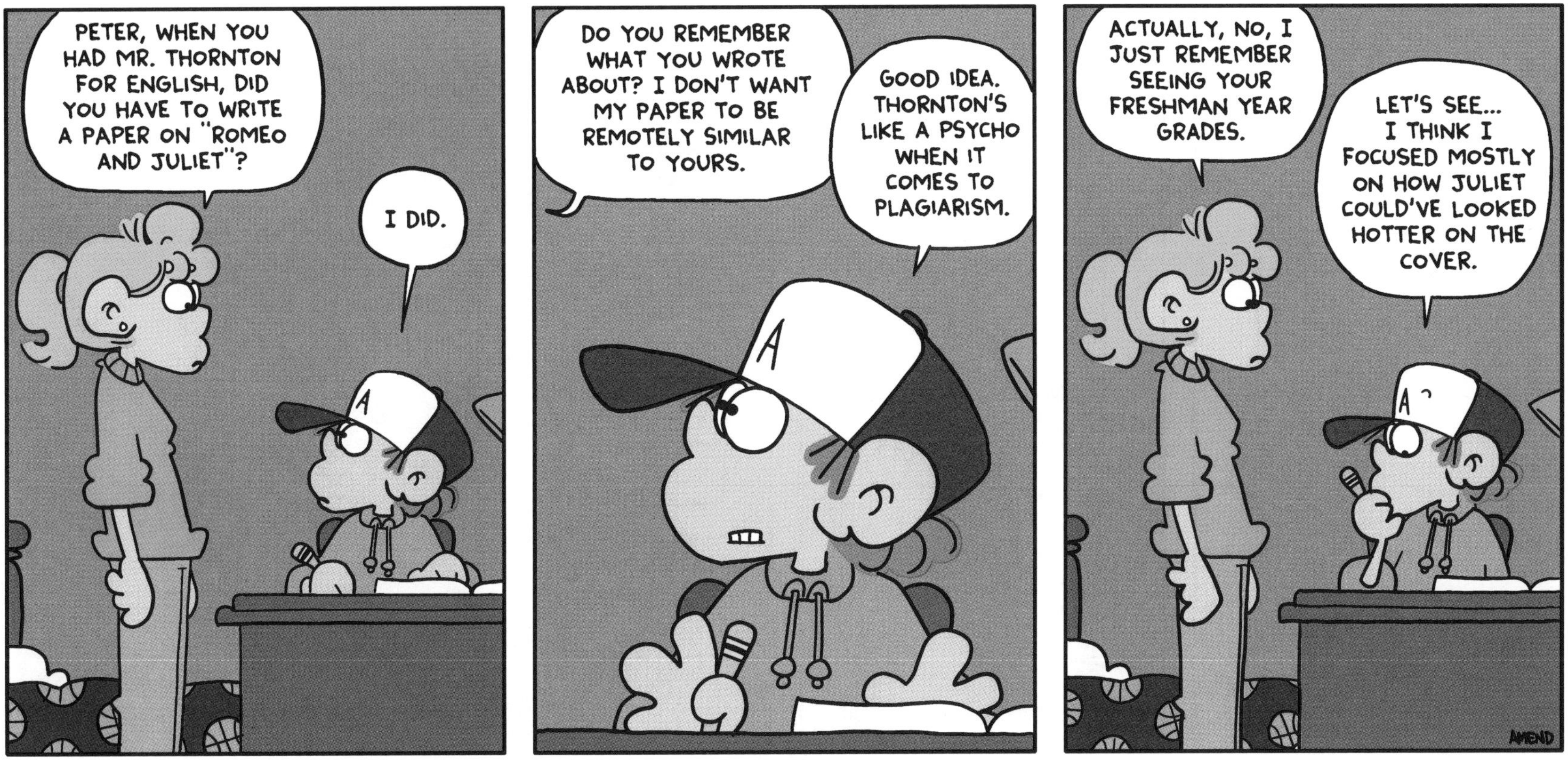
PETER, WHEN YOU HAD MR. THORNTON FOR ENGLISH, DID YOU HAVE TO WRITE A PAPER ON "ROMEO AND JULIET"?
I DID.
DO YOU REMEMBER WHAT YOU WROTE ABOUT? I DON'T WANT MY PAPER TO BE REMOTELY SIMILAR TO YOURS.
GOOD IDEA. THORNTON'S LIKE A PSYCHO WHEN IT COMES TO PLAGIARISM.
ACTUALLY, NO, I JUST REMEMBER SEEING YOUR FRESHMAN YEAR GRADES.
LET'S SEE... I THINK I FOCUSED MOSTLY ON HOW JULIET COULD'VE LOOKED HOTTER ON THE COVER.
AMEND

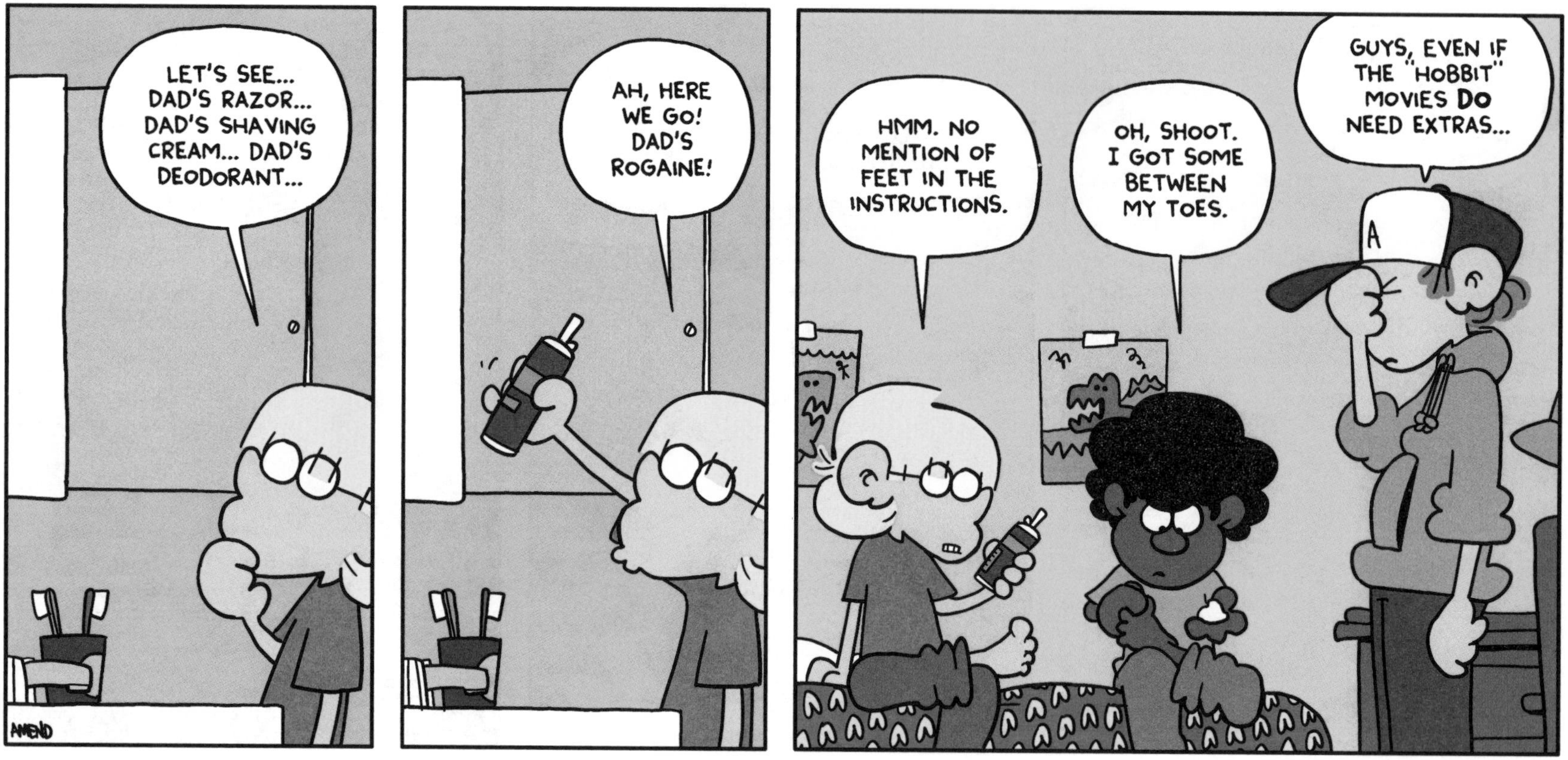
LET'S SEE... DAD'S RAZOR... DAD'S SHAVING CREAM... DAD'S DEODORANT...
AMEND
AH, HERE WE GO! DAD'S ROGAINE!
HMM. NO MENTION OF FEET IN THE INSTRUCTIONS.
OH, SHOOT. I GOT SOME BETWEEN MY TOES.
GUYS, EVEN IF THE "HOBBIT" MOVIES DO NEED EXTRAS...
A

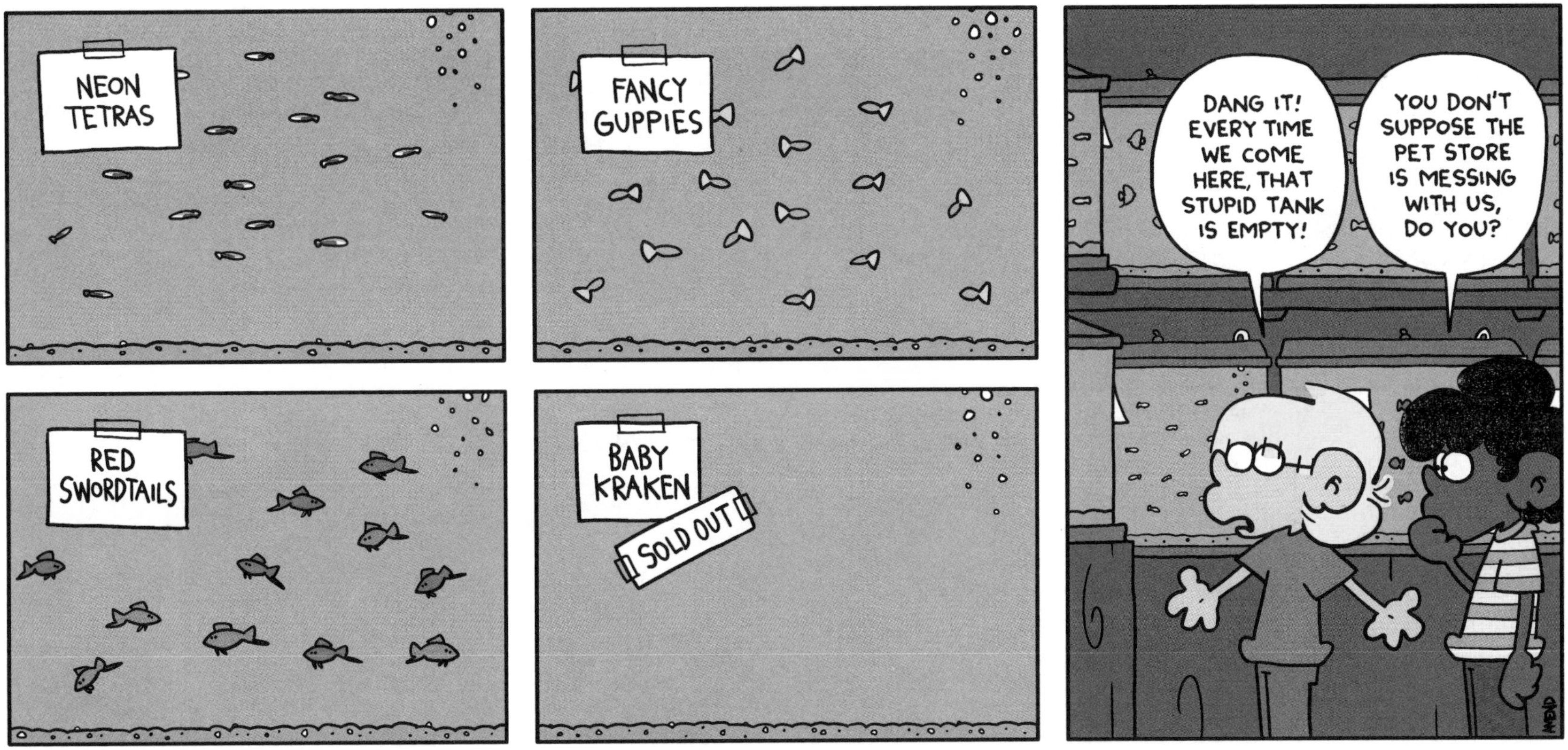
NEON TETRAS
FANCY GUPPIES
RED SWORDTAILS
BABY KRAKEN
SOLD OUT
DANG IT! EVERY TIME WE COME HERE, THAT STUPID TANK IS EMPTY!
YOU DON'T SUPPOSE THE PET STORE IS MESSING WITH US, DO YOU?

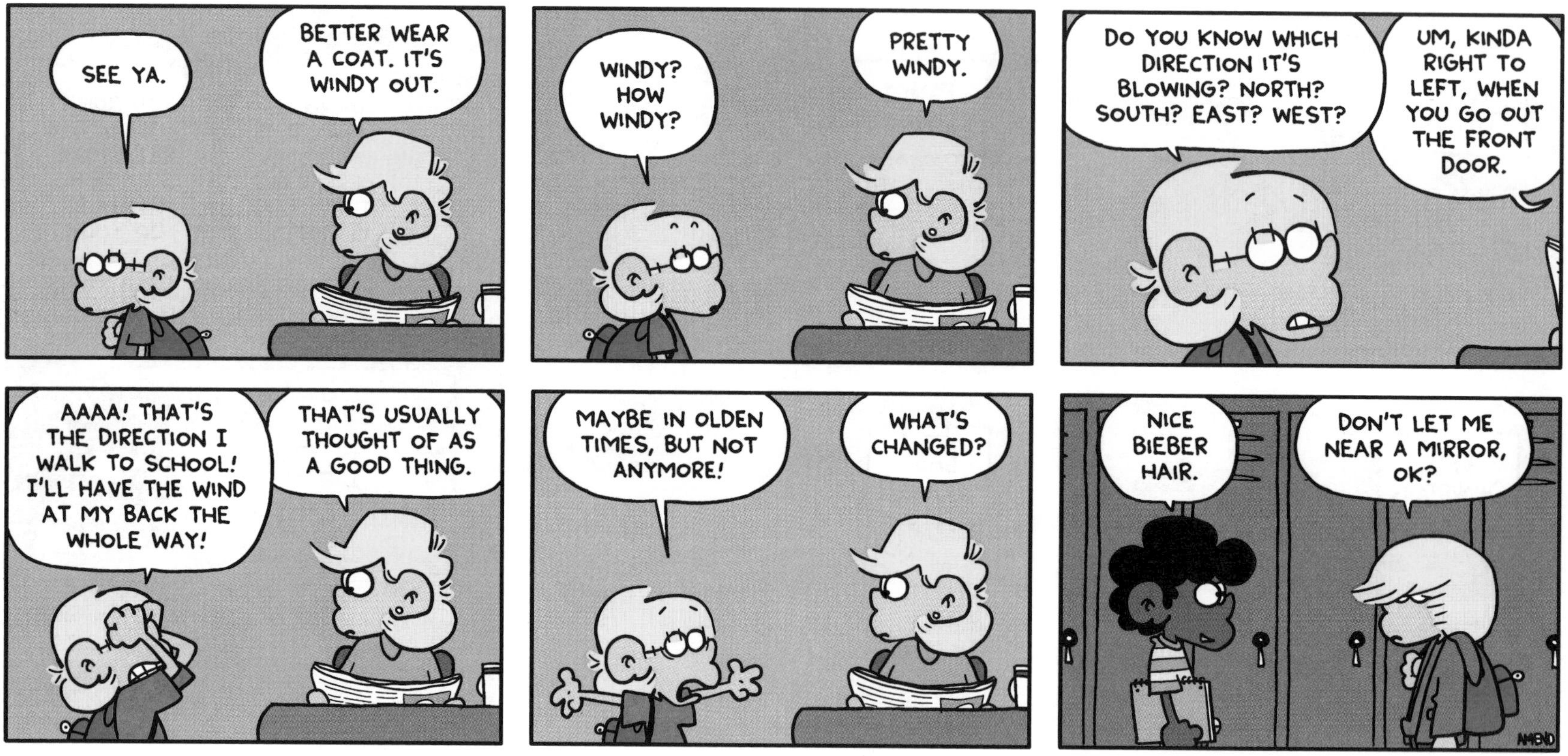
SEE YA.
BETTER WEAR A COAT. IT'S WINDY OUT.
WINDY? HOW WINDY?
PRETTY WINDY.
DO YOU KNOW WHICH DIRECTION IT'S BLOWING? NORTH? SOUTH? EAST? WEST?
UM, KINDA RIGHT TO LEFT, WHEN YOU GO OUT THE FRONT DOOR.
AAAA! THAT'S THE DIRECTION I WALK TO SCHOOL! I'LL HAVE THE WIND AT MY BACK THE WHOLE WAY!
THAT'S USUALLY THOUGHT OF AS A GOOD THING.
MAYBE IN OLDEN TIMES, BUT NOT ANYMORE!
WHAT'S CHANGED?
NICE BIEBER HAIR.
DON'T LET ME NEAR A MIRROR, OK?
AMEND

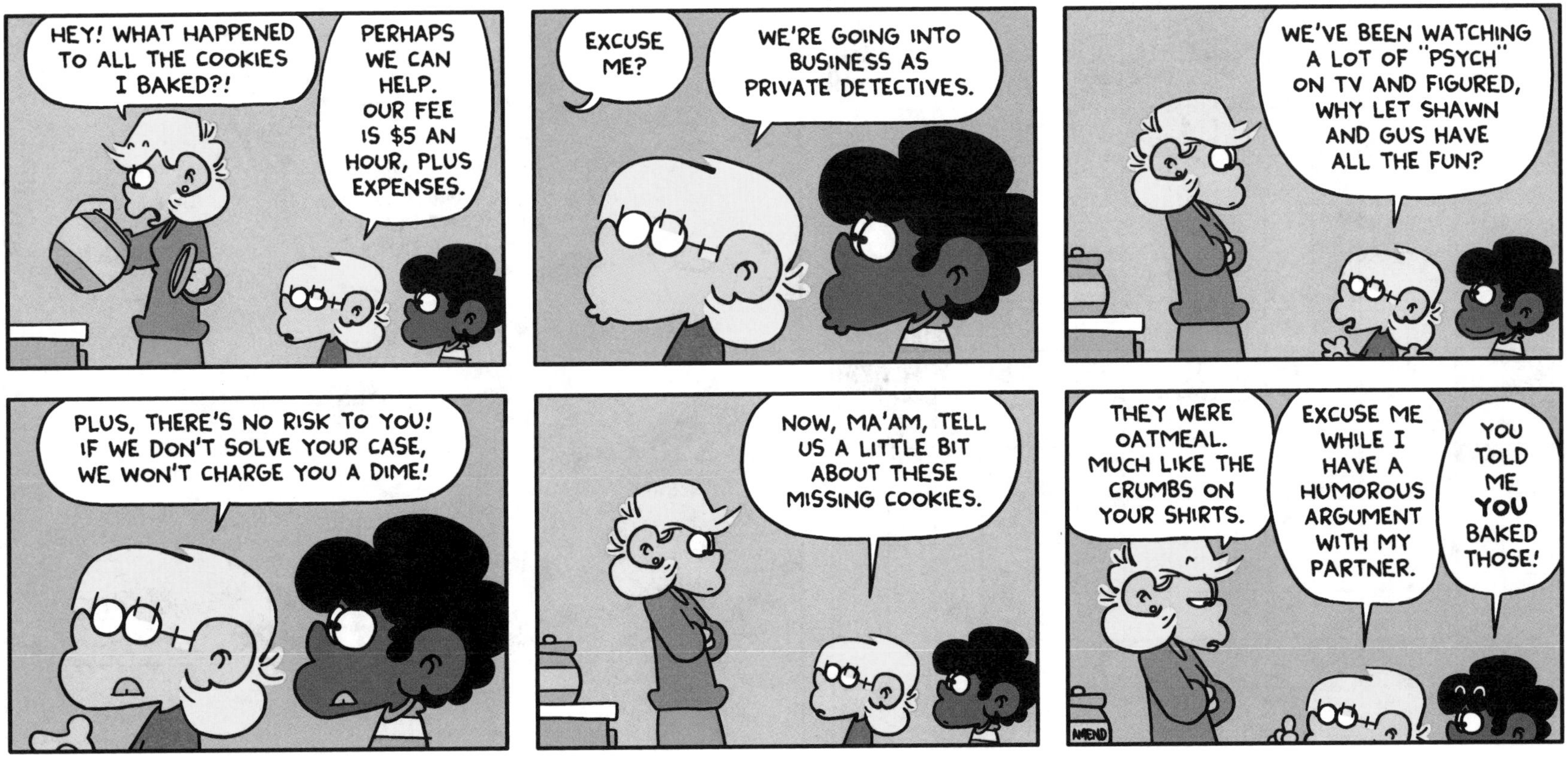
HEY! WHAT HAPPENED TO ALL THE COOKIES I BAKED?!
PERHAPS WE CAN HELP. OUR FEE IS $5 AN HOUR, PLUS EXPENSES.
EXCUSE ME?
WE'RE GOING INTO BUSINESS AS PRIVATE DETECTIVES.
WE'VE BEEN WATCHING A LOT OF "PSYCH" ON TV AND FIGURED, WHY LET SHAWN AND GUS HAVE ALL THE FUN?
PLUS, THERE'S NO RISK TO YOU! IF WE DON'T SOLVE YOUR CASE, WE WON'T CHARGE YOU A DIME!
NOW, MA'AM, TELL US A LITTLE BIT ABOUT THESE MISSING COOKIES.
THEY WERE OATMEAL. MUCH LIKE THE CRUMBS ON YOUR SHIRTS.
EXCUSE ME WHILE I HAVE A HUMOROUS ARGUMENT WITH MY PARTNER.
YOU TOLD ME **YOU** BAKED THOSE!
AMEND

MOTHER
HATES
SEEING
OUR
CHILDREN
HAVING
FUN
CUTE.
FOR THE RECORD, WHEN WE SUGGESTED FAMILY GAME NIGHT, WE MEANT PLAYING "CALL OF DUTY."
IF I HAVE A BLANK TILE, CAN I USE IT AS A BAZOOKA?
AMEND

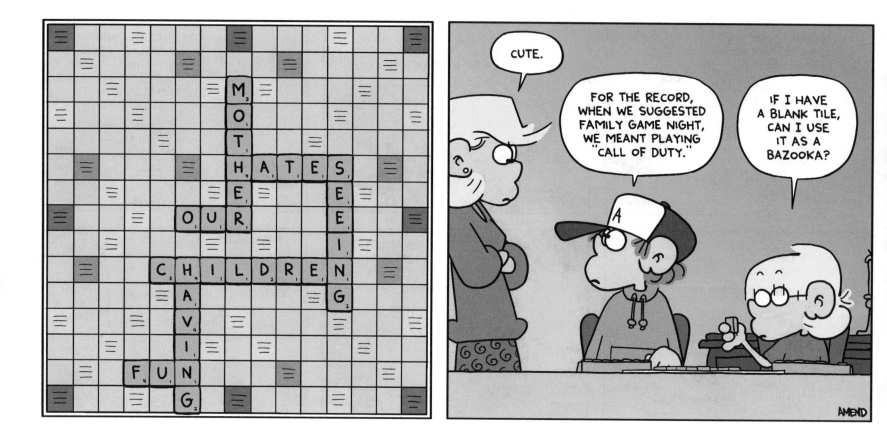

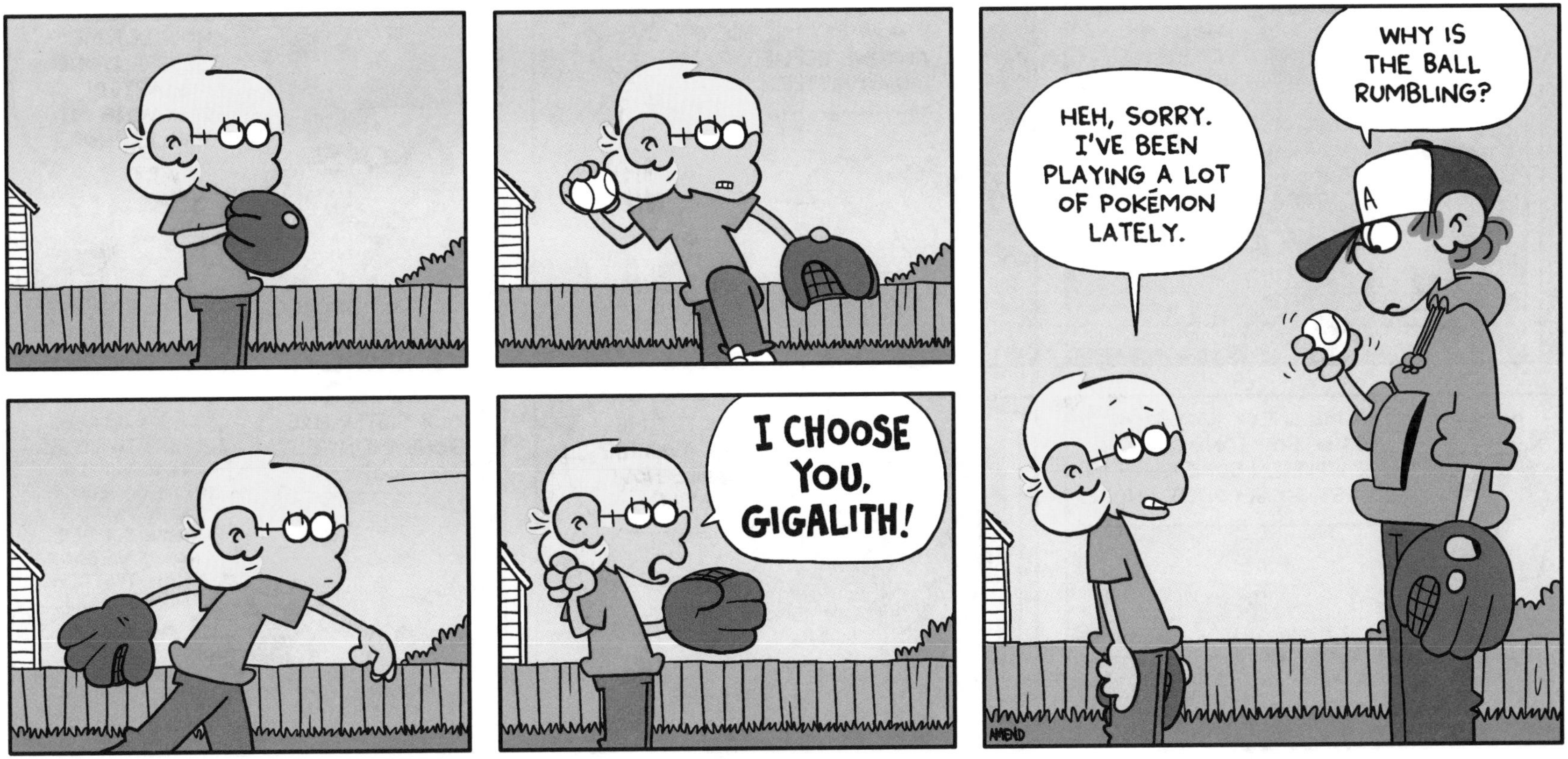
I CHOOSE YOU, GIGALITH!
WHY IS THE BALL RUMBLING?
HEH, SORRY. I'VE BEEN PLAYING A LOT OF POKÉMON LATELY.
AMEND

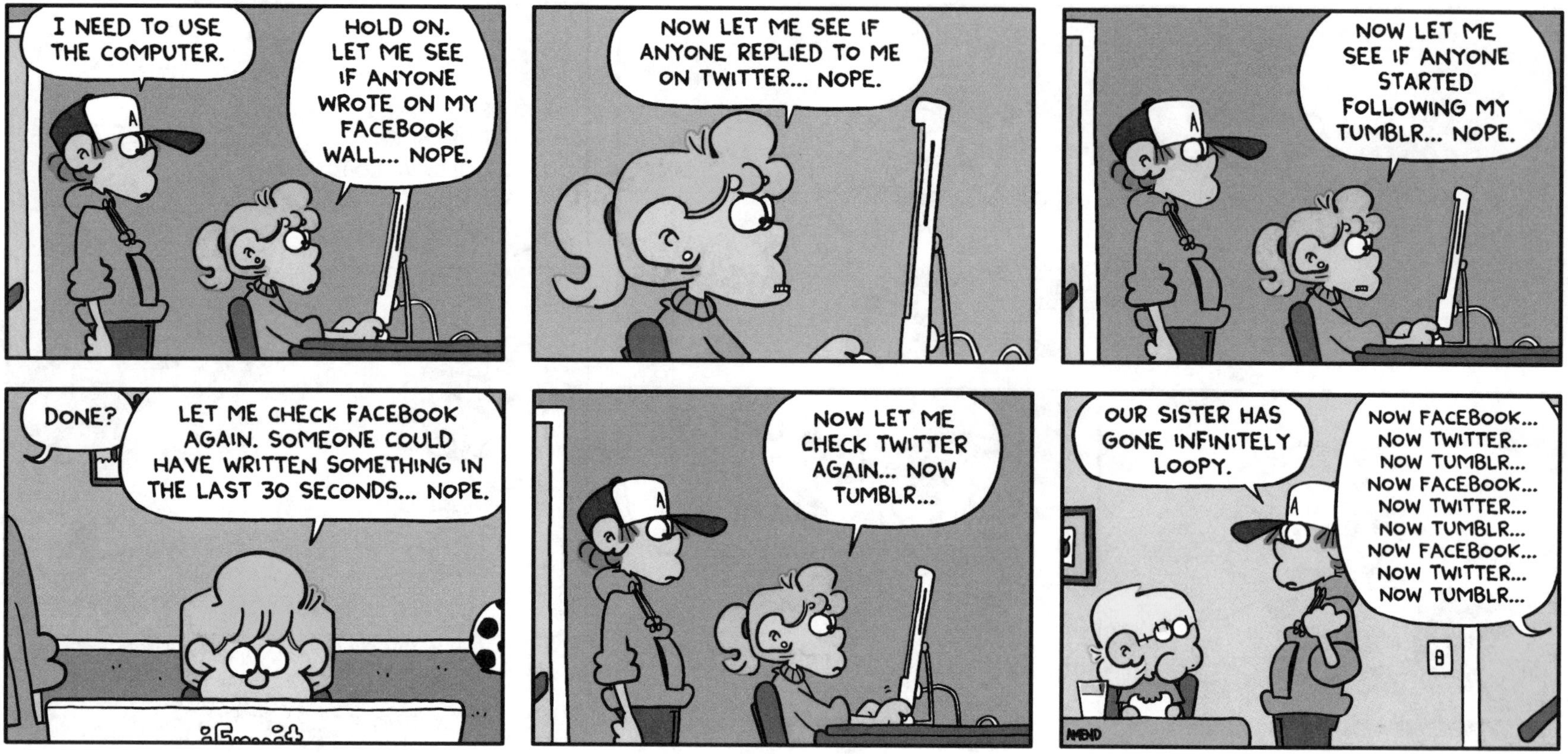
I NEED TO USE THE COMPUTER.
HOLD ON. LET ME SEE IF ANYONE WROTE ON MY FACEBOOK WALL... NOPE.
NOW LET ME SEE IF ANYONE REPLIED TO ME ON TWITTER... NOPE.
NOW LET ME SEE IF ANYONE STARTED FOLLOWING MY TUMBLR... NOPE.
DONE?
LET ME CHECK FACEBOOK AGAIN. SOMEONE COULD HAVE WRITTEN SOMETHING IN THE LAST 30 SECONDS... NOPE.
NOW LET ME CHECK TWITTER AGAIN... NOW TUMBLR...
OUR SISTER HAS GONE INFINITELY LOOPY.
NOW FACEBOOK... NOW TWITTER... NOW TUMBLR... NOW FACEBOOK... NOW TWITTER... NOW TUMBLR... NOW FACEBOOK... NOW TWITTER... NOW TUMBLR...
AMEND

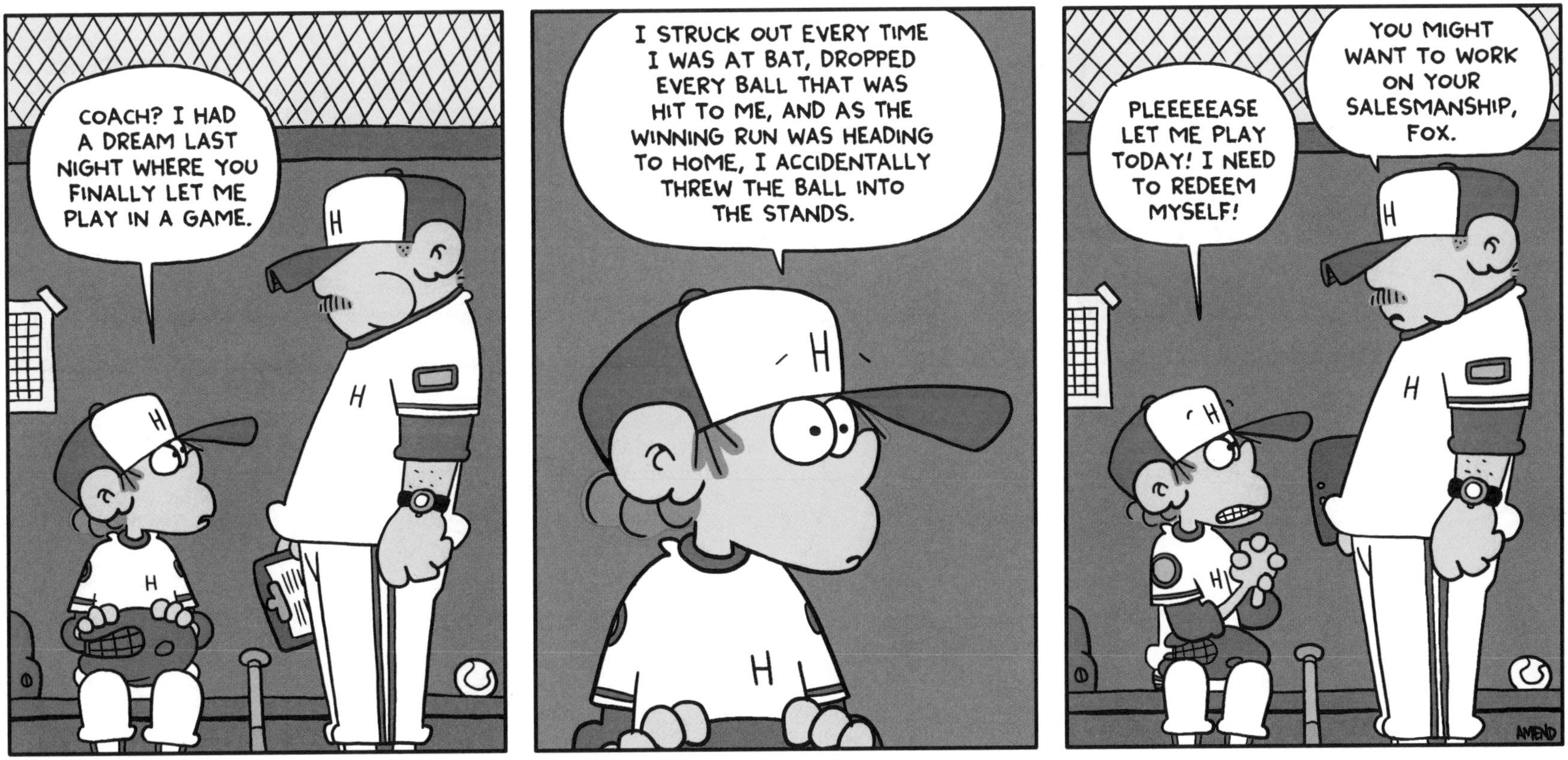
COACH? I HAD A DREAM LAST NIGHT WHERE YOU FINALLY LET ME PLAY IN A GAME.
I STRUCK OUT EVERY TIME I WAS AT BAT, DROPPED EVERY BALL THAT WAS HIT TO ME, AND AS THE WINNING RUN WAS HEADING TO HOME, I ACCIDENTALLY THREW THE BALL INTO THE STANDS.
PLEEEEEASE LET ME PLAY TODAY! I NEED TO REDEEM MYSELF!
YOU MIGHT WANT TO WORK ON YOUR SALESMANSHIP, FOX.
AMEND

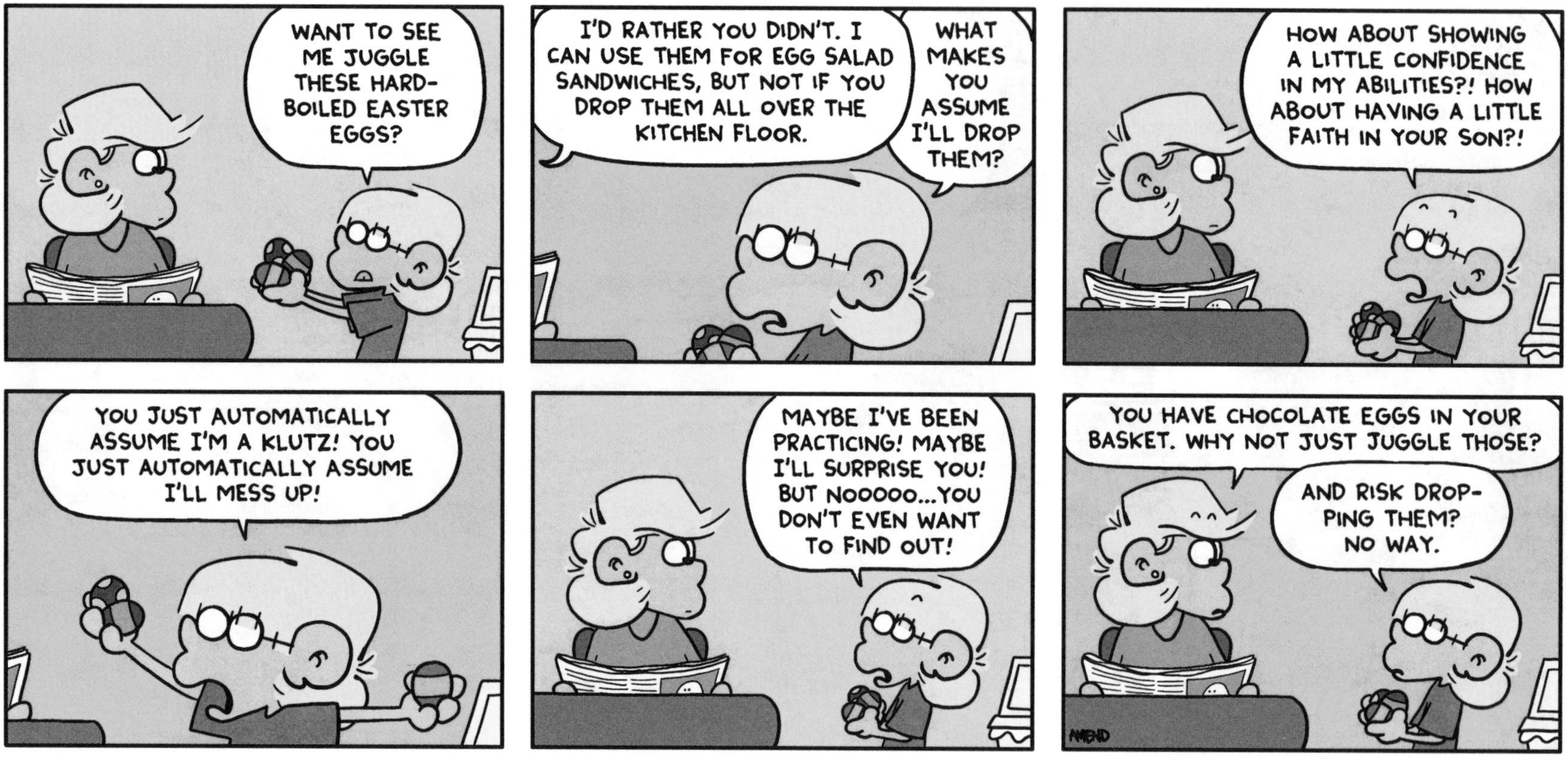
WANT TO SEE ME JUGGLE THESE HARD-BOILED EASTER EGGS?
I'D RATHER YOU DIDN'T. I CAN USE THEM FOR EGG SALAD SANDWICHES, BUT NOT IF YOU DROP THEM ALL OVER THE KITCHEN FLOOR.
WHAT MAKES YOU ASSUME I'LL DROP THEM?
HOW ABOUT SHOWING A LITTLE CONFIDENCE IN MY ABILITIES?! HOW ABOUT HAVING A LITTLE FAITH IN YOUR SON?!
YOU JUST AUTOMATICALLY ASSUME I'M A KLUTZ! YOU JUST AUTOMATICALLY ASSUME I'LL MESS UP!
MAYBE I'VE BEEN PRACTICING! MAYBE I'LL SURPRISE YOU! BUT NOOOOO...YOU DON'T EVEN WANT TO FIND OUT!
YOU HAVE CHOCOLATE EGGS IN YOUR BASKET. WHY NOT JUST JUGGLE THOSE?
AND RISK DROPPING THEM? NO WAY.
AMEND

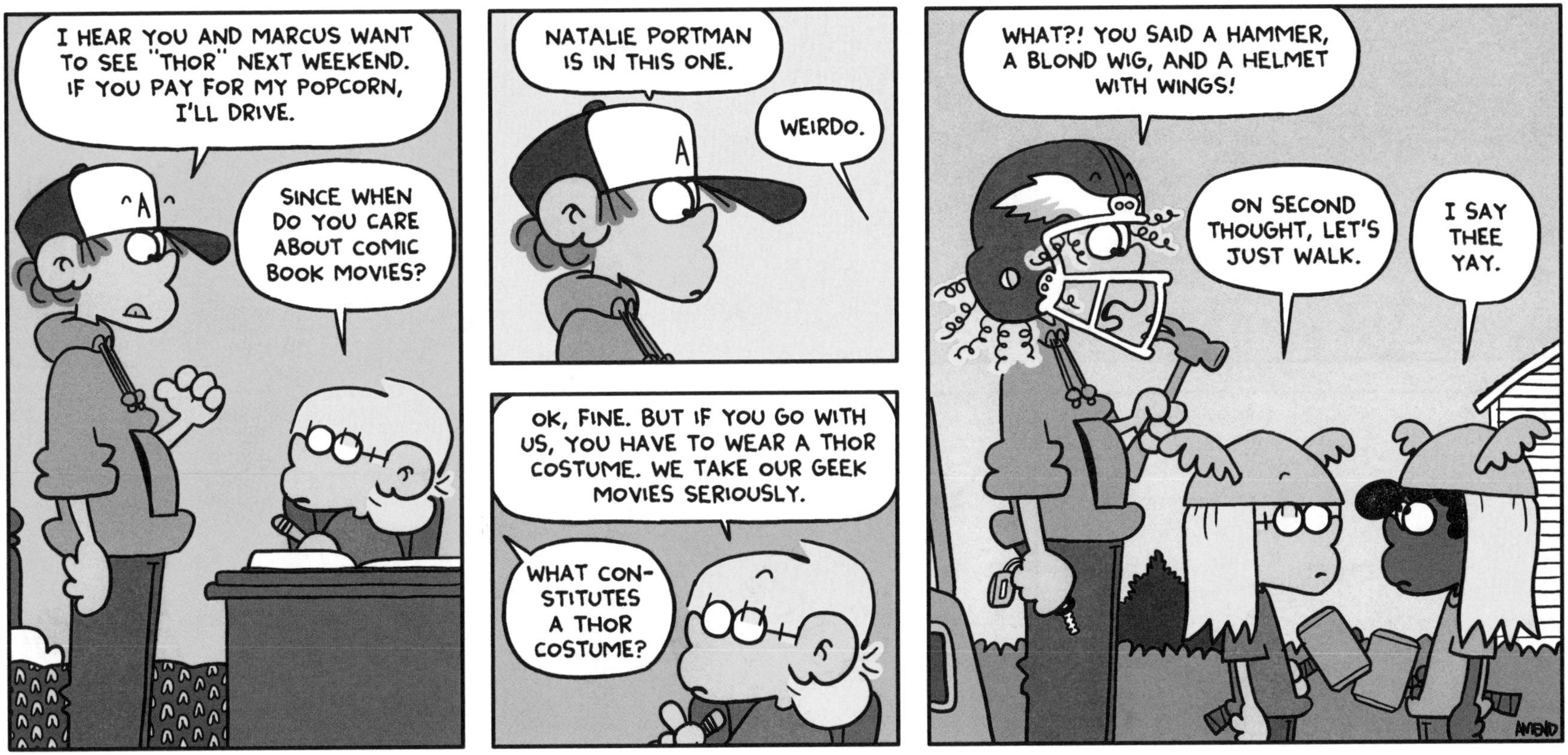
I HEAR YOU AND MARCUS WANT TO SEE "THOR" NEXT WEEKEND. IF YOU PAY FOR MY POPCORN, I'LL DRIVE.
SINCE WHEN DO YOU CARE ABOUT COMIC BOOK MOVIES?
NATALIE PORTMAN IS IN THIS ONE.
WEIRDO.
OK, FINE. BUT IF YOU GO WITH US, YOU HAVE TO WEAR A THOR COSTUME. WE TAKE OUR GEEK MOVIES SERIOUSLY.
WHAT CON-STITUTES A THOR COSTUME?
WHAT?! YOU SAID A HAMMER, A BLOND WIG, AND A HELMET WITH WINGS!
ON SECOND THOUGHT, LET'S JUST WALK.
I SAY THEE YAY.
AMEND

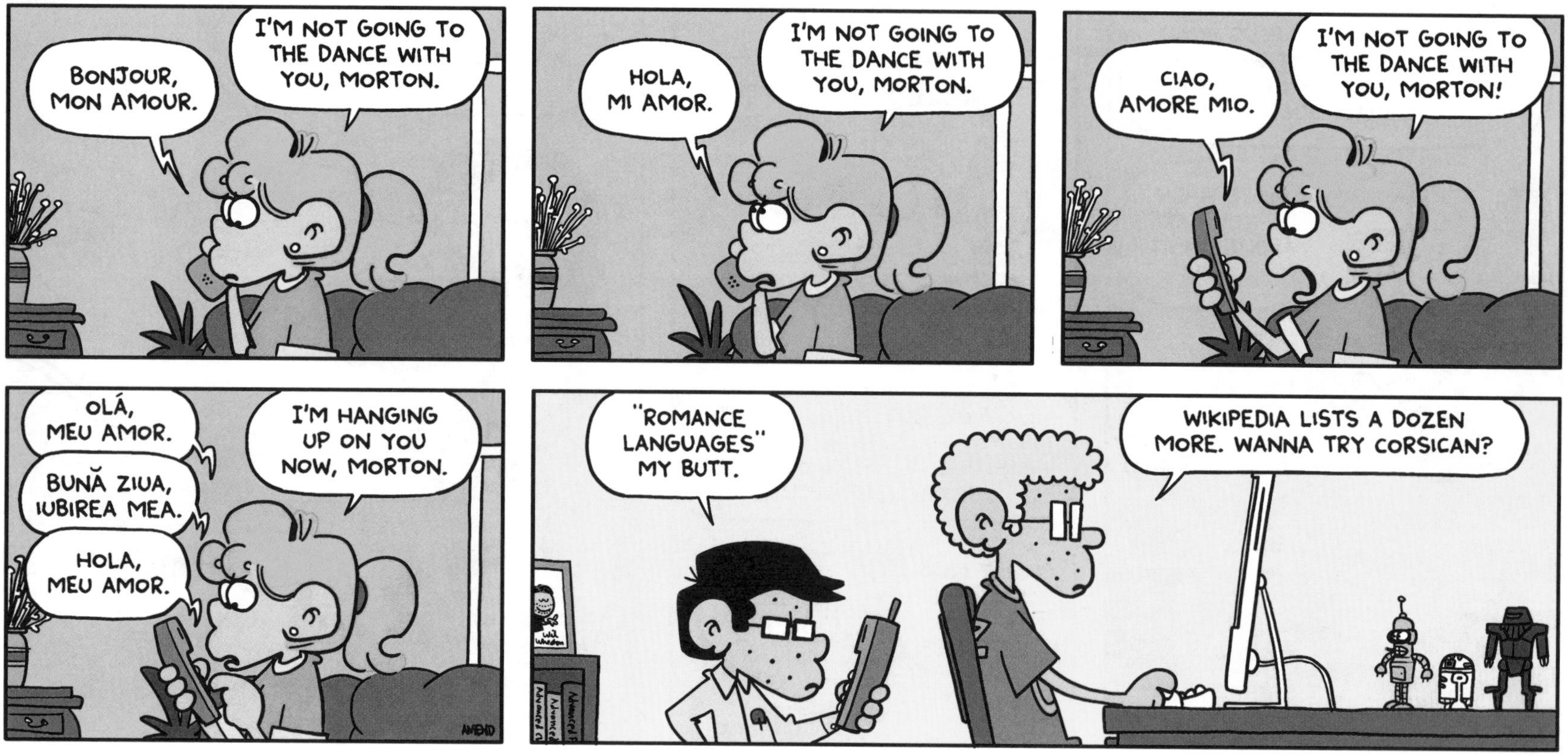
BONJOUR, MON AMOUR.
I'M NOT GOING TO THE DANCE WITH YOU, MORTON.
HOLA, MI AMOR.
I'M NOT GOING TO THE DANCE WITH YOU, MORTON.
CIAO, AMORE MIO.
I'M NOT GOING TO THE DANCE WITH YOU, MORTON!
OLÁ, MEU AMOR.
BUNĂ ZIUA, IUBIREA MEA.
HOLA, MEU AMOR.
I'M HANGING UP ON YOU NOW, MORTON.
AMEND
"ROMANCE LANGUAGES" MY BUTT.
WIKIPEDIA LISTS A DOZEN MORE. WANNA TRY CORSICAN?

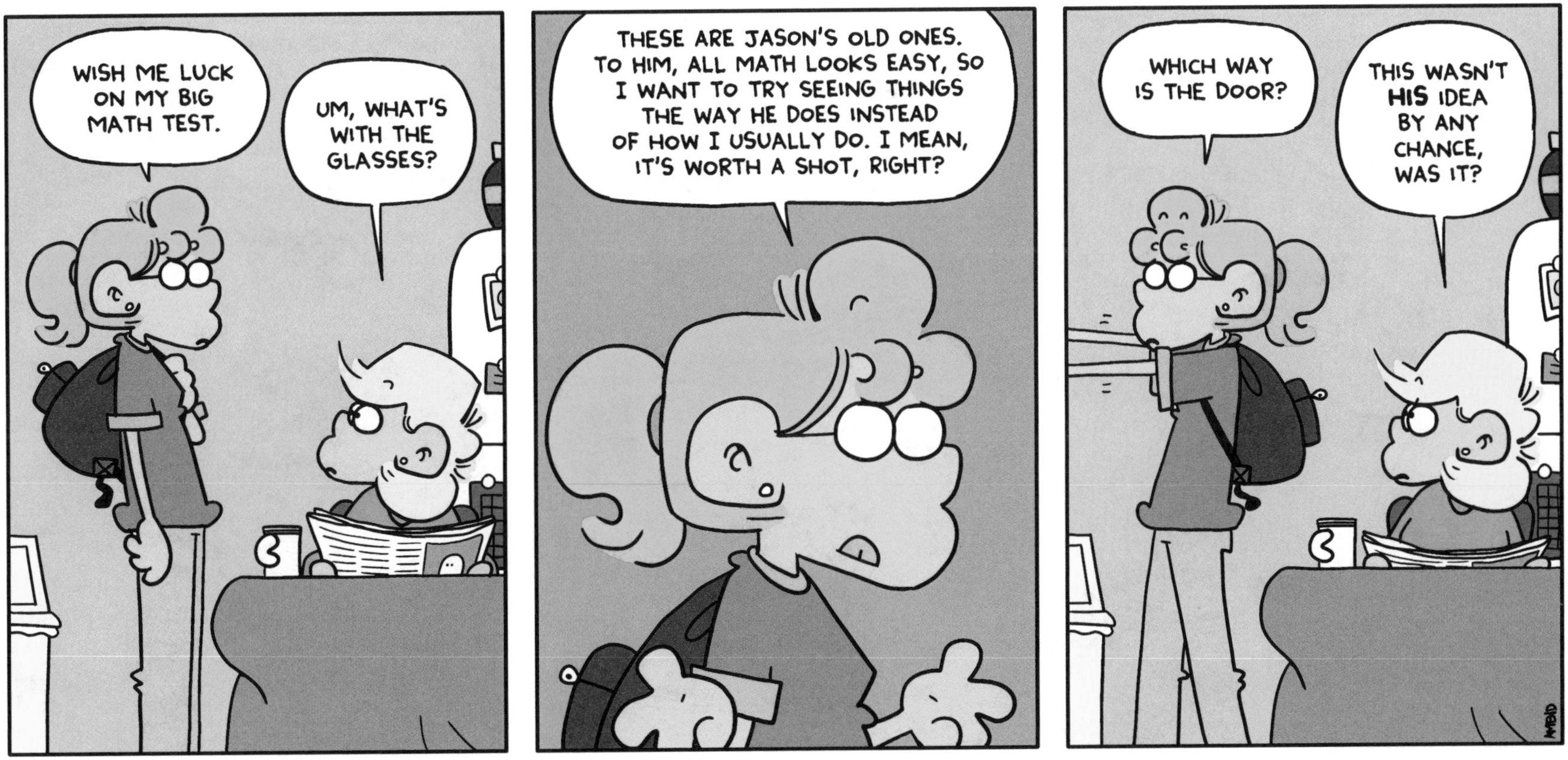
WISH ME LUCK ON MY BIG MATH TEST.
UM, WHAT'S WITH THE GLASSES?
THESE ARE JASON'S OLD ONES. TO HIM, ALL MATH LOOKS EASY, SO I WANT TO TRY SEEING THINGS THE WAY HE DOES INSTEAD OF HOW I USUALLY DO. I MEAN, IT'S WORTH A SHOT, RIGHT?
WHICH WAY IS THE DOOR?
THIS WASN'T **HIS** IDEA BY ANY CHANCE, WAS IT?
AMEND

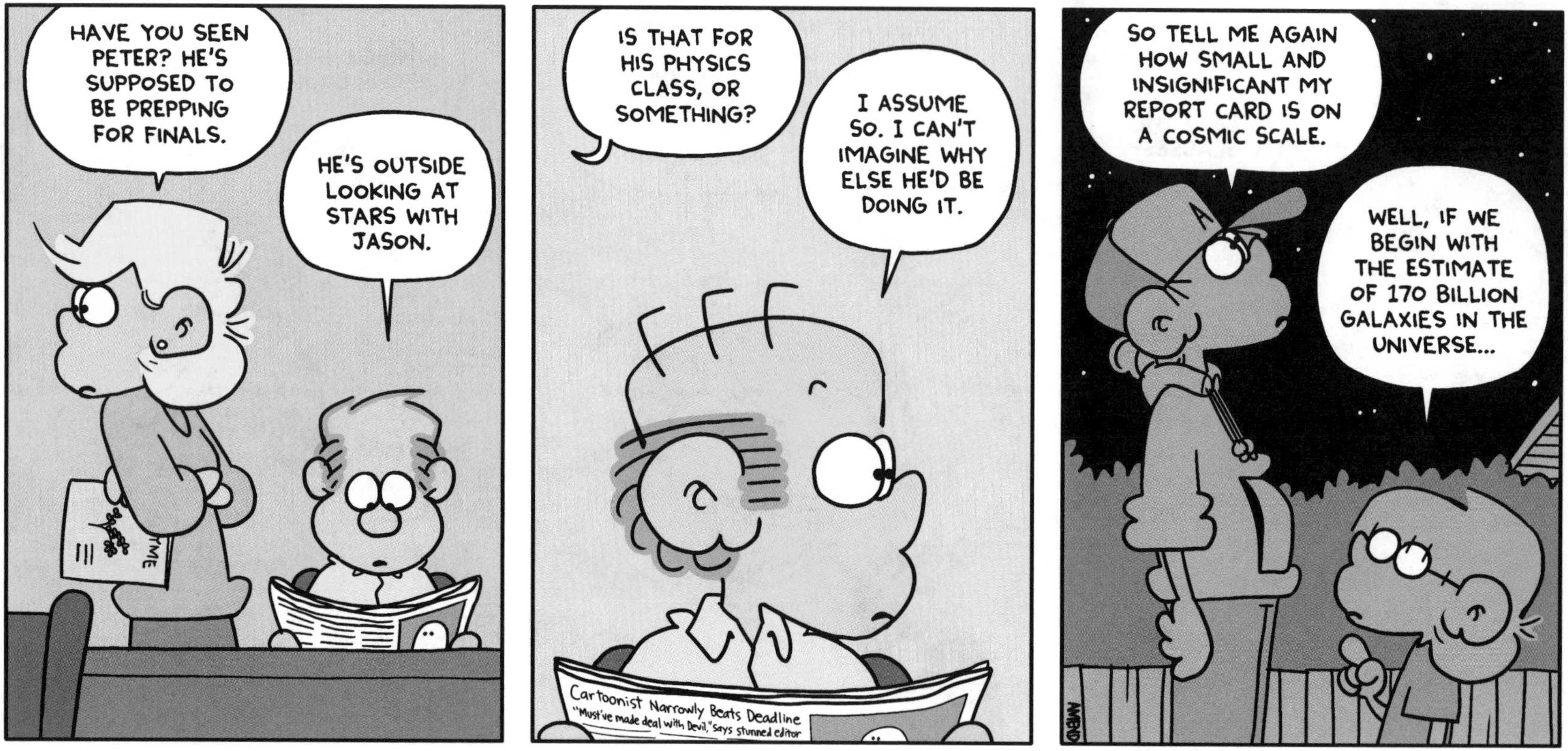
HAVE YOU SEEN PETER? HE'S SUPPOSED TO BE PREPPING FOR FINALS.
HE'S OUTSIDE LOOKING AT STARS WITH JASON.
IS THAT FOR HIS PHYSICS CLASS, OR SOMETHING?
I ASSUME SO. I CAN'T IMAGINE WHY ELSE HE'D BE DOING IT.
Cartoonist Narrowly Beats Deadline
"Must've made deal with Devil," says stunned editor
SO TELL ME AGAIN HOW SMALL AND INSIGNIFICANT MY REPORT CARD IS ON A COSMIC SCALE.
WELL, IF WE BEGIN WITH THE ESTIMATE OF 170 BILLION GALAXIES IN THE UNIVERSE...
AMEND

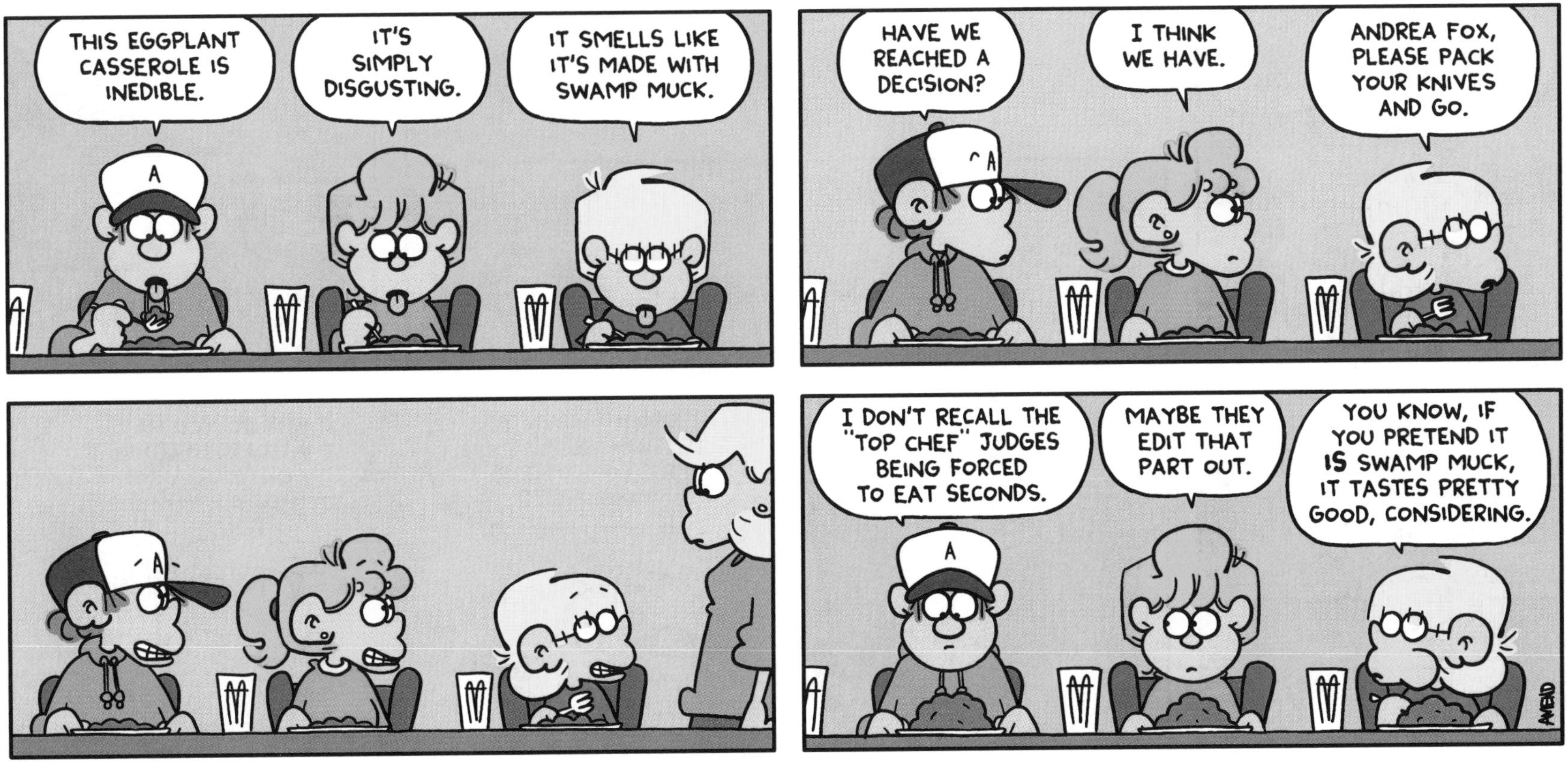
THIS EGGPLANT CASSEROLE IS INEDIBLE.
IT'S SIMPLY DISGUSTING.
IT SMELLS LIKE IT'S MADE WITH SWAMP MUCK.
HAVE WE REACHED A DECISION?
I THINK WE HAVE.
ANDREA FOX, PLEASE PACK YOUR KNIVES AND GO.
I DON'T RECALL THE "TOP CHEF" JUDGES BEING FORCED TO EAT SECONDS.
MAYBE THEY EDIT THAT PART OUT.
YOU KNOW, IF YOU PRETEND IT **IS** SWAMP MUCK, IT TASTES PRETTY GOOD, CONSIDERING.

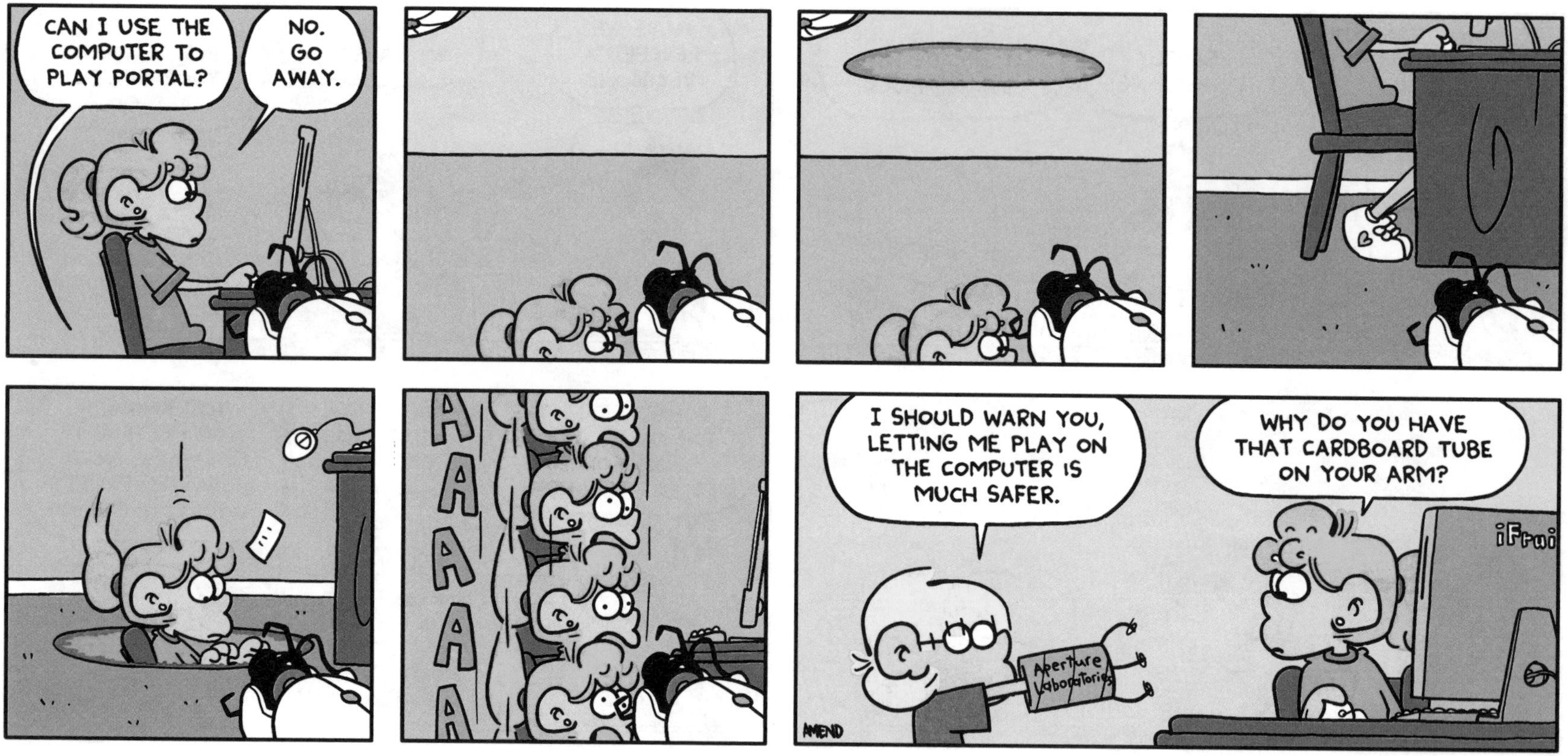
CAN I USE THE COMPUTER TO PLAY PORTAL?
NO. GO AWAY.
AAAAAA
I SHOULD WARN YOU, LETTING ME PLAY ON THE COMPUTER IS MUCH SAFER.
WHY DO YOU HAVE THAT CARDBOARD TUBE ON YOUR ARM?
Aperture Laboratories
iFrui
AMEND

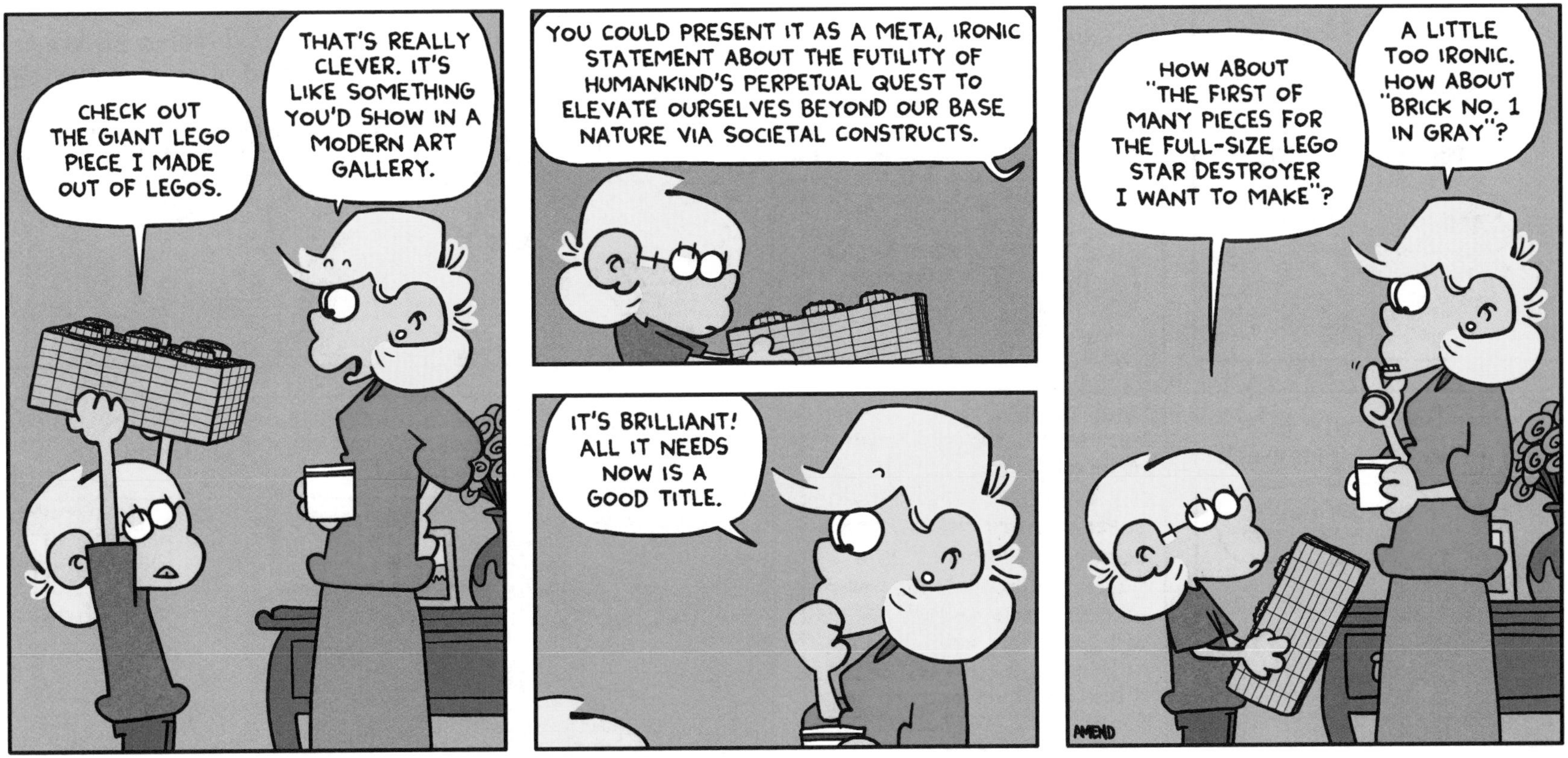
CHECK OUT THE GIANT LEGO PIECE I MADE OUT OF LEGOS.
THAT'S REALLY CLEVER. IT'S LIKE SOMETHING YOU'D SHOW IN A MODERN ART GALLERY.
YOU COULD PRESENT IT AS A META, IRONIC STATEMENT ABOUT THE FUTILITY OF HUMANKIND'S PERPETUAL QUEST TO ELEVATE OURSELVES BEYOND OUR BASE NATURE VIA SOCIETAL CONSTRUCTS.
IT'S BRILLIANT! ALL IT NEEDS NOW IS A GOOD TITLE.
HOW ABOUT "THE FIRST OF MANY PIECES FOR THE FULL-SIZE LEGO STAR DESTROYER I WANT TO MAKE"?
A LITTLE TOO IRONIC. HOW ABOUT "BRICK NO. 1 IN GRAY"?
AMEND

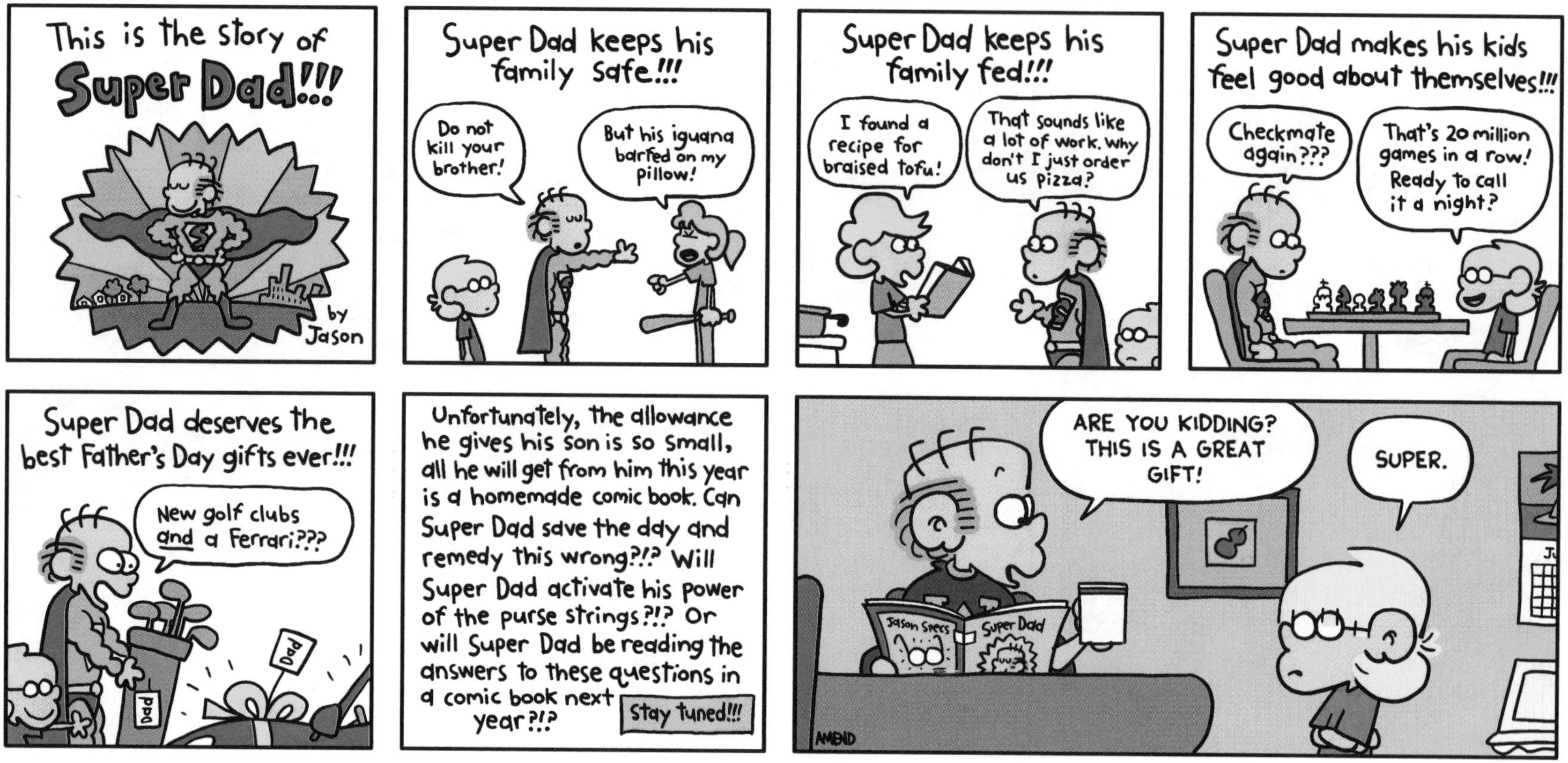

This is the story of Super Dad!!!...
by Jason
Super Dad keeps his family safe!!!
Do not kill your brother!
But his iguana barfed on my pillow!
Super Dad keeps his family fed!!!
I found a recipe for braised tofu!
That sounds like a lot of work. Why don't I just order us pizza?
Super Dad makes his kids feel good about themselves!!!
Checkmate again???
That's 20 million games in a row! Ready to call it a night?
Super Dad deserves the best Father's Day gifts ever!!!
New golf clubs and a Ferrari???
Dad
Dad
Unfortunately, the allowance he gives his son is so small, all he will get from him this year is a homemade comic book. Can Super Dad save the day and remedy this wrong?!? Will Super Dad activate his power of the purse strings?!? Or will Super Dad be reading the answers to these questions in a comic book next year?!?
Stay tuned!!!
Jason Specs
Super Dad
ARE YOU KIDDING? THIS IS A GREAT GIFT!
SUPER.
AMEND

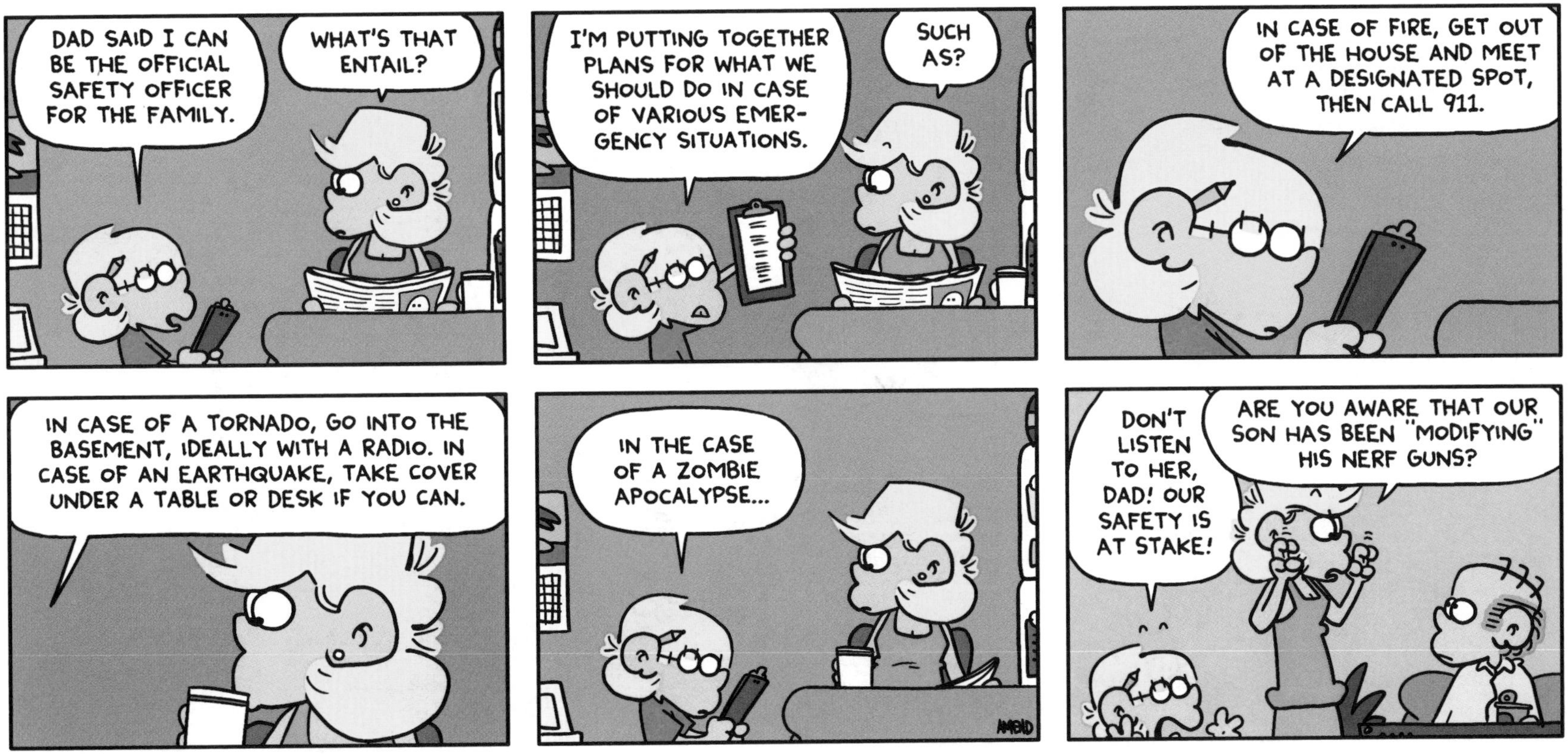
DAD SAID I CAN BE THE OFFICIAL SAFETY OFFICER FOR THE FAMILY.
WHAT'S THAT ENTAIL?
I'M PUTTING TOGETHER PLANS FOR WHAT WE SHOULD DO IN CASE OF VARIOUS EMERGENCY SITUATIONS.
SUCH AS?
IN CASE OF FIRE, GET OUT OF THE HOUSE AND MEET AT A DESIGNATED SPOT, THEN CALL 911.
IN CASE OF A TORNADO, GO INTO THE BASEMENT, IDEALLY WITH A RADIO. IN CASE OF AN EARTHQUAKE, TAKE COVER UNDER A TABLE OR DESK IF YOU CAN.
IN THE CASE OF A ZOMBIE APOCALYPSE...
ARE YOU AWARE THAT OUR SON HAS BEEN "MODIFYING" HIS NERF GUNS?
DON'T LISTEN TO HER, DAD! OUR SAFETY IS AT STAKE!
AMEND

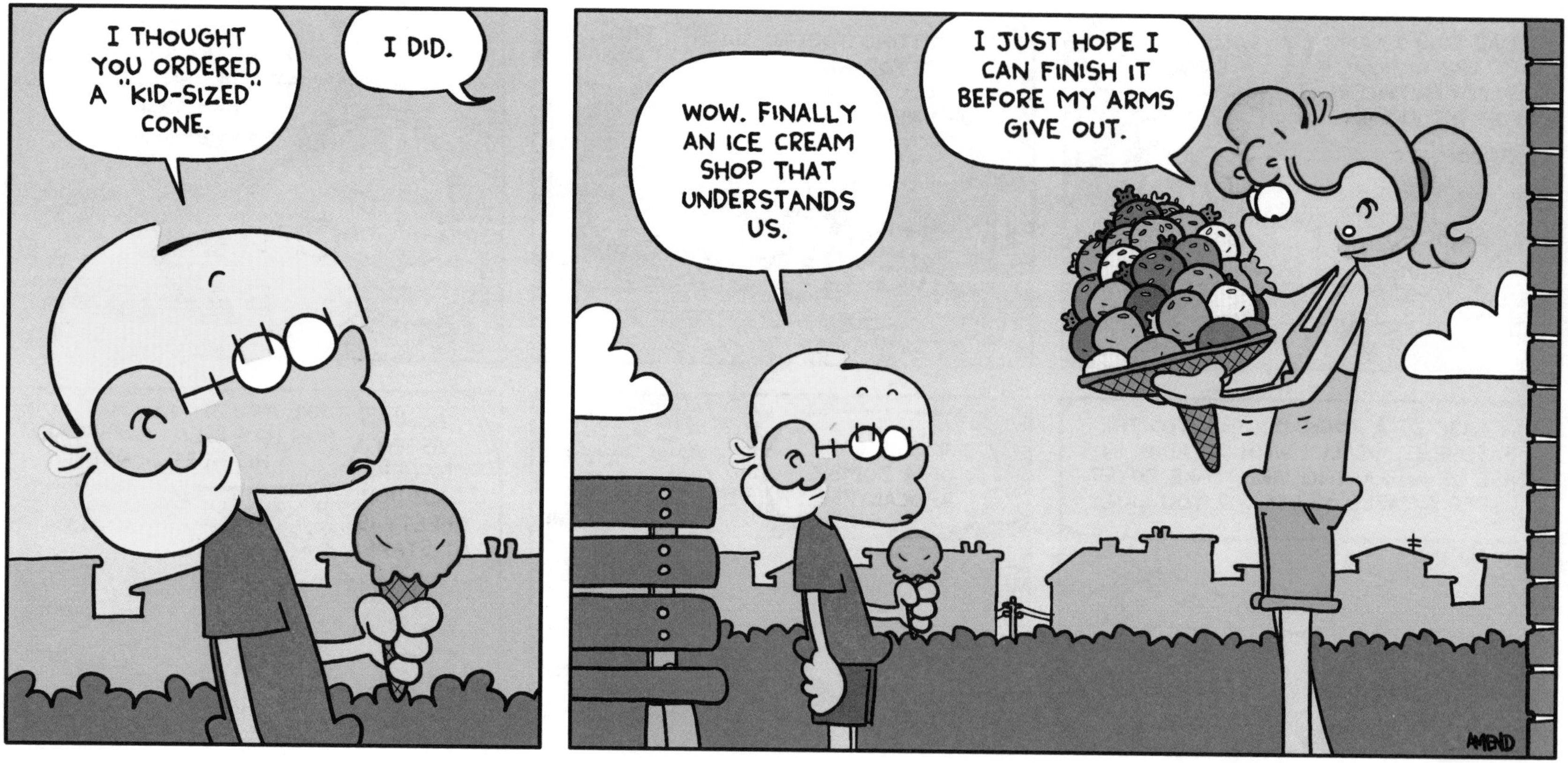
I THOUGHT YOU ORDERED A "KID-SIZED" CONE.
I DID.
WOW. FINALLY AN ICE CREAM SHOP THAT UNDERSTANDS US.
I JUST HOPE I CAN FINISH IT BEFORE MY ARMS GIVE OUT.
AMEND

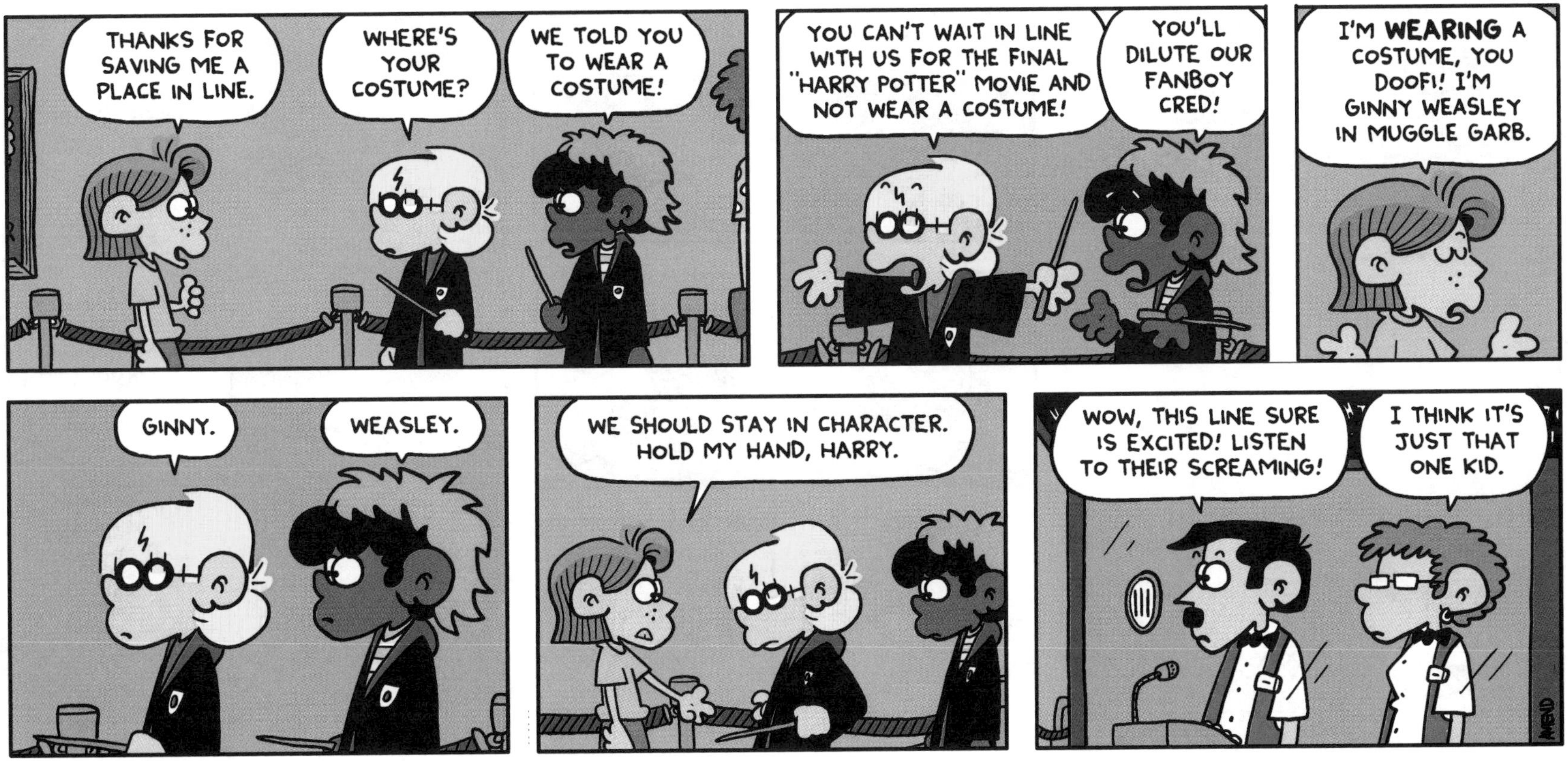
THANKS FOR SAVING ME A PLACE IN LINE.
WHERE'S YOUR COSTUME?
WE TOLD YOU TO WEAR A COSTUME!
YOU CAN'T WAIT IN LINE WITH US FOR THE FINAL "HARRY POTTER" MOVIE AND NOT WEAR A COSTUME!
YOU'LL DILUTE OUR FANBOY CRED!
I'M **WEARING** A COSTUME, YOU DOOF!! I'M GINNY WEASLEY IN MUGGLE GARB.
GINNY.
WEASLEY.
WE SHOULD STAY IN CHARACTER. HOLD MY HAND, HARRY.
WOW, THIS LINE SURE IS EXCITED! LISTEN TO THEIR SCREAMING!
I THINK IT'S JUST THAT ONE KID.
AMEND

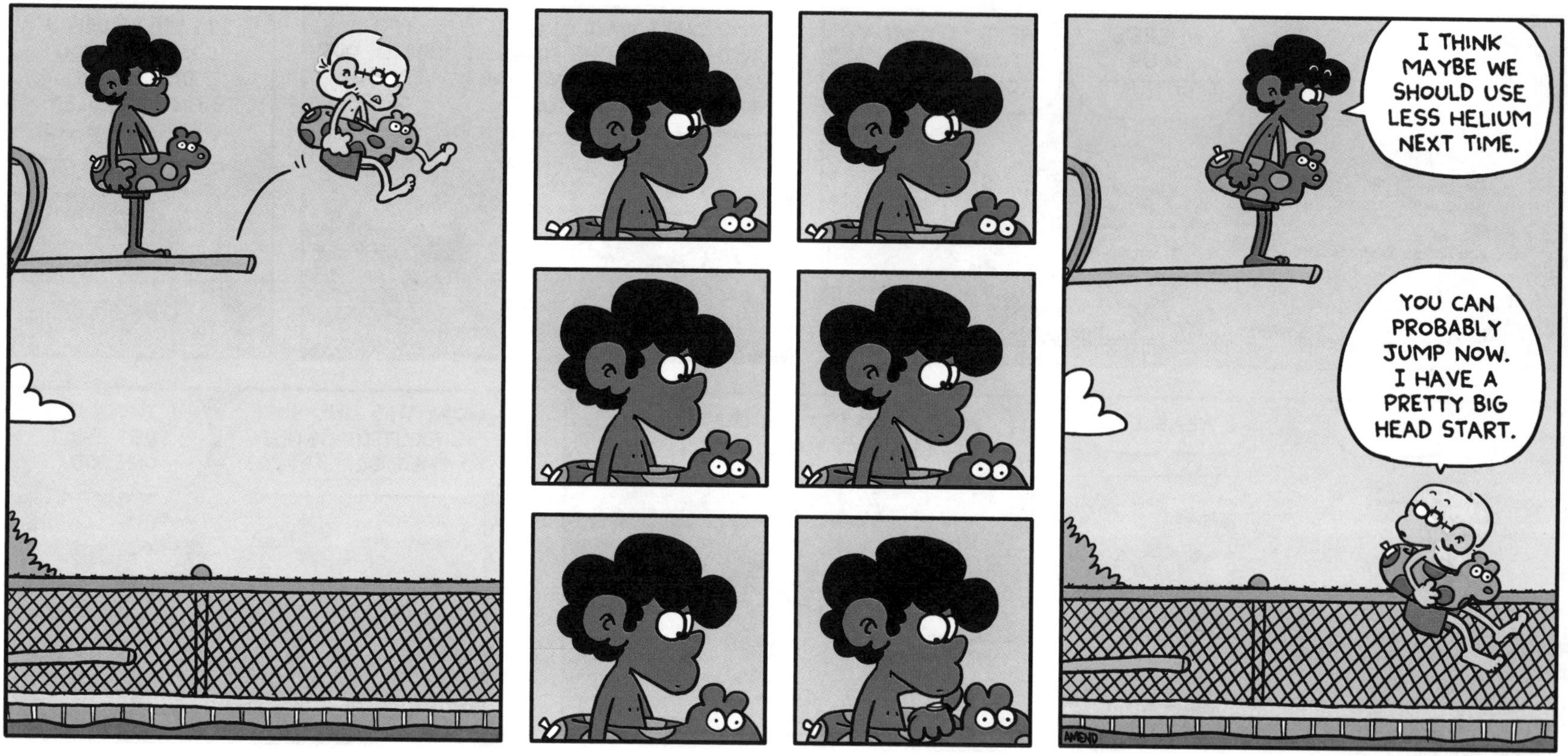
I THINK MAYBE WE SHOULD USE LESS HELIUM NEXT TIME.
YOU CAN PROBABLY JUMP NOW. I HAVE A PRETTY BIG HEAD START.
AMEND

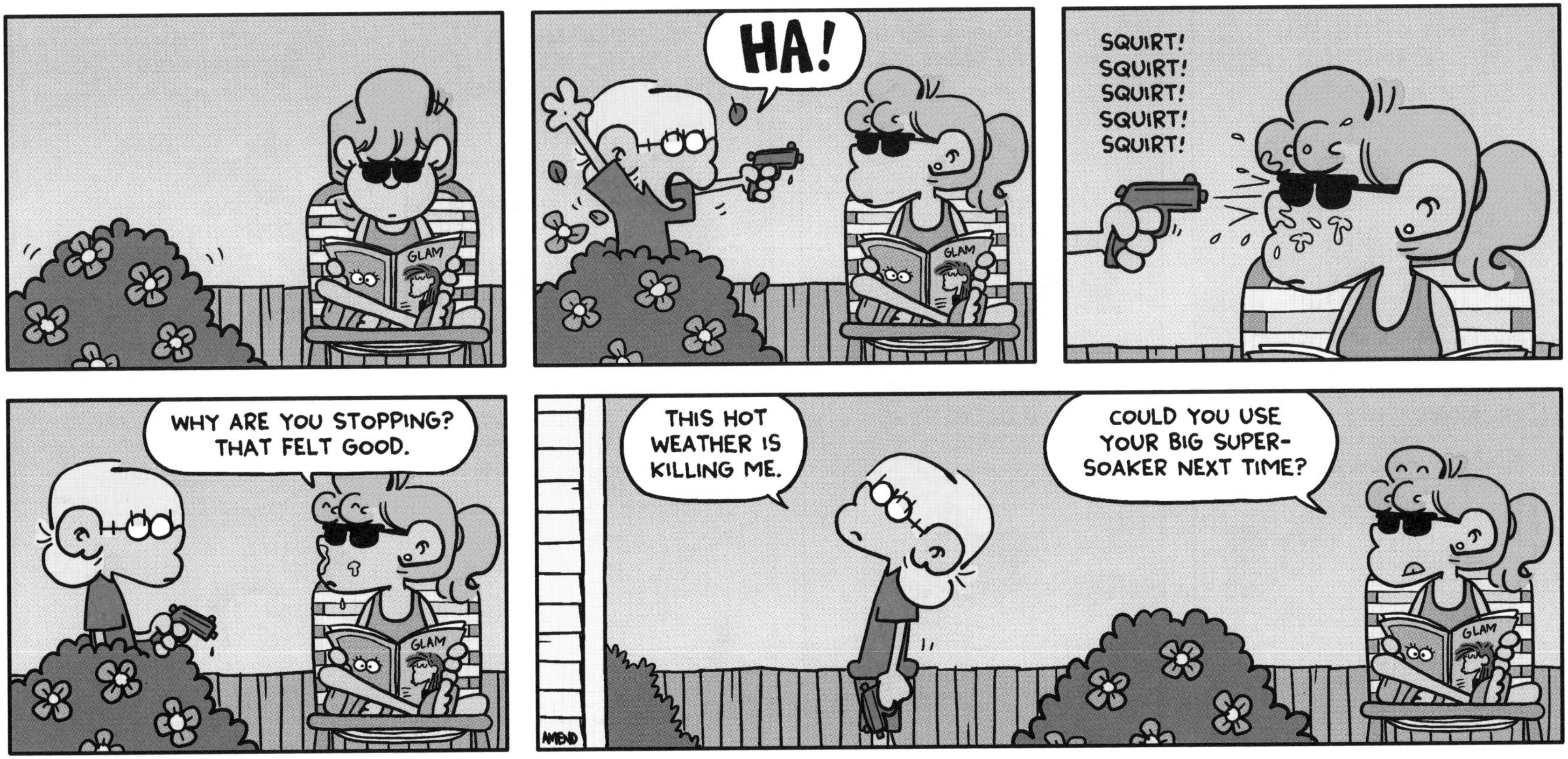
HA!
SQUIRT! SQUIRT! SQUIRT! SQUIRT! SQUIRT!
WHY ARE YOU STOPPING? THAT FELT GOOD.
THIS HOT WEATHER IS KILLING ME.
COULD YOU USE YOUR BIG SUPER-SOAKER NEXT TIME?
AMEND

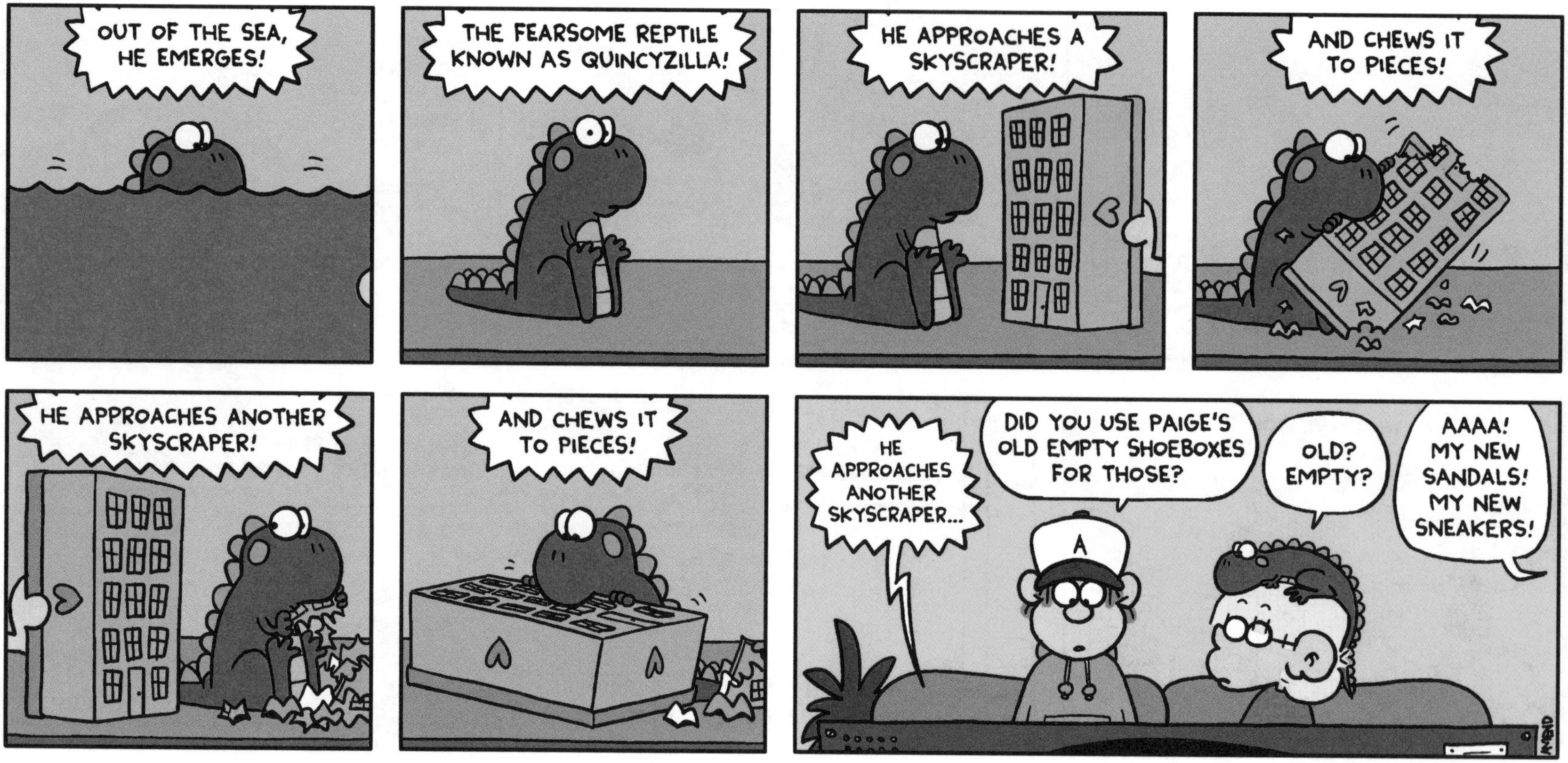
OUT OF THE SEA, HE EMERGES!
THE FEARSOME REPTILE KNOWN AS QUINCYZILLA!
HE APPROACHES A SKYSCRAPER!
AND CHEWS IT TO PIECES!
HE APPROACHES ANOTHER SKYSCRAPER!
AND CHEWS IT TO PIECES!
HE APPROACHES ANOTHER SKYSCRAPER...
DID YOU USE PAIGE'S OLD EMPTY SHOEBOXES FOR THOSE?
OLD? EMPTY?
AAAA! MY NEW SANDALS! MY NEW SNEAKERS!

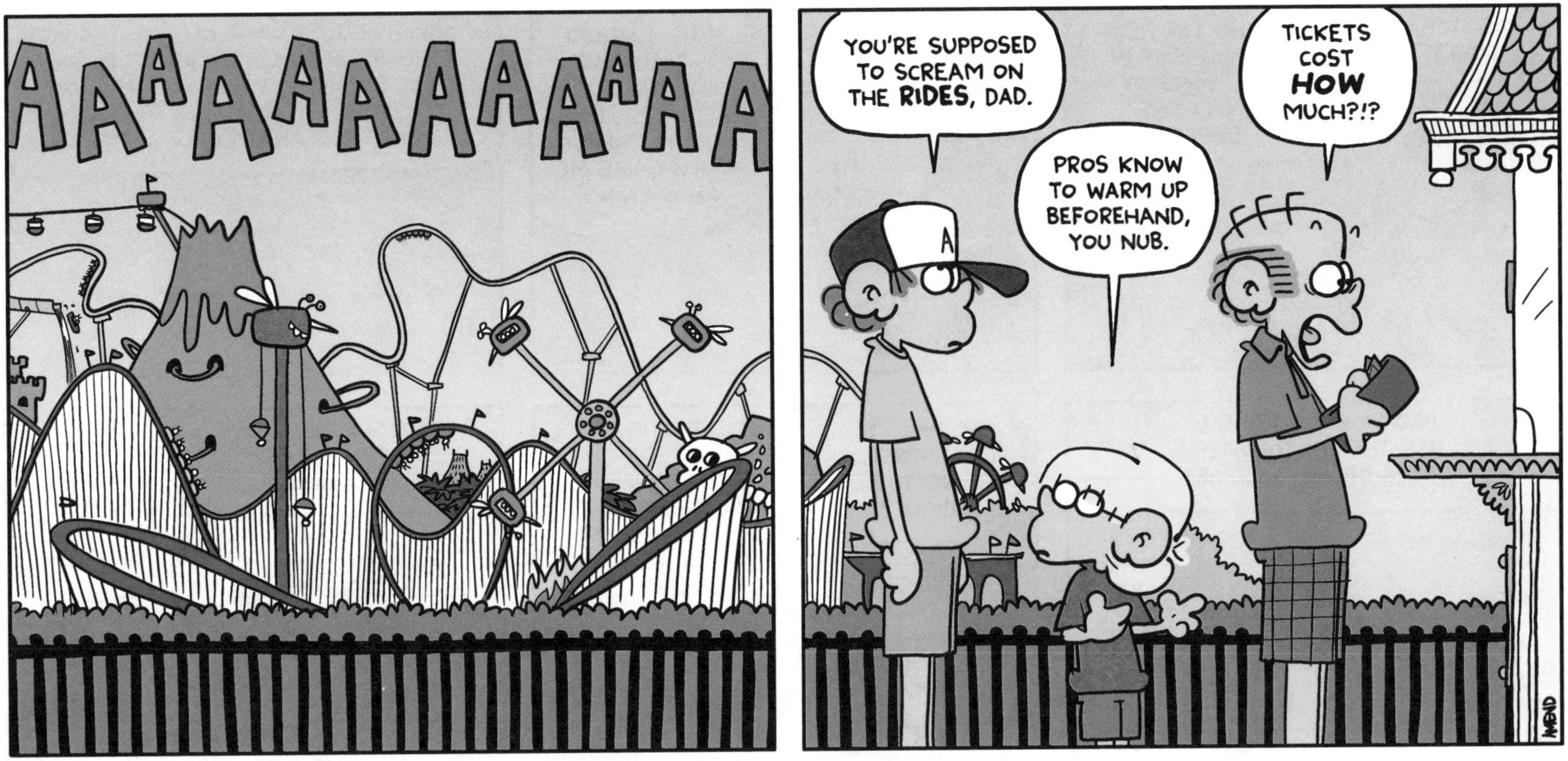
AAAAAAAAAAAA
YOU'RE SUPPOSED TO SCREAM ON THE RIDES, DAD.
PROS KNOW TO WARM UP BEFOREHAND, YOU NUB.
TICKETS COST HOW MUCH?!?
AMEND

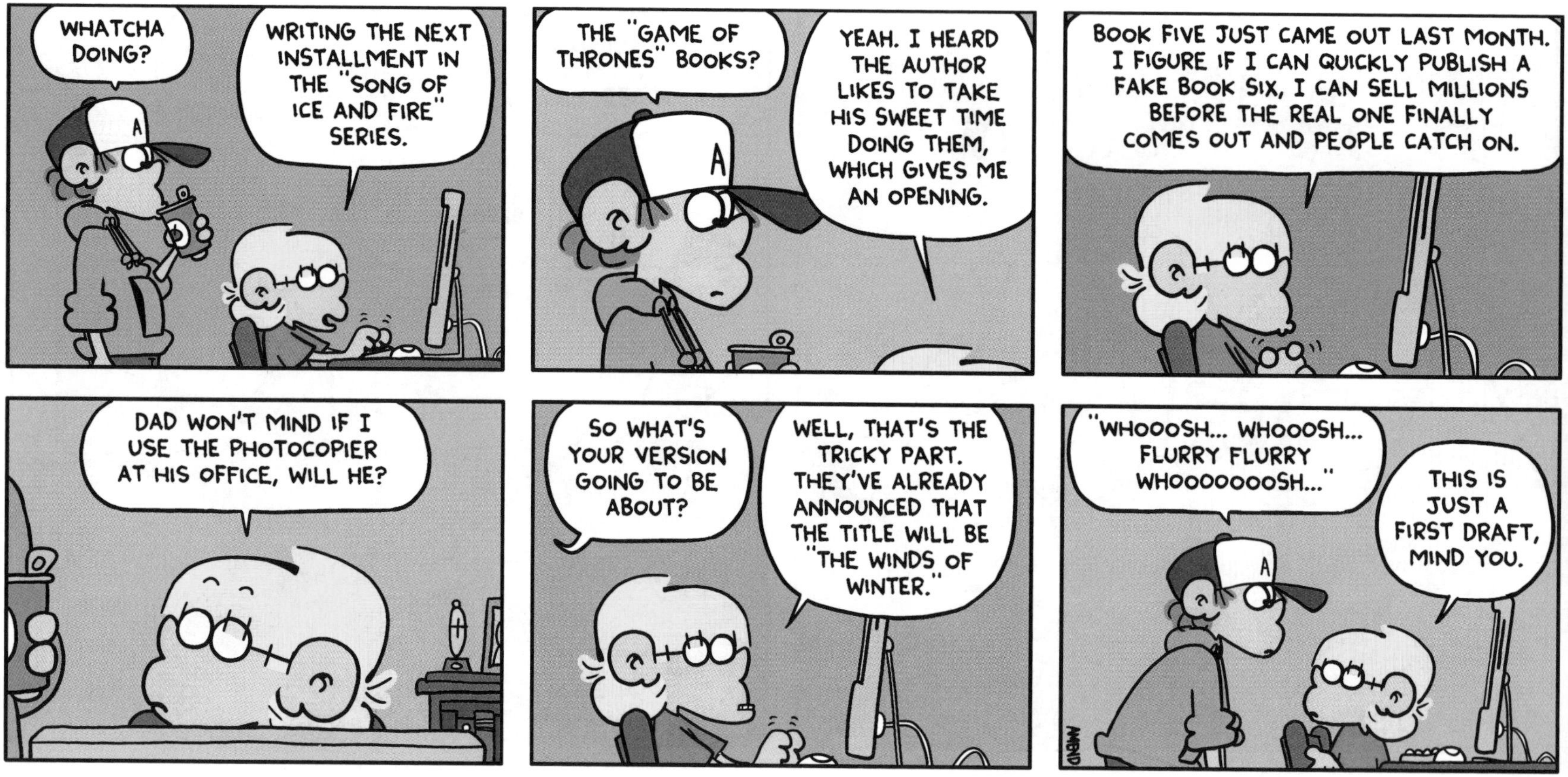
WHATCHA DOING?
WRITING THE NEXT INSTALLMENT IN THE "SONG OF ICE AND FIRE" SERIES.
THE "GAME OF THRONES" BOOKS?
YEAH. I HEARD THE AUTHOR LIKES TO TAKE HIS SWEET TIME DOING THEM, WHICH GIVES ME AN OPENING.
BOOK FIVE JUST CAME OUT LAST MONTH. I FIGURE IF I CAN QUICKLY PUBLISH A FAKE BOOK SIX, I CAN SELL MILLIONS BEFORE THE REAL ONE FINALLY COMES OUT AND PEOPLE CATCH ON.
DAD WON'T MIND IF I USE THE PHOTOCOPIER AT HIS OFFICE, WILL HE?
SO WHAT'S YOUR VERSION GOING TO BE ABOUT?
WELL, THAT'S THE TRICKY PART. THEY'VE ALREADY ANNOUNCED THAT THE TITLE WILL BE "THE WINDS OF WINTER."
"WHOOOSH... WHOOOSH... FLURRY FLURRY WHOOOOOOOSH..."
THIS IS JUST A FIRST DRAFT, MIND YOU.
AMEND

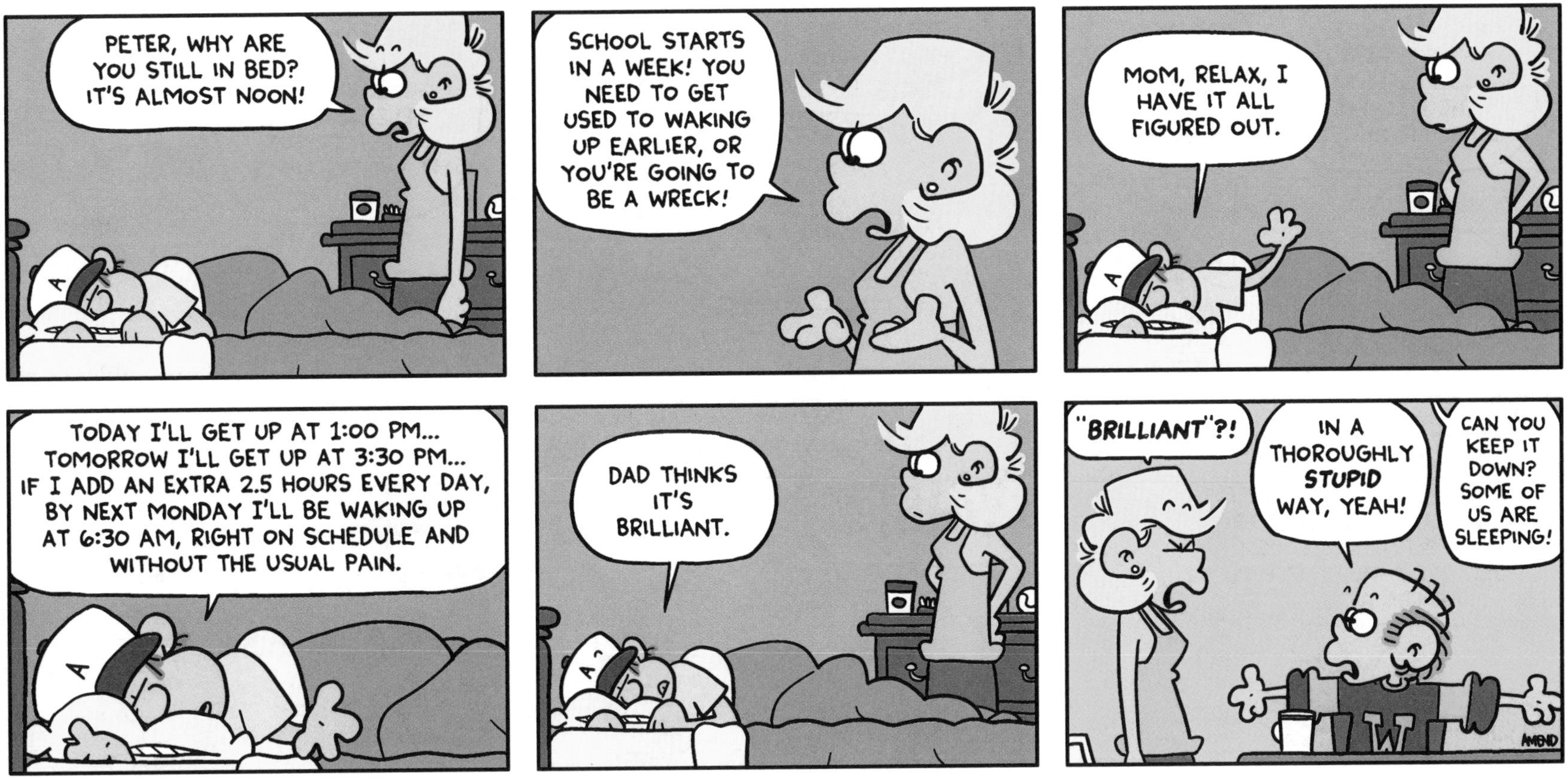
PETER, WHY ARE YOU STILL IN BED? IT'S ALMOST NOON!
SCHOOL STARTS IN A WEEK! YOU NEED TO GET USED TO WAKING UP EARLIER, OR YOU'RE GOING TO BE A WRECK!
MOM, RELAX, I HAVE IT ALL FIGURED OUT.
TODAY I'LL GET UP AT 1:00 PM... TOMORROW I'LL GET UP AT 3:30 PM... IF I ADD AN EXTRA 2.5 HOURS EVERY DAY, BY NEXT MONDAY I'LL BE WAKING UP AT 6:30 AM, RIGHT ON SCHEDULE AND WITHOUT THE USUAL PAIN.
DAD THINKS IT'S BRILLIANT.
"BRILLIANT"?!
IN A THOROUGHLY STUPID WAY, YEAH!
CAN YOU KEEP IT DOWN? SOME OF US ARE SLEEPING!
AMEND

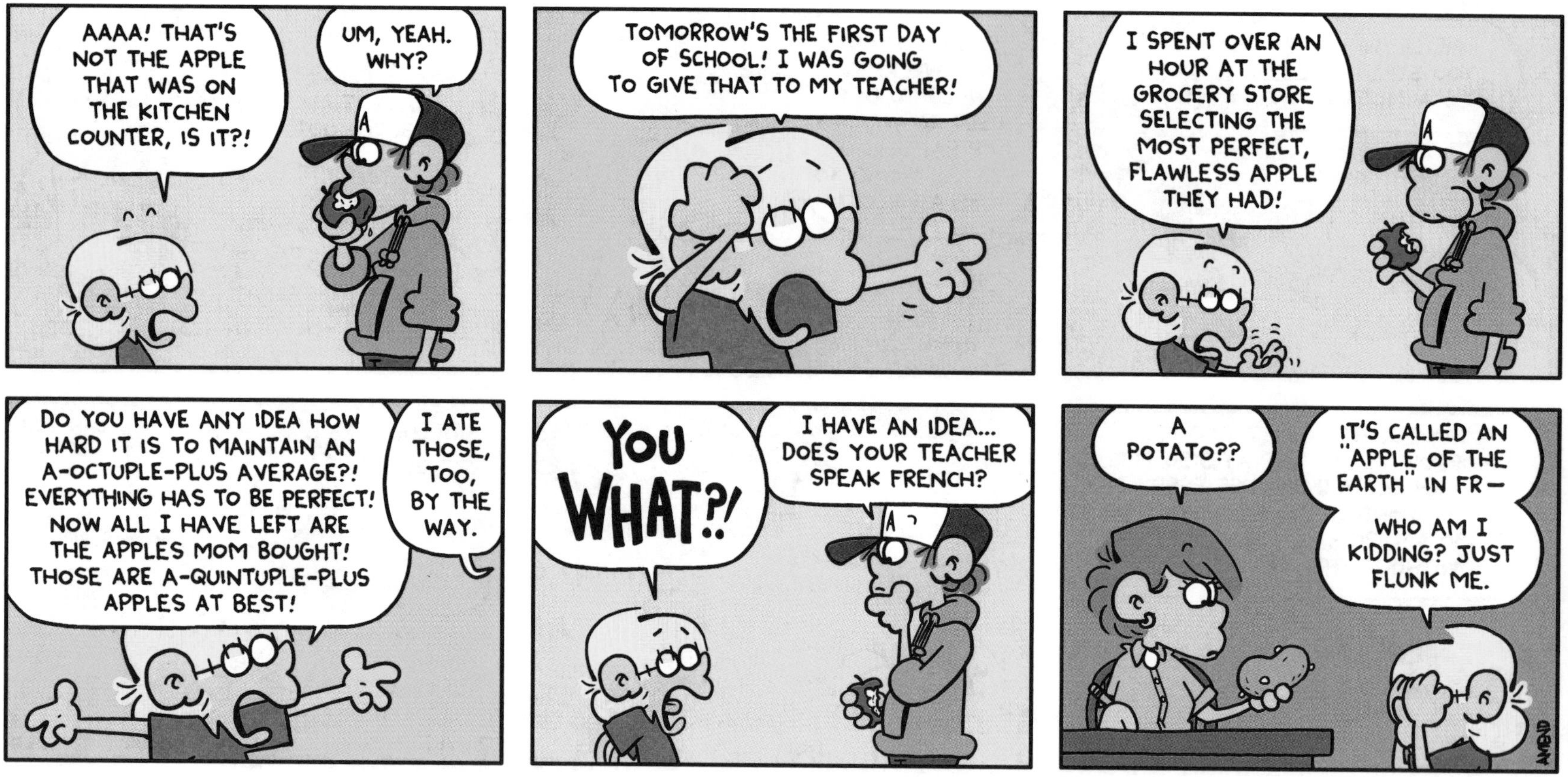
AAAA! THAT'S NOT THE APPLE THAT WAS ON THE KITCHEN COUNTER, IS IT?!
UM, YEAH. WHY?
TOMORROW'S THE FIRST DAY OF SCHOOL! I WAS GOING TO GIVE THAT TO MY TEACHER!
I SPENT OVER AN HOUR AT THE GROCERY STORE SELECTING THE MOST PERFECT, FLAWLESS APPLE THEY HAD!
DO YOU HAVE ANY IDEA HOW HARD IT IS TO MAINTAIN AN A-OCTUPLE-PLUS AVERAGE?! EVERYTHING HAS TO BE PERFECT! NOW ALL I HAVE LEFT ARE THE APPLES MOM BOUGHT! THOSE ARE A-QUINTUPLE-PLUS APPLES AT BEST!
I ATE THOSE, TOO, BY THE WAY.
YOU WHAT?!
I HAVE AN IDEA... DOES YOUR TEACHER SPEAK FRENCH?
A POTATO??
IT'S CALLED AN "APPLE OF THE EARTH" IN FR—
WHO AM I KIDDING? JUST FLUNK ME.
AMEND

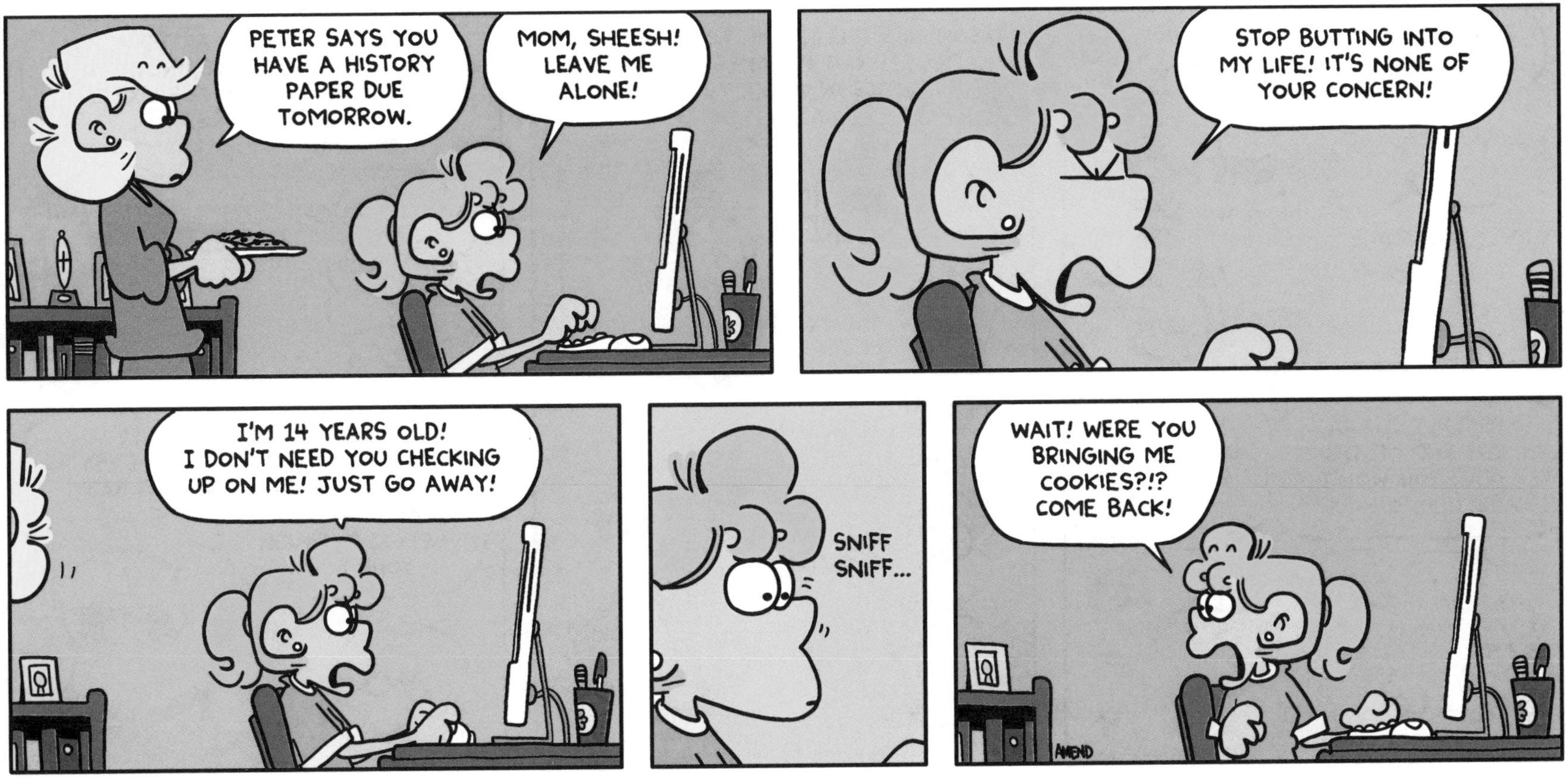
PETER SAYS YOU HAVE A HISTORY PAPER DUE TOMORROW.
MOM, SHEESH! LEAVE ME ALONE!
STOP BUTTING INTO MY LIFE! IT'S NONE OF YOUR CONCERN!
I'M 14 YEARS OLD! I DON'T NEED YOU CHECKING UP ON ME! JUST GO AWAY!
SNIFF SNIFF...
WAIT! WERE YOU BRINGING ME COOKIES?!? COME BACK!
AMEND

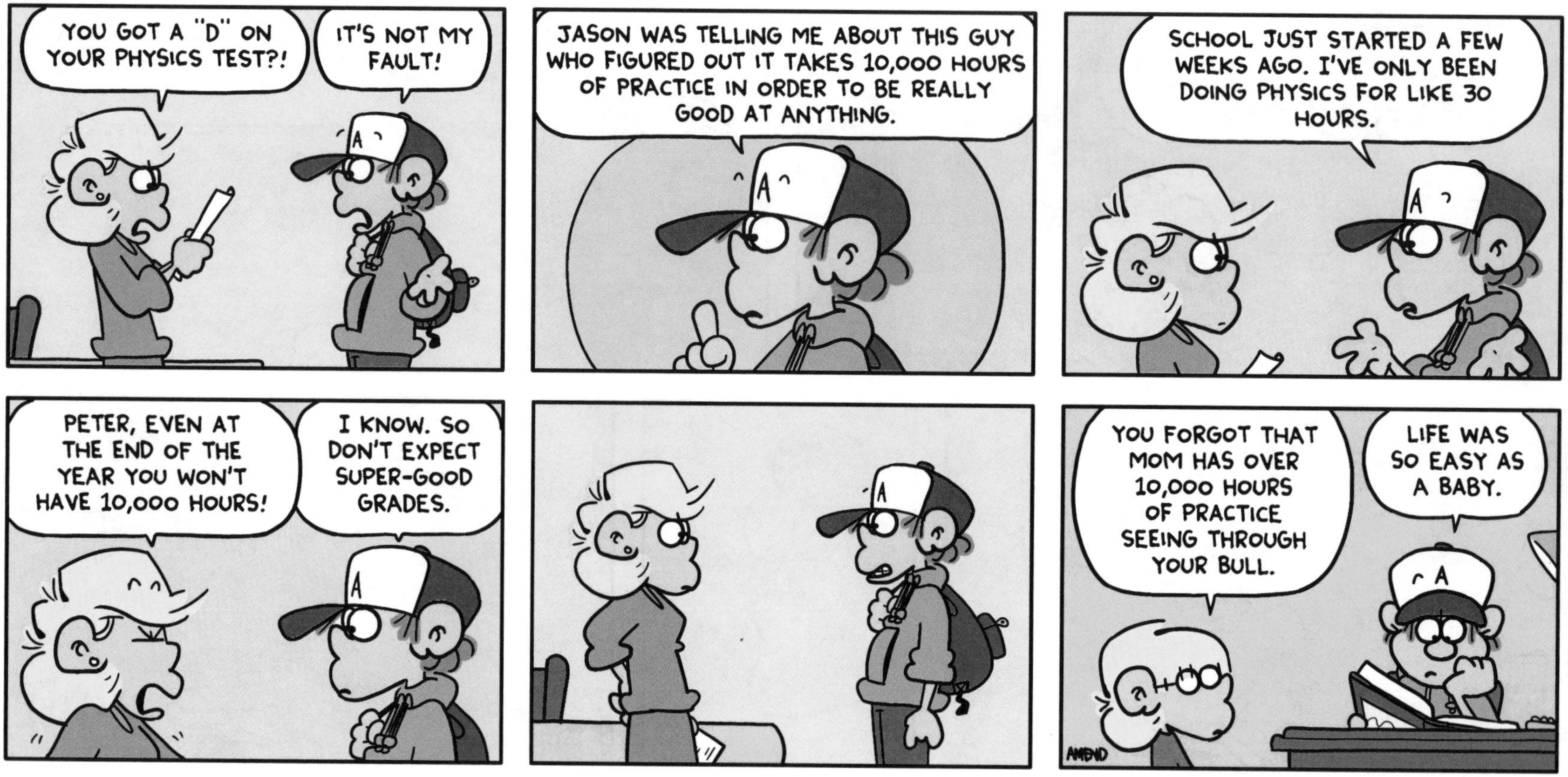
YOU GOT A "D" ON YOUR PHYSICS TEST?!
IT'S NOT MY FAULT!
JASON WAS TELLING ME ABOUT THIS GUY WHO FIGURED OUT IT TAKES 10,000 HOURS OF PRACTICE IN ORDER TO BE REALLY GOOD AT ANYTHING.
SCHOOL JUST STARTED A FEW WEEKS AGO. I'VE ONLY BEEN DOING PHYSICS FOR LIKE 30 HOURS.
PETER, EVEN AT THE END OF THE YEAR YOU WON'T HAVE 10,000 HOURS!
I KNOW. SO DON'T EXPECT SUPER-GOOD GRADES.
YOU FORGOT THAT MOM HAS OVER 10,000 HOURS OF PRACTICE SEEING THROUGH YOUR BULL.
LIFE WAS SO EASY AS A BABY.
AMEND

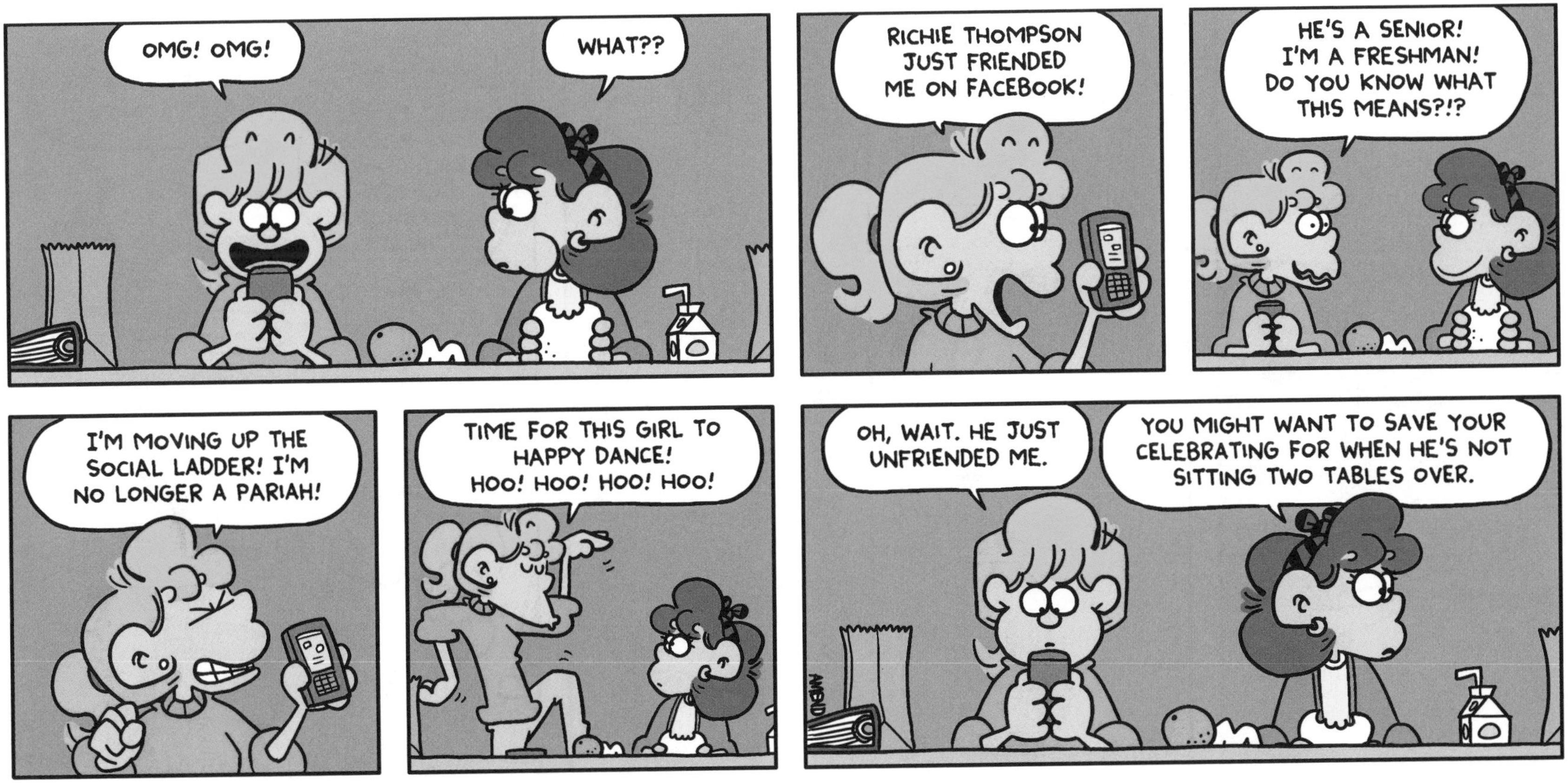
OMG! OMG!
WHAT??
RICHIE THOMPSON JUST FRIENDED ME ON FACEBOOK!
HE'S A SENIOR! I'M A FRESHMAN! DO YOU KNOW WHAT THIS MEANS?!?
I'M MOVING UP THE SOCIAL LADDER! I'M NO LONGER A PARIAH!
TIME FOR THIS GIRL TO HAPPY DANCE! HOO! HOO! HOO! HOO!
OH, WAIT. HE JUST UNFRIENDED ME.
YOU MIGHT WANT TO SAVE YOUR CELEBRATING FOR WHEN HE'S NOT SITTING TWO TABLES OVER.

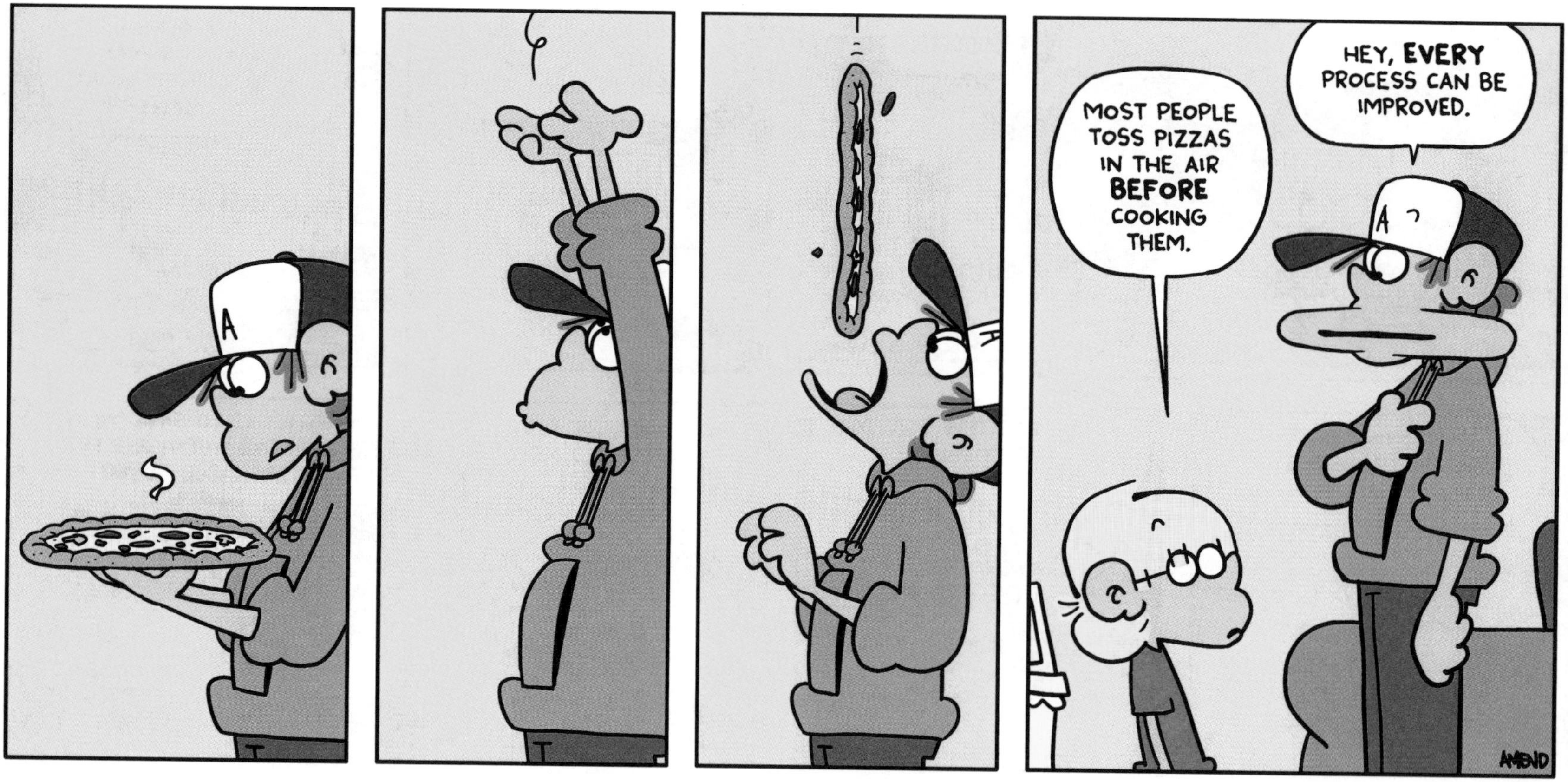
MOST PEOPLE TOSS PIZZAS IN THE AIR **BEFORE** COOKING THEM.
HEY, **EVERY** PROCESS CAN BE IMPROVED.
AMEND

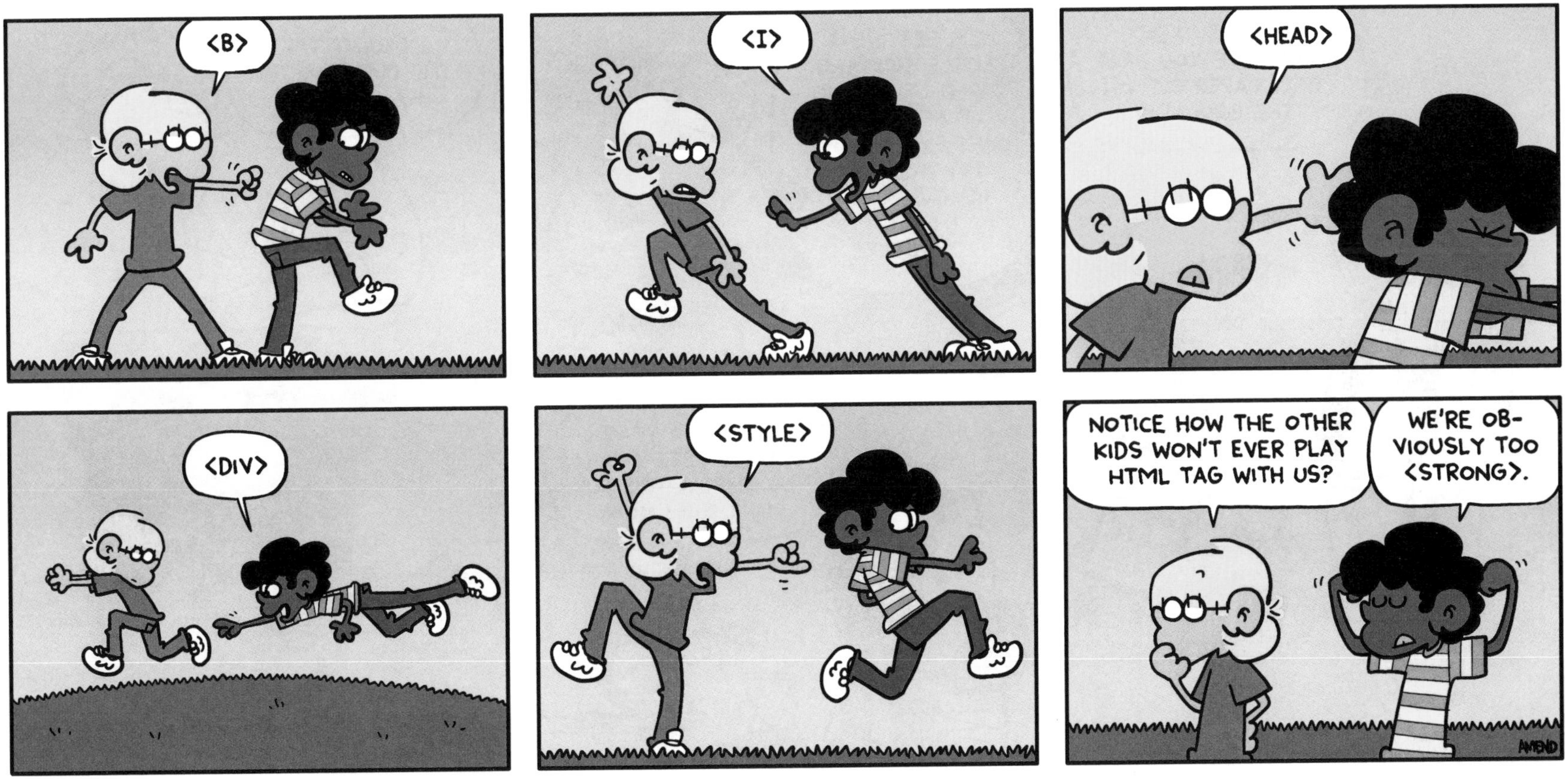
<B>
<I>
<HEAD>
<DIV>
<STYLE>
NOTICE HOW THE OTHER KIDS WON'T EVER PLAY HTML TAG WITH US?
WE'RE OB-VIOUSLY TOO <STRONG>.
AMEND

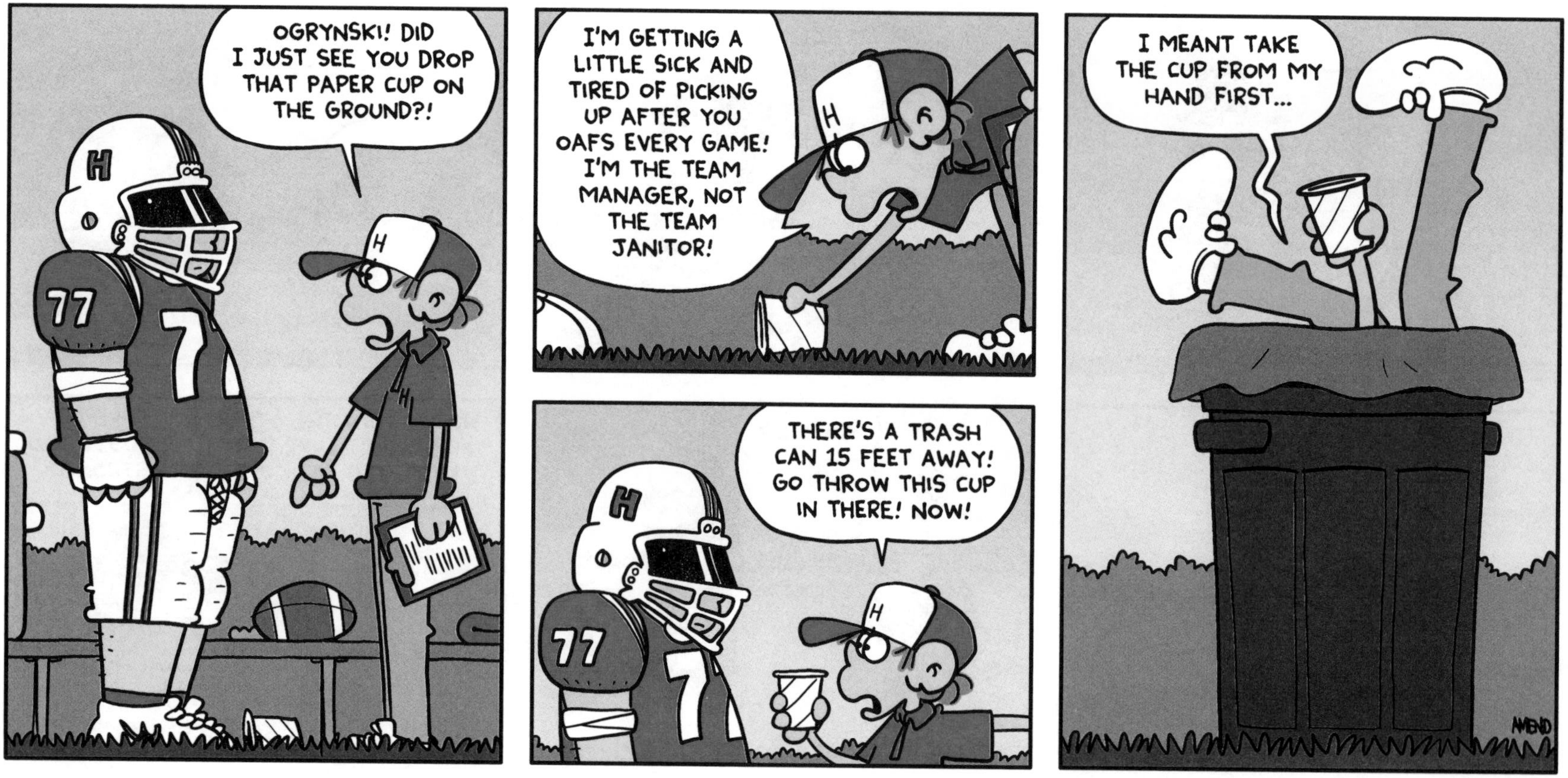
OGRYNSKI! DID I JUST SEE YOU DROP THAT PAPER CUP ON THE GROUND?!
I'M GETTING A LITTLE SICK AND TIRED OF PICKING UP AFTER YOU OAFS EVERY GAME! I'M THE TEAM MANAGER, NOT THE TEAM JANITOR!
THERE'S A TRASH CAN 15 FEET AWAY! GO THROW THIS CUP IN THERE! NOW!
I MEANT TAKE THE CUP FROM MY HAND FIRST...
AMEND

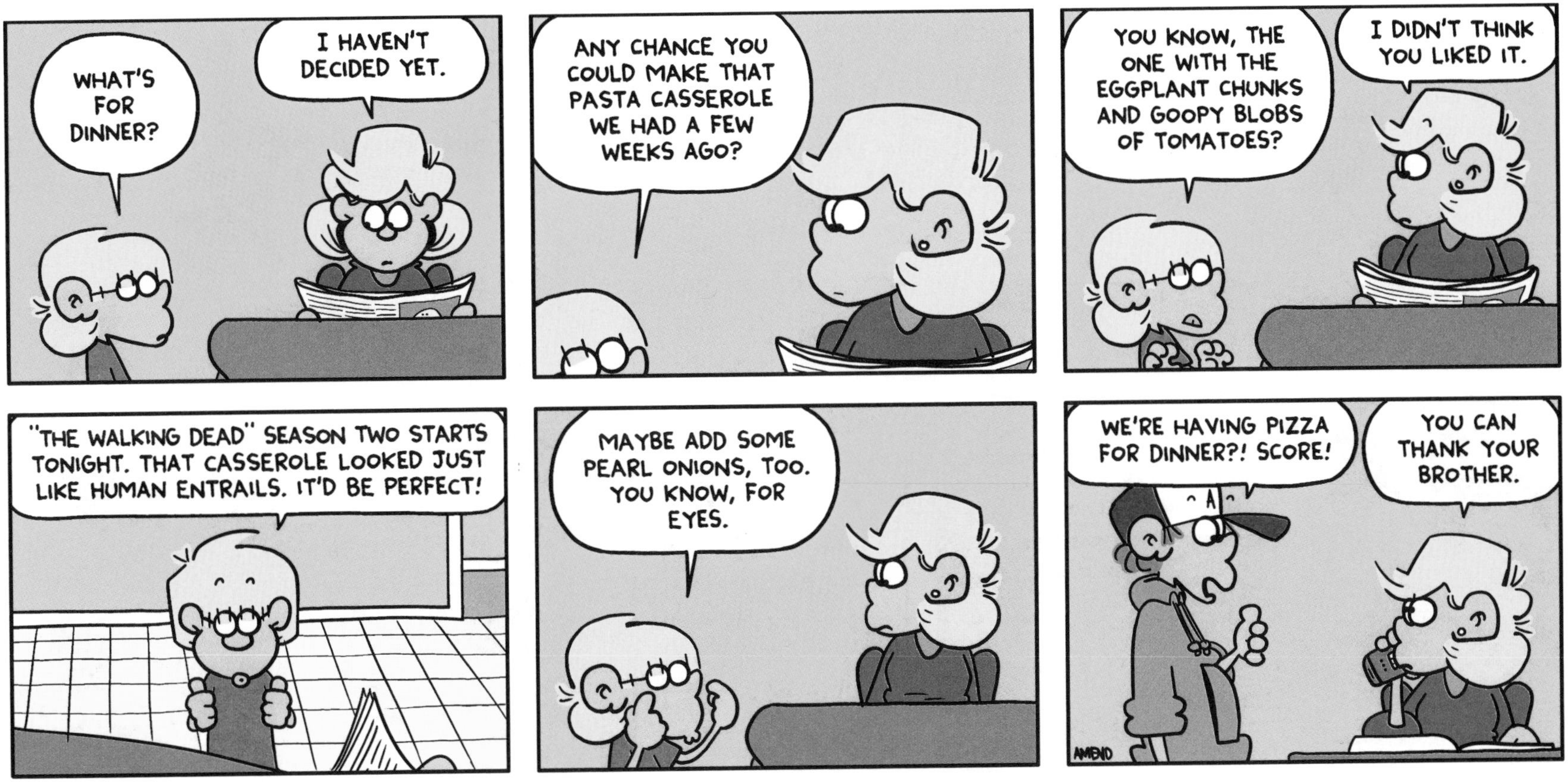
WHAT'S FOR DINNER?
I HAVEN'T DECIDED YET.
ANY CHANCE YOU COULD MAKE THAT PASTA CASSEROLE WE HAD A FEW WEEKS AGO?
YOU KNOW, THE ONE WITH THE EGGPLANT CHUNKS AND GOOPY BLOBS OF TOMATOES?
I DIDN'T THINK YOU LIKED IT.
"THE WALKING DEAD" SEASON TWO STARTS TONIGHT. THAT CASSEROLE LOOKED JUST LIKE HUMAN ENTRAILS. IT'D BE PERFECT!
MAYBE ADD SOME PEARL ONIONS, TOO. YOU KNOW, FOR EYES.
WE'RE HAVING PIZZA FOR DINNER?! SCORE!
YOU CAN THANK YOUR BROTHER.
AMEND

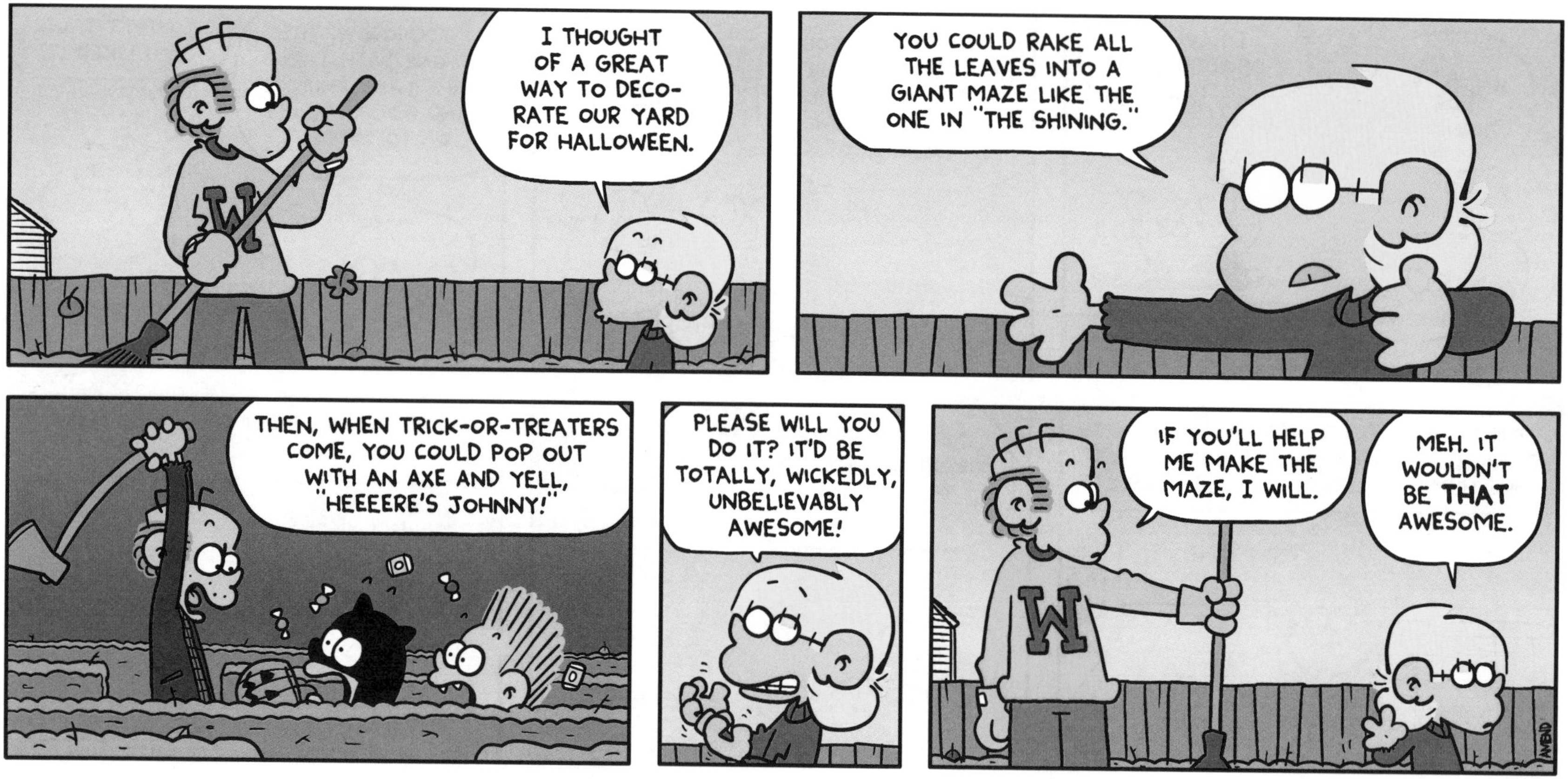
I THOUGHT OF A GREAT WAY TO DECO-RATE OUR YARD FOR HALLOWEEN.
YOU COULD RAKE ALL THE LEAVES INTO A GIANT MAZE LIKE THE ONE IN "THE SHINING."
THEN, WHEN TRICK-OR-TREATERS COME, YOU COULD POP OUT WITH AN AXE AND YELL, "HEEEERE'S JOHNNY!"
PLEASE WILL YOU DO IT? IT'D BE TOTALLY, WICKEDLY, UNBELIEVABLY AWESOME!
IF YOU'LL HELP ME MAKE THE MAZE, I WILL.
MEH. IT WOULDN'T BE **THAT** AWESOME.
AMEND

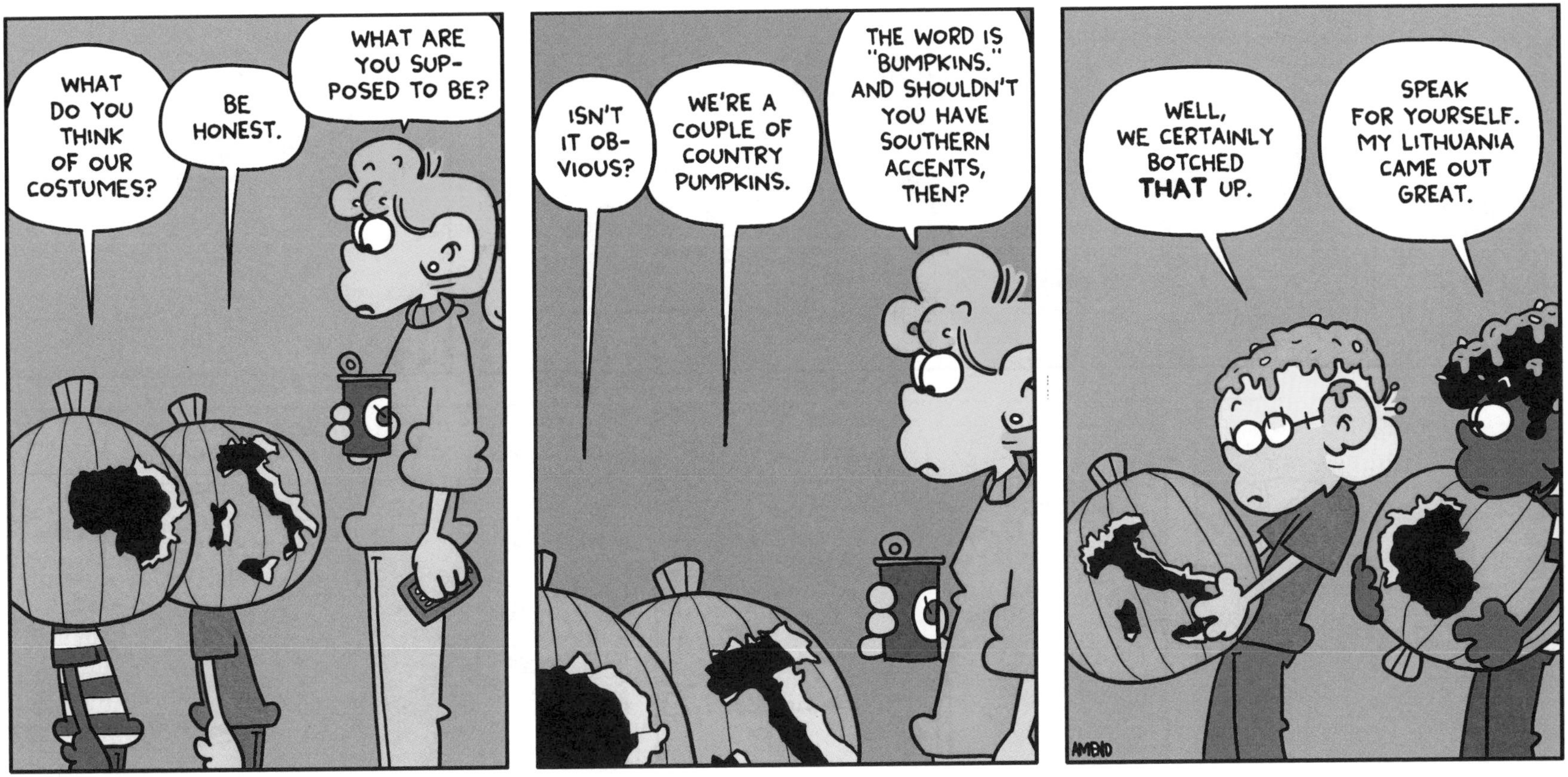
WHAT DO YOU THINK OF OUR COSTUMES?
BE HONEST.
WHAT ARE YOU SUP-POSED TO BE?
ISN'T IT OB-VIOUS?
WE'RE A COUPLE OF COUNTRY PUMPKINS.
THE WORD IS "BUMPKINS." AND SHOULDN'T YOU HAVE SOUTHERN ACCENTS, THEN?
WELL, WE CERTAINLY BOTCHED THAT UP.
SPEAK FOR YOURSELF. MY LITHUANIA CAME OUT GREAT.
AMEND

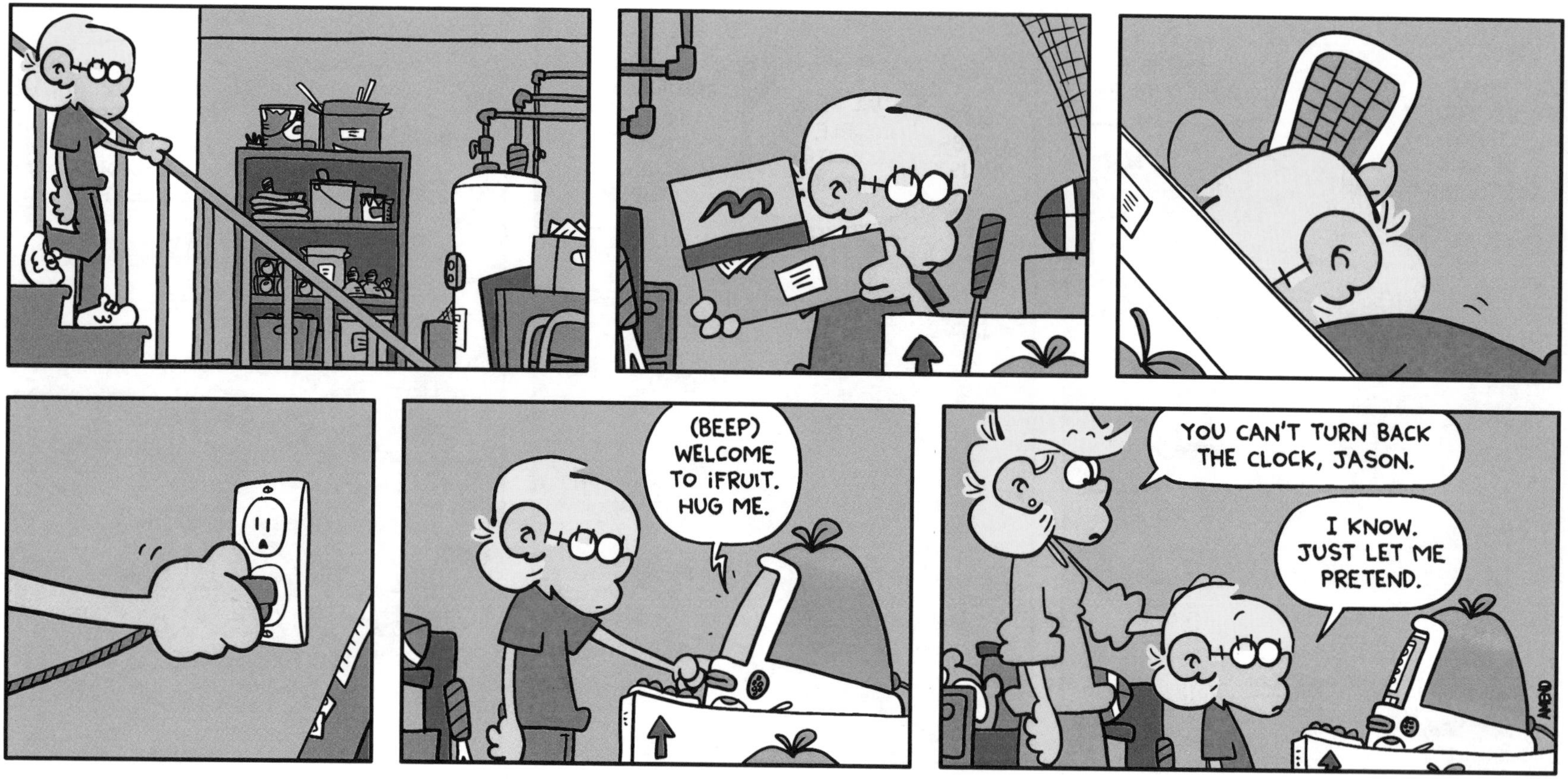
(BEEP) WELCOME TO iFRUIT. HUG ME.
YOU CAN'T TURN BACK THE CLOCK, JASON.
I KNOW. JUST LET ME PRETEND.
AMEND

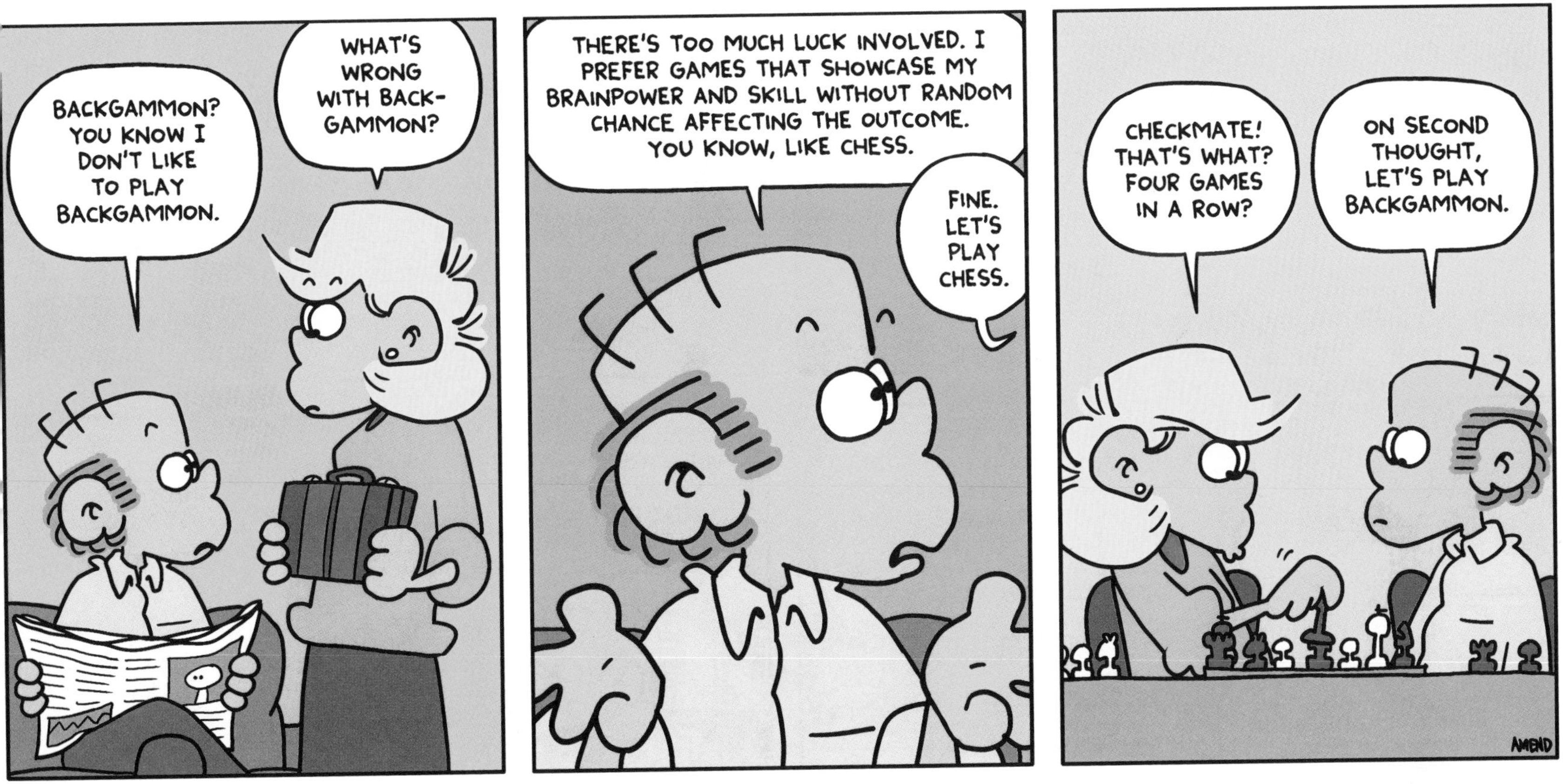
BACKGAMMON? YOU KNOW I DON'T LIKE TO PLAY BACKGAMMON.
WHAT'S WRONG WITH BACK-GAMMON?
THERE'S TOO MUCH LUCK INVOLVED. I PREFER GAMES THAT SHOWCASE MY BRAINPOWER AND SKILL WITHOUT RANDOM CHANCE AFFECTING THE OUTCOME. YOU KNOW, LIKE CHESS.
FINE. LET'S PLAY CHESS.
CHECKMATE! THAT'S WHAT? FOUR GAMES IN A ROW?
ON SECOND THOUGHT, LET'S PLAY BACKGAMMON.
AMEND

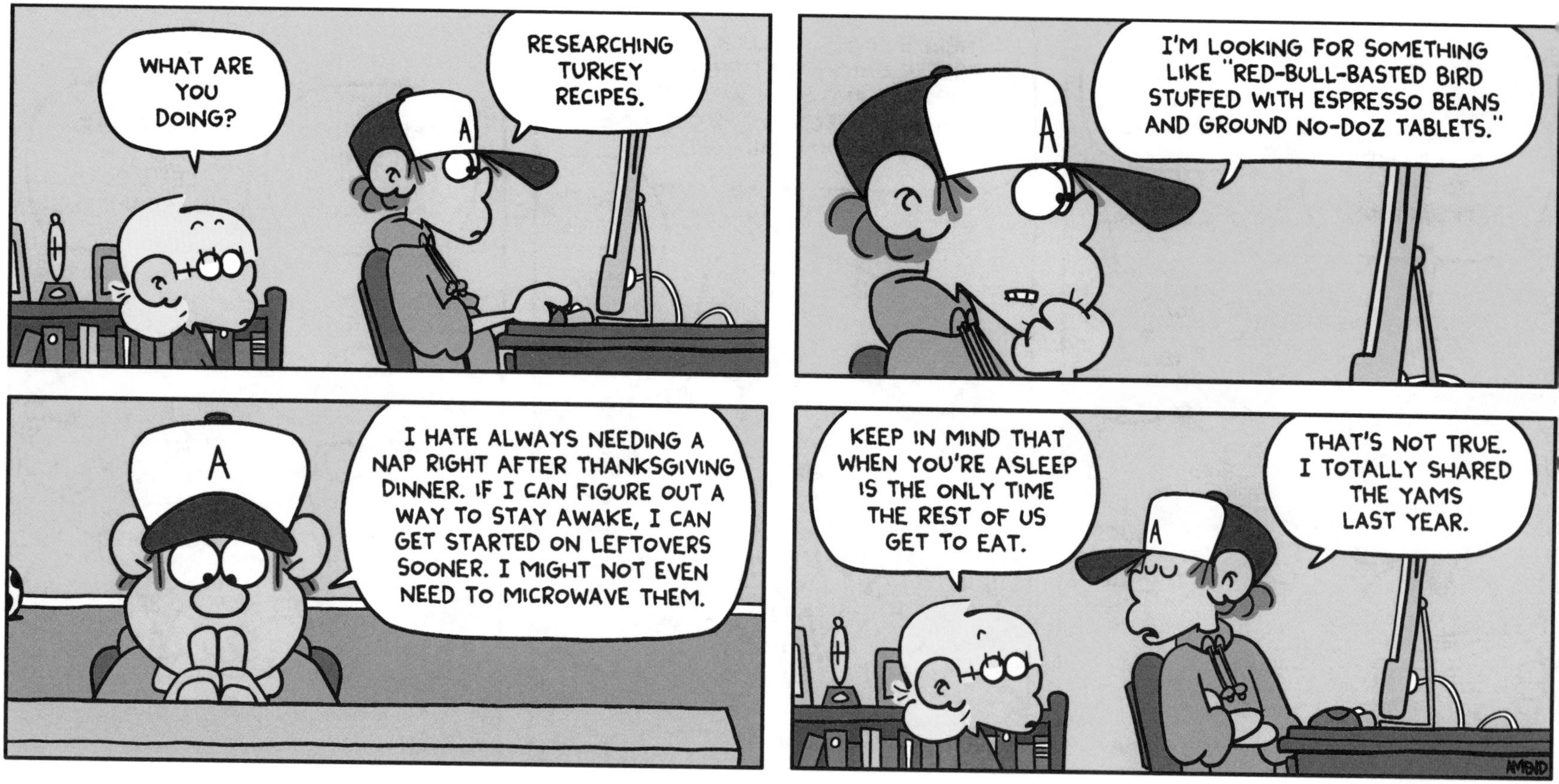
WHAT ARE YOU DOING?
RESEARCHING TURKEY RECIPES.
I'M LOOKING FOR SOMETHING LIKE "RED-BULL-BASTED BIRD STUFFED WITH ESPRESSO BEANS AND GROUND NO-DOZ TABLETS."
I HATE ALWAYS NEEDING A NAP RIGHT AFTER THANKSGIVING DINNER. IF I CAN FIGURE OUT A WAY TO STAY AWAKE, I CAN GET STARTED ON LEFTOVERS SOONER. I MIGHT NOT EVEN NEED TO MICROWAVE THEM.
KEEP IN MIND THAT WHEN YOU'RE ASLEEP IS THE ONLY TIME THE REST OF US GET TO EAT.
THAT'S NOT TRUE. I TOTALLY SHARED THE YAMS LAST YEAR.
AMEND

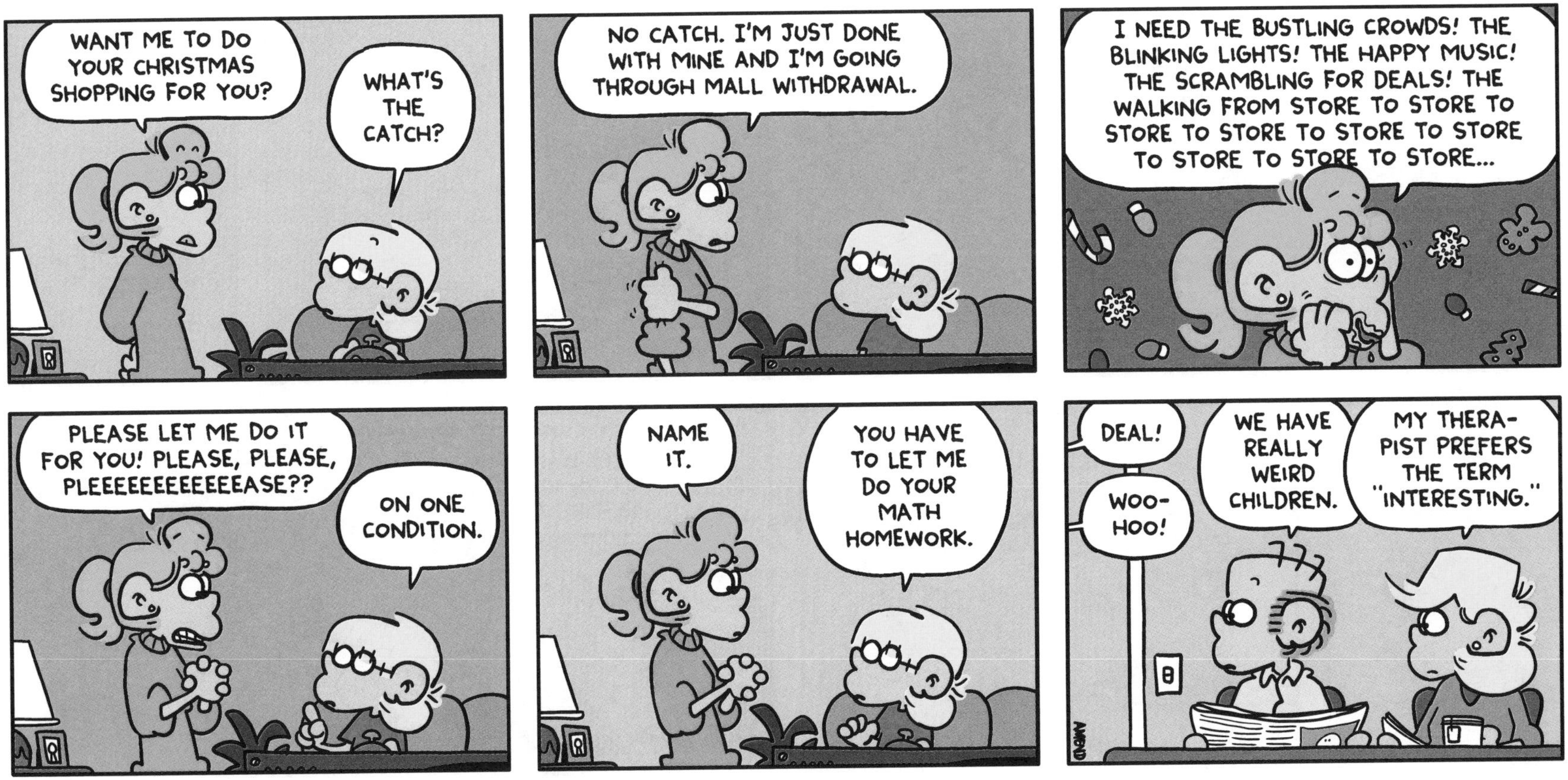
WANT ME TO DO YOUR CHRISTMAS SHOPPING FOR YOU?
WHAT'S THE CATCH?
NO CATCH. I'M JUST DONE WITH MINE AND I'M GOING THROUGH MALL WITHDRAWAL.
I NEED THE BUSTLING CROWDS! THE BLINKING LIGHTS! THE HAPPY MUSIC! THE SCRAMBLING FOR DEALS! THE WALKING FROM STORE TO STORE TO STORE TO STORE TO STORE TO STORE TO STORE TO STORE TO STORE...
PLEASE LET ME DO IT FOR YOU! PLEASE, PLEASE, PLEEEEEEEEEEEEASE??
ON ONE CONDITION.
NAME IT.
YOU HAVE TO LET ME DO YOUR MATH HOMEWORK.
DEAL!
WOO-HOO!
WE HAVE REALLY WEIRD CHILDREN.
MY THERA-PIST PREFERS THE TERM "INTERESTING."
AMEND

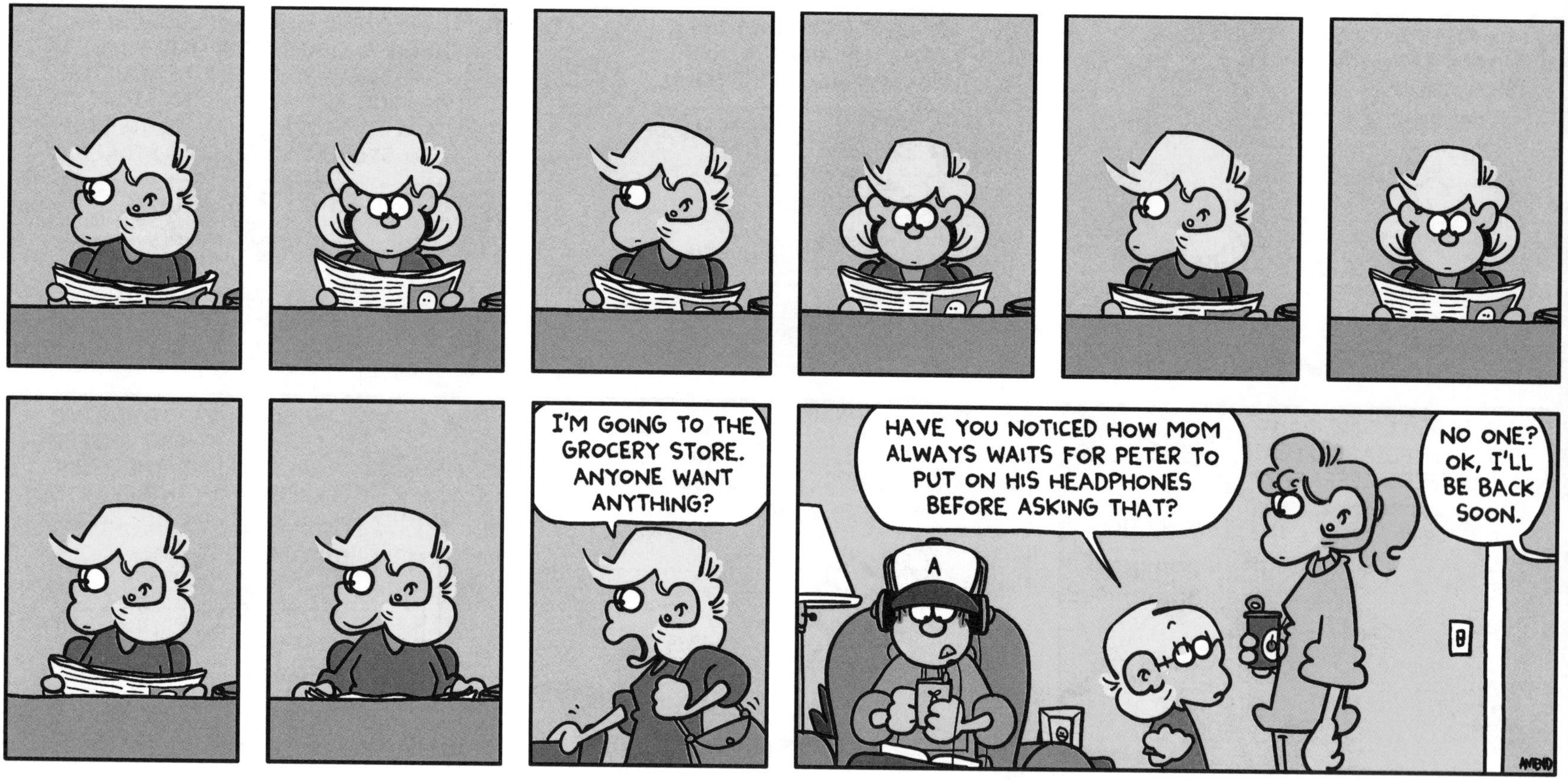
I'M GOING TO THE GROCERY STORE. ANYONE WANT ANYTHING?
HAVE YOU NOTICED HOW MOM ALWAYS WAITS FOR PETER TO PUT ON HIS HEADPHONES BEFORE ASKING THAT?
NO ONE? OK, I'LL BE BACK SOON.

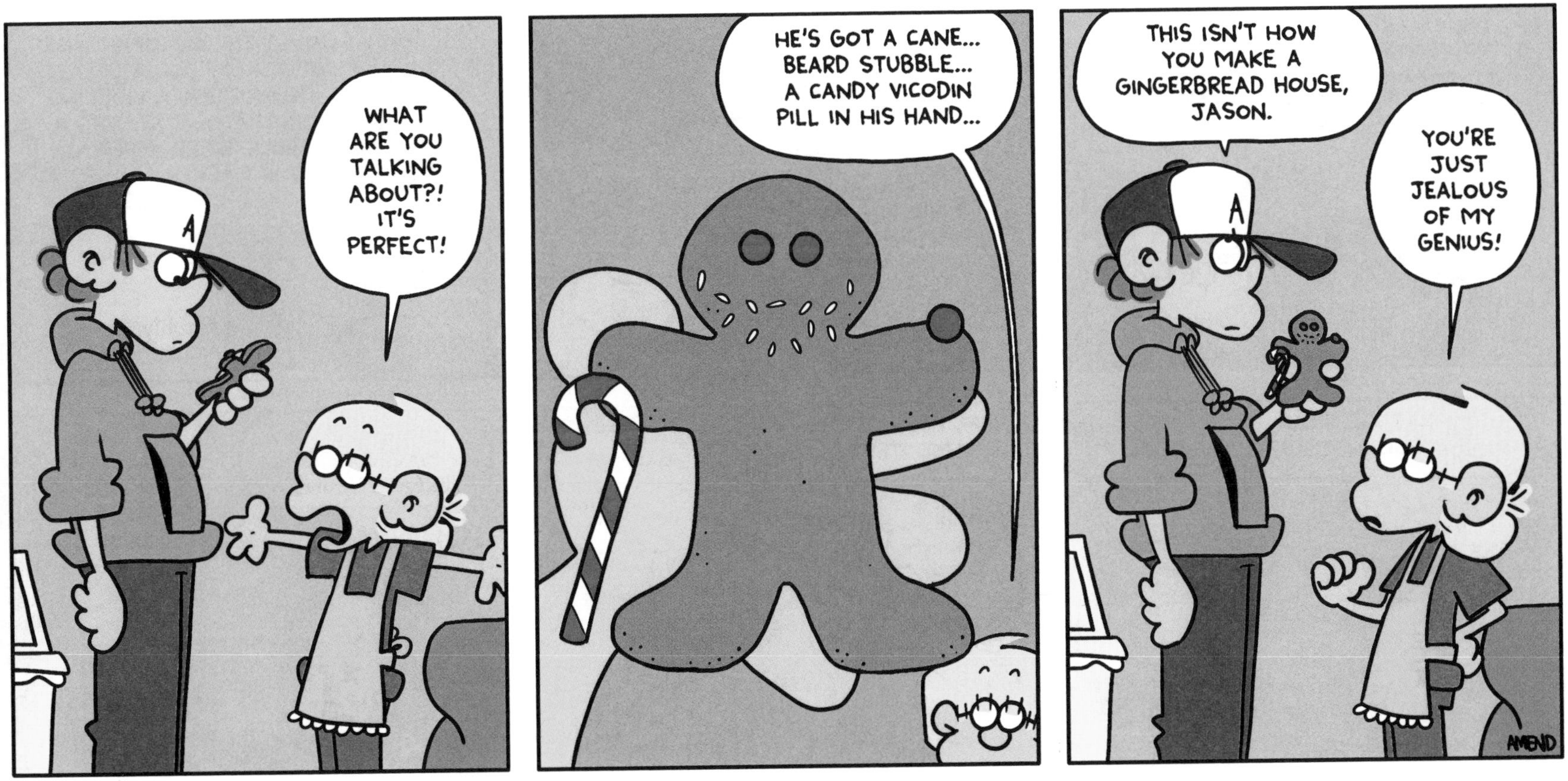
WHAT ARE YOU TALKING ABOUT?! IT'S PERFECT!
HE'S GOT A CANE... BEARD STUBBLE... A CANDY VICODIN PILL IN HIS HAND...
THIS ISN'T HOW YOU MAKE A GINGERBREAD HOUSE, JASON.
YOU'RE JUST JEALOUS OF MY GENIUS!
AMEND

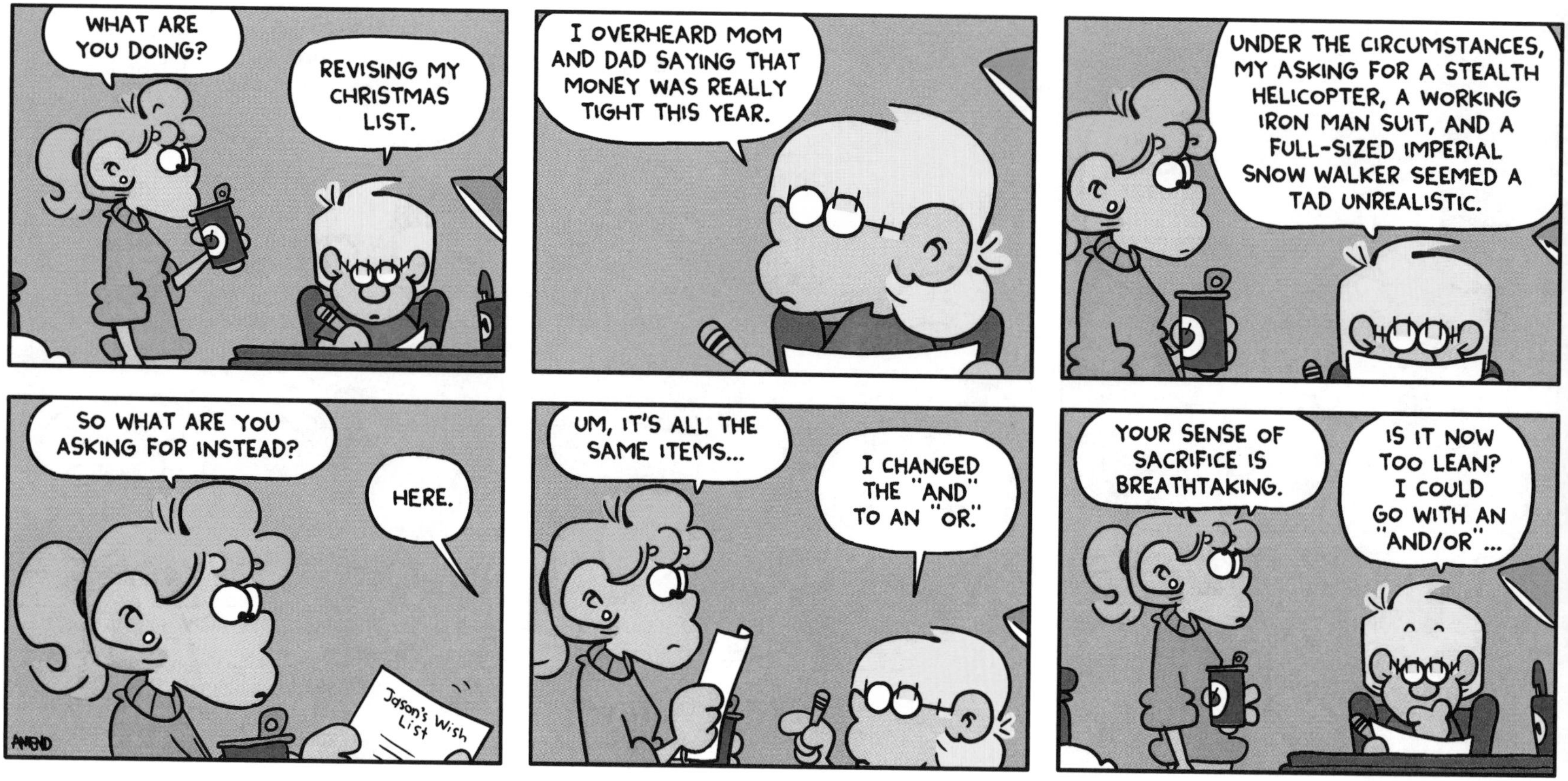
WHAT ARE YOU DOING?
REVISING MY CHRISTMAS LIST.
I OVERHEARD MOM AND DAD SAYING THAT MONEY WAS REALLY TIGHT THIS YEAR.
UNDER THE CIRCUMSTANCES, MY ASKING FOR A STEALTH HELICOPTER, A WORKING IRON MAN SUIT, AND A FULL-SIZED IMPERIAL SNOW WALKER SEEMED A TAD UNREALISTIC.
SO WHAT ARE YOU ASKING FOR INSTEAD?
HERE.
Jason's Wish List
AMEND
UM, IT'S ALL THE SAME ITEMS...
I CHANGED THE "AND" TO AN "OR."
YOUR SENSE OF SACRIFICE IS BREATHTAKING.
IS IT NOW TOO LEAN? I COULD GO WITH AN "AND/OR"...

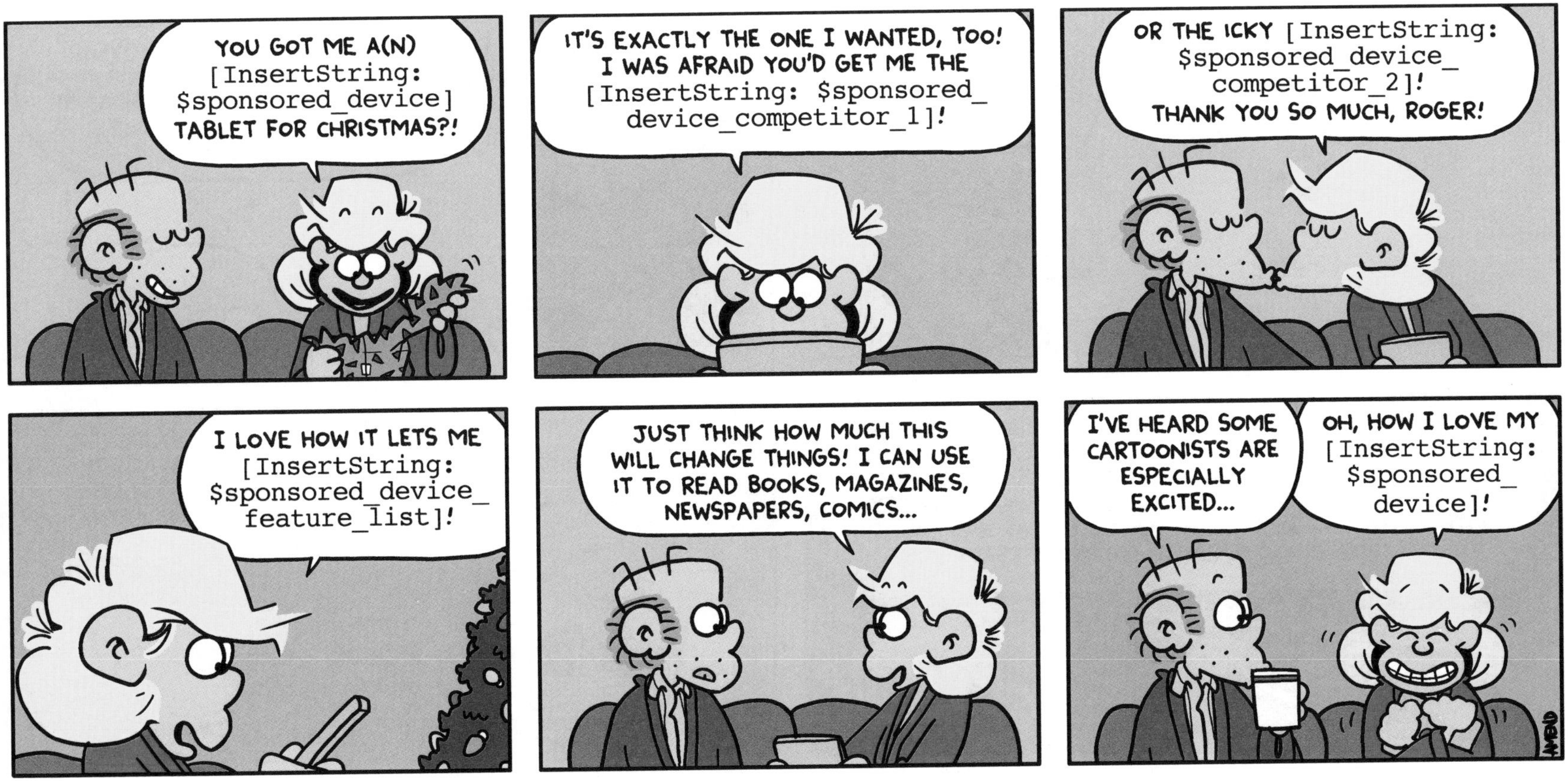
YOU GOT ME A(N) [InsertString: $sponsored_device] TABLET FOR CHRISTMAS?!
IT'S EXACTLY THE ONE I WANTED, TOO! I WAS AFRAID YOU'D GET ME THE [InsertString: $sponsored_device_competitor_1]!
OR THE ICKY [InsertString: $sponsored_device_competitor_2]! THANK YOU SO MUCH, ROGER!
I LOVE HOW IT LETS ME [InsertString: $sponsored_device_feature_list]!
JUST THINK HOW MUCH THIS WILL CHANGE THINGS! I CAN USE IT TO READ BOOKS, MAGAZINES, NEWSPAPERS, COMICS...
I'VE HEARD SOME CARTOONISTS ARE ESPECIALLY EXCITED...
OH, HOW I LOVE MY [InsertString: $sponsored_device]!

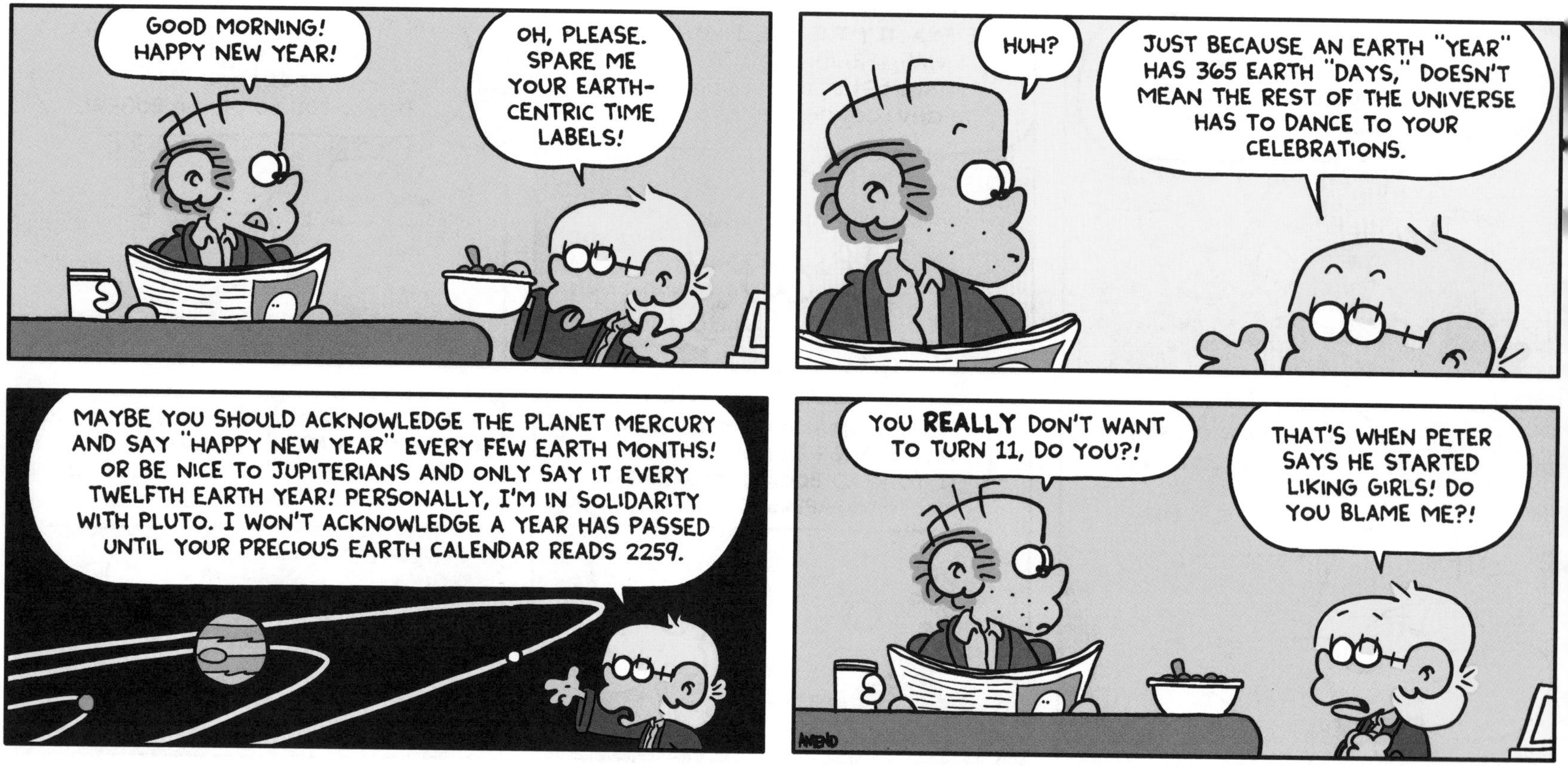
GOOD MORNING! HAPPY NEW YEAR!
OH, PLEASE. SPARE ME YOUR EARTH-CENTRIC TIME LABELS!
HUH?
JUST BECAUSE AN EARTH "YEAR" HAS 365 EARTH "DAYS," DOESN'T MEAN THE REST OF THE UNIVERSE HAS TO DANCE TO YOUR CELEBRATIONS.
MAYBE YOU SHOULD ACKNOWLEDGE THE PLANET MERCURY AND SAY "HAPPY NEW YEAR" EVERY FEW EARTH MONTHS! OR BE NICE TO JUPITERIANS AND ONLY SAY IT EVERY TWELFTH EARTH YEAR! PERSONALLY, I'M IN SOLIDARITY WITH PLUTO. I WON'T ACKNOWLEDGE A YEAR HAS PASSED UNTIL YOUR PRECIOUS EARTH CALENDAR READS 2259.
YOU **REALLY** DON'T WANT TO TURN 11, DO YOU?!
THAT'S WHEN PETER SAYS HE STARTED LIKING GIRLS! DO YOU BLAME ME?!
AMEND

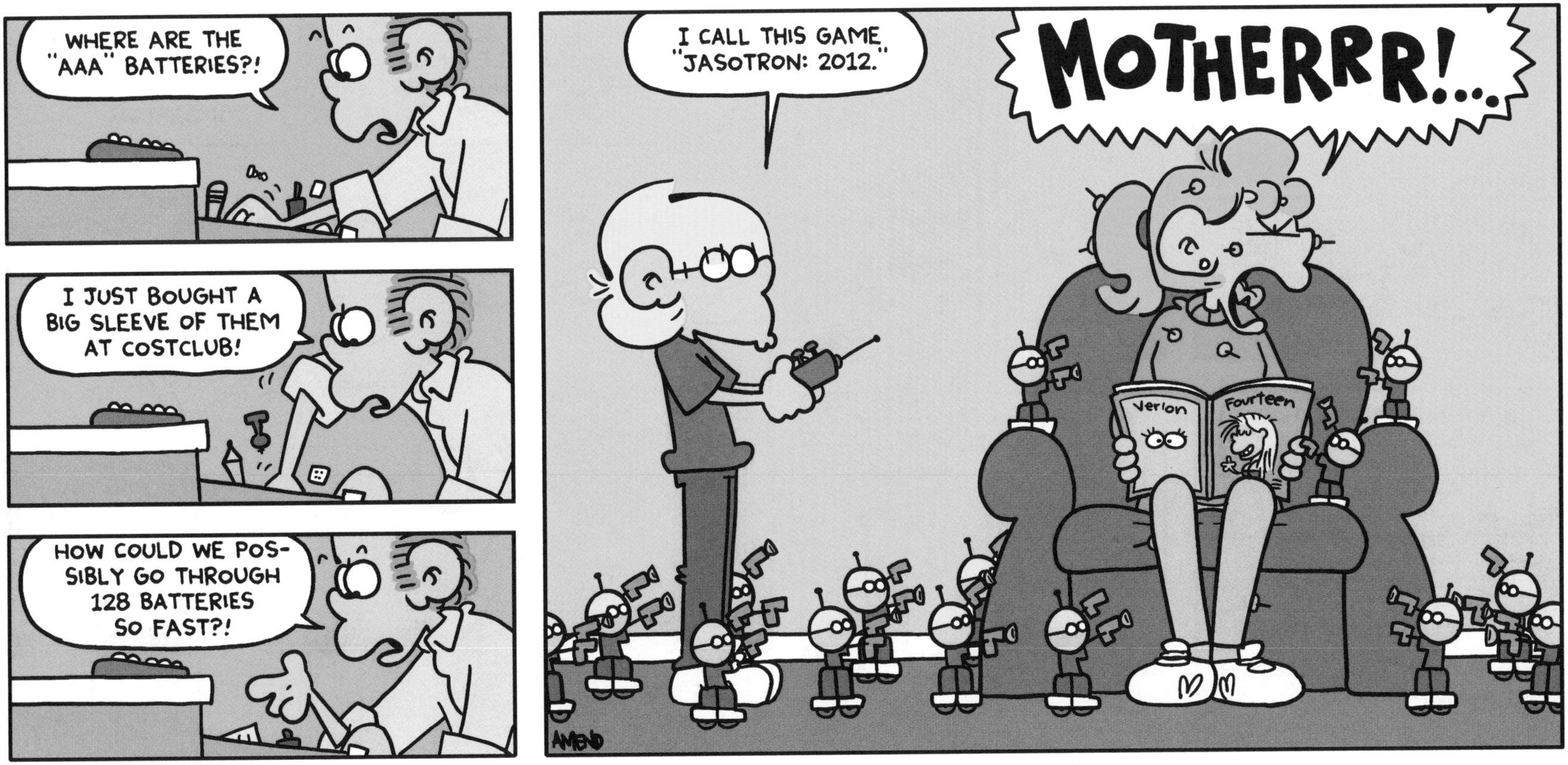

WHERE ARE THE "AAA" BATTERIES?!
I JUST BOUGHT A BIG SLEEVE OF THEM AT COSTCLUB!
HOW COULD WE POSSIBLY GO THROUGH 128 BATTERIES SO FAST?!
I CALL THIS GAME "JASOTRON: 2012."
MOTHERRR!...
Verlon
Fourteen
AMEND

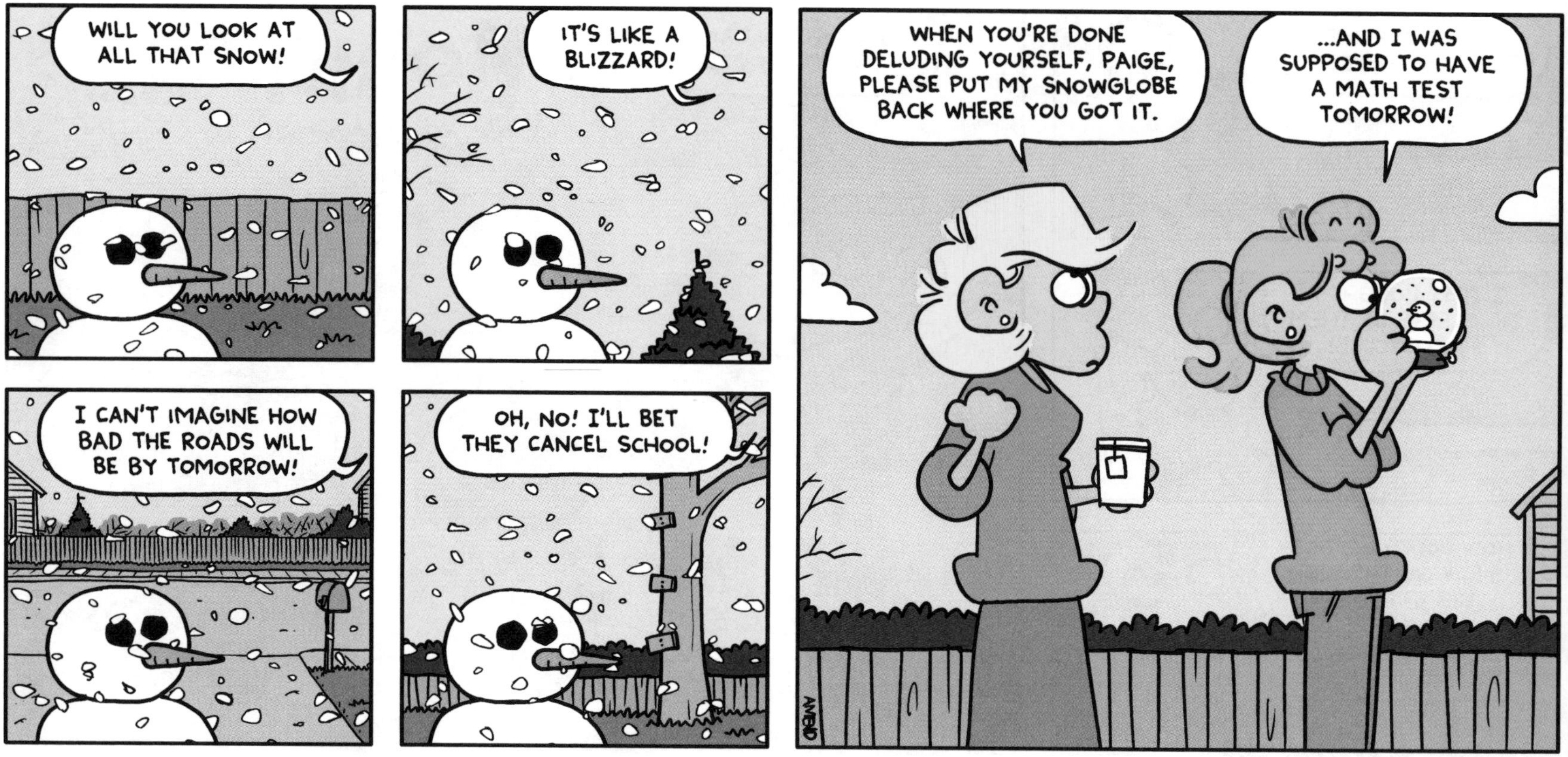
WILL YOU LOOK AT ALL THAT SNOW!
IT'S LIKE A BLIZZARD!
I CAN'T IMAGINE HOW BAD THE ROADS WILL BE BY TOMORROW!
OH, NO! I'LL BET THEY CANCEL SCHOOL!
WHEN YOU'RE DONE DELUDING YOURSELF, PAIGE, PLEASE PUT MY SNOWGLOBE BACK WHERE YOU GOT IT.
...AND I WAS SUPPOSED TO HAVE A MATH TEST TOMORROW!
AMEND

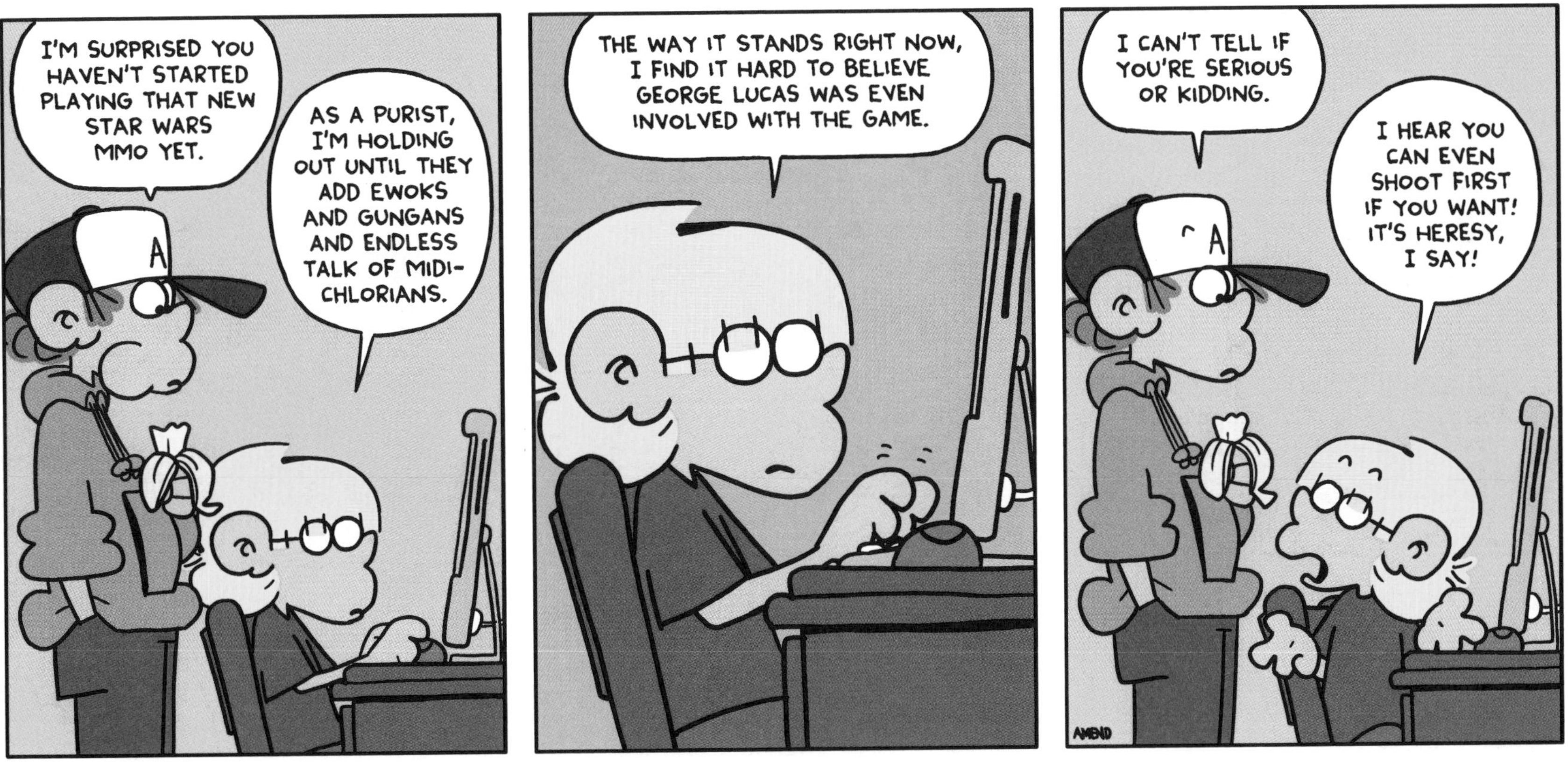
I'M SURPRISED YOU HAVEN'T STARTED PLAYING THAT NEW STAR WARS MMO YET.
AS A PURIST, I'M HOLDING OUT UNTIL THEY ADD EWOKS AND GUNGANS AND ENDLESS TALK OF MIDI-CHLORIANS.
THE WAY IT STANDS RIGHT NOW, I FIND IT HARD TO BELIEVE GEORGE LUCAS WAS EVEN INVOLVED WITH THE GAME.
I CAN'T TELL IF YOU'RE SERIOUS OR KIDDING.
I HEAR YOU CAN EVEN SHOOT FIRST IF YOU WANT! IT'S HERESY, I SAY!
AMEND

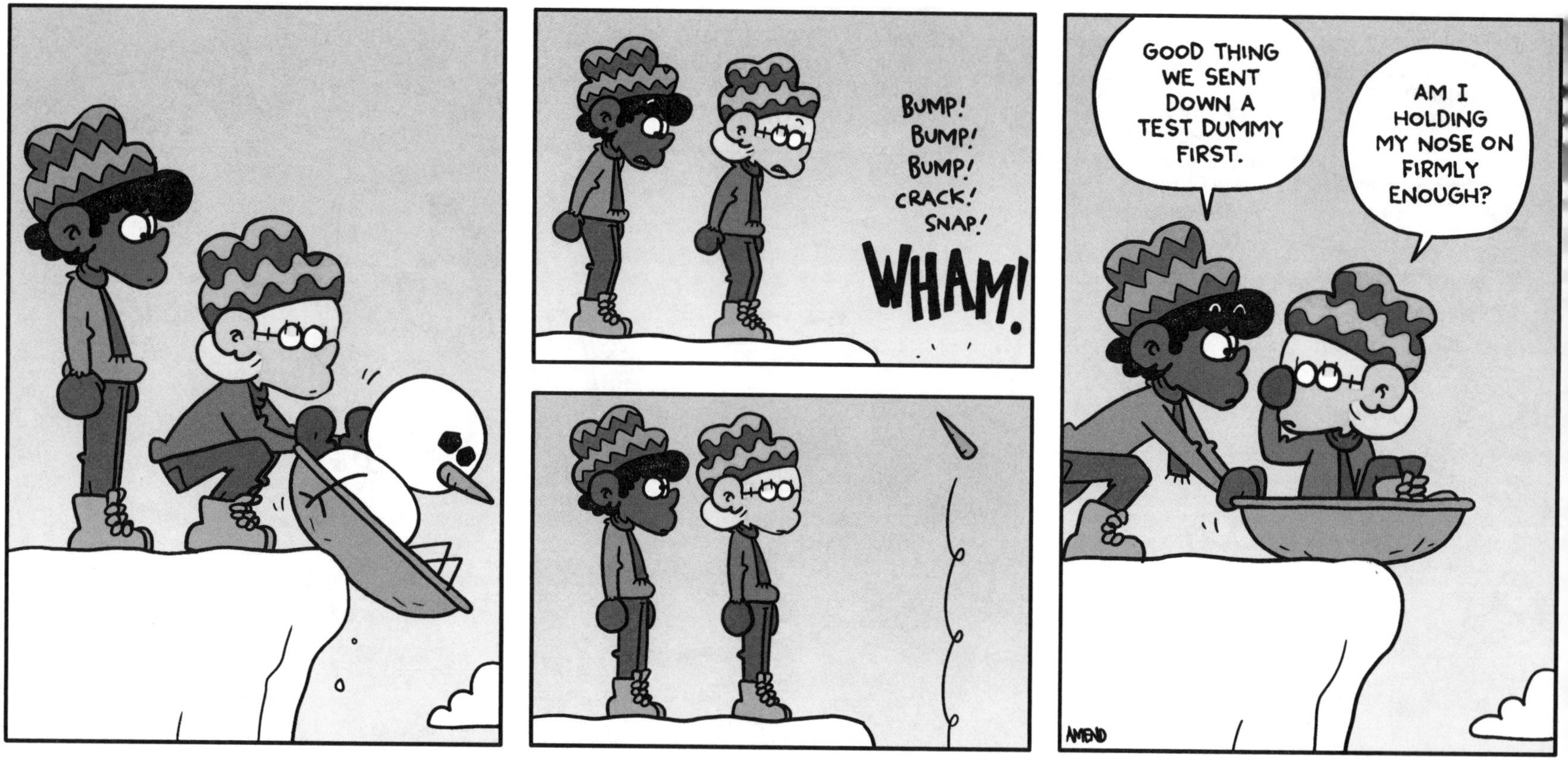
BUMP!
BUMP!
BUMP!
CRACK!
SNAP!
WHAM!
GOOD THING WE SENT DOWN A TEST DUMMY FIRST.
AM I HOLDING MY NOSE ON FIRMLY ENOUGH?
AMEND

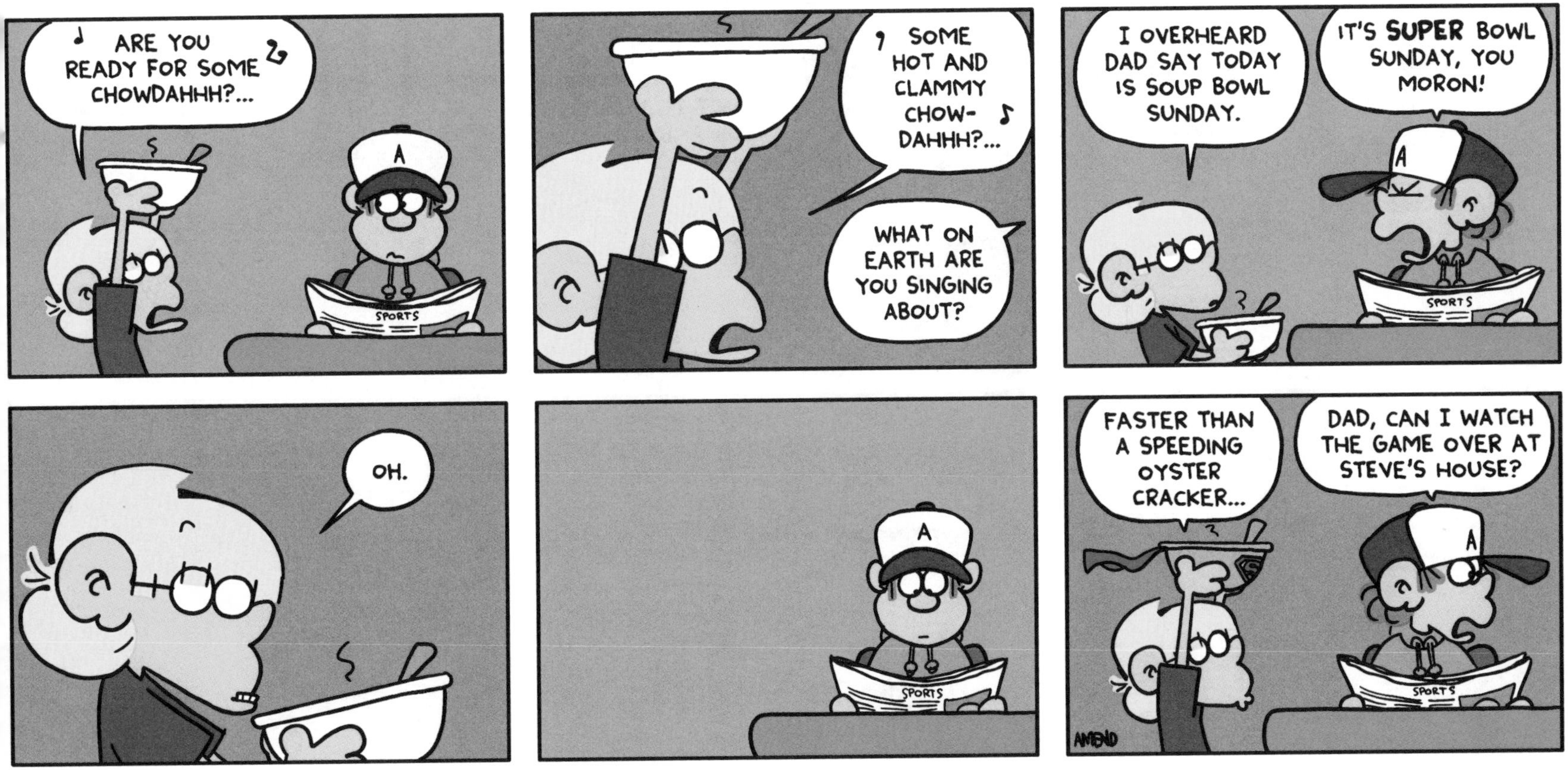
ARE YOU READY FOR SOME CHOWDAHHH?...
SOME HOT AND CLAMMY CHOW-DAHHH?...
WHAT ON EARTH ARE YOU SINGING ABOUT?
I OVERHEARD DAD SAY TODAY IS SOUP BOWL SUNDAY.
IT'S **SUPER** BOWL SUNDAY, YOU MORON!
OH.
FASTER THAN A SPEEDING OYSTER CRACKER...
DAD, CAN I WATCH THE GAME OVER AT STEVE'S HOUSE?
SPORTS
AMEND

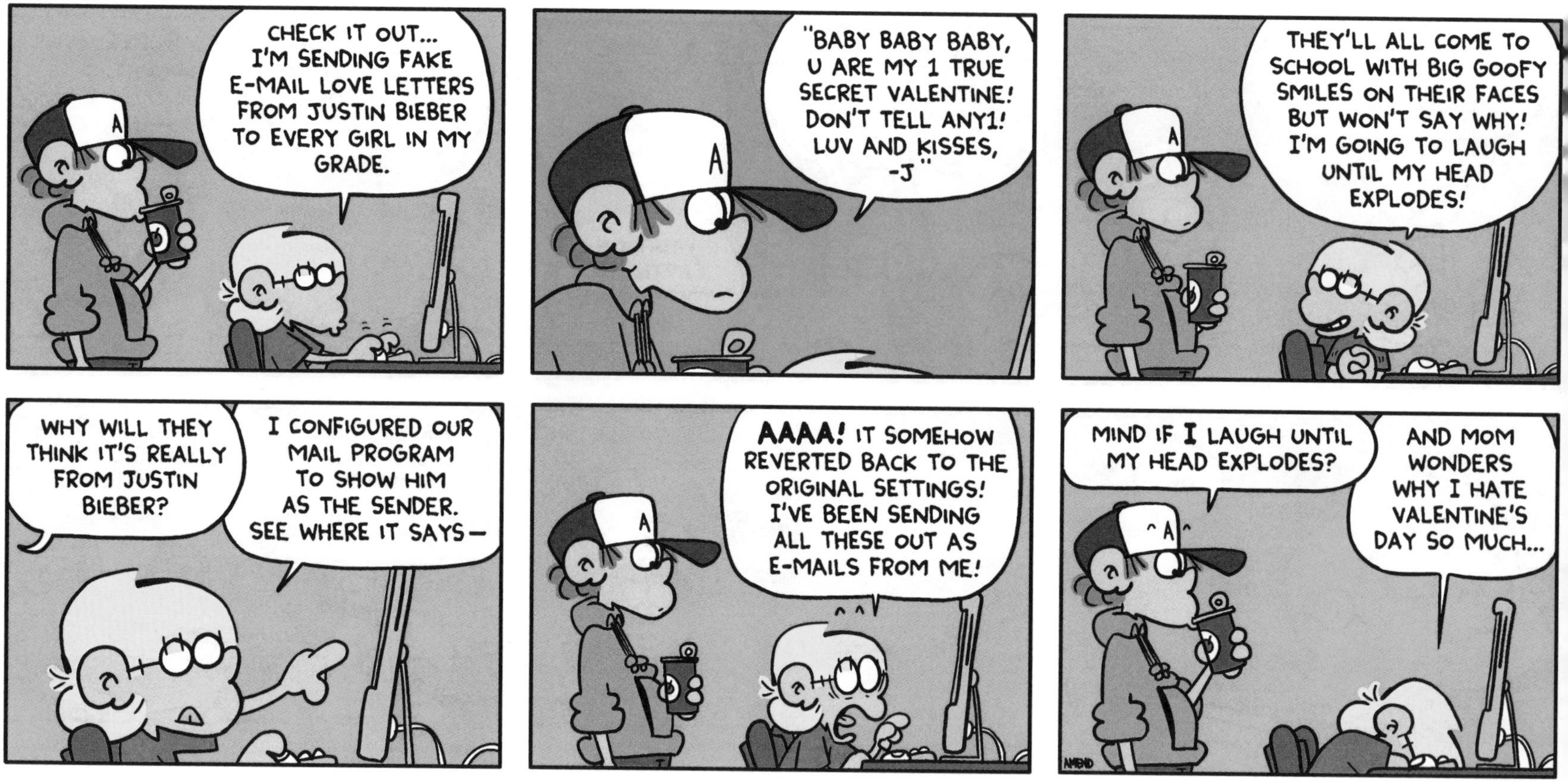
CHECK IT OUT... I'M SENDING FAKE E-MAIL LOVE LETTERS FROM JUSTIN BIEBER TO EVERY GIRL IN MY GRADE.
"BABY BABY BABY, U ARE MY 1 TRUE SECRET VALENTINE! DON'T TELL ANY1! LUV AND KISSES, -J"
THEY'LL ALL COME TO SCHOOL WITH BIG GOOFY SMILES ON THEIR FACES BUT WON'T SAY WHY! I'M GOING TO LAUGH UNTIL MY HEAD EXPLODES!
WHY WILL THEY THINK IT'S REALLY FROM JUSTIN BIEBER?
I CONFIGURED OUR MAIL PROGRAM TO SHOW HIM AS THE SENDER. SEE WHERE IT SAYS—
AAAA! IT SOMEHOW REVERTED BACK TO THE ORIGINAL SETTINGS! I'VE BEEN SENDING ALL THESE OUT AS E-MAILS FROM ME!
MIND IF I LAUGH UNTIL MY HEAD EXPLODES?
AND MOM WONDERS WHY I HATE VALENTINE'S DAY SO MUCH...
AMEND

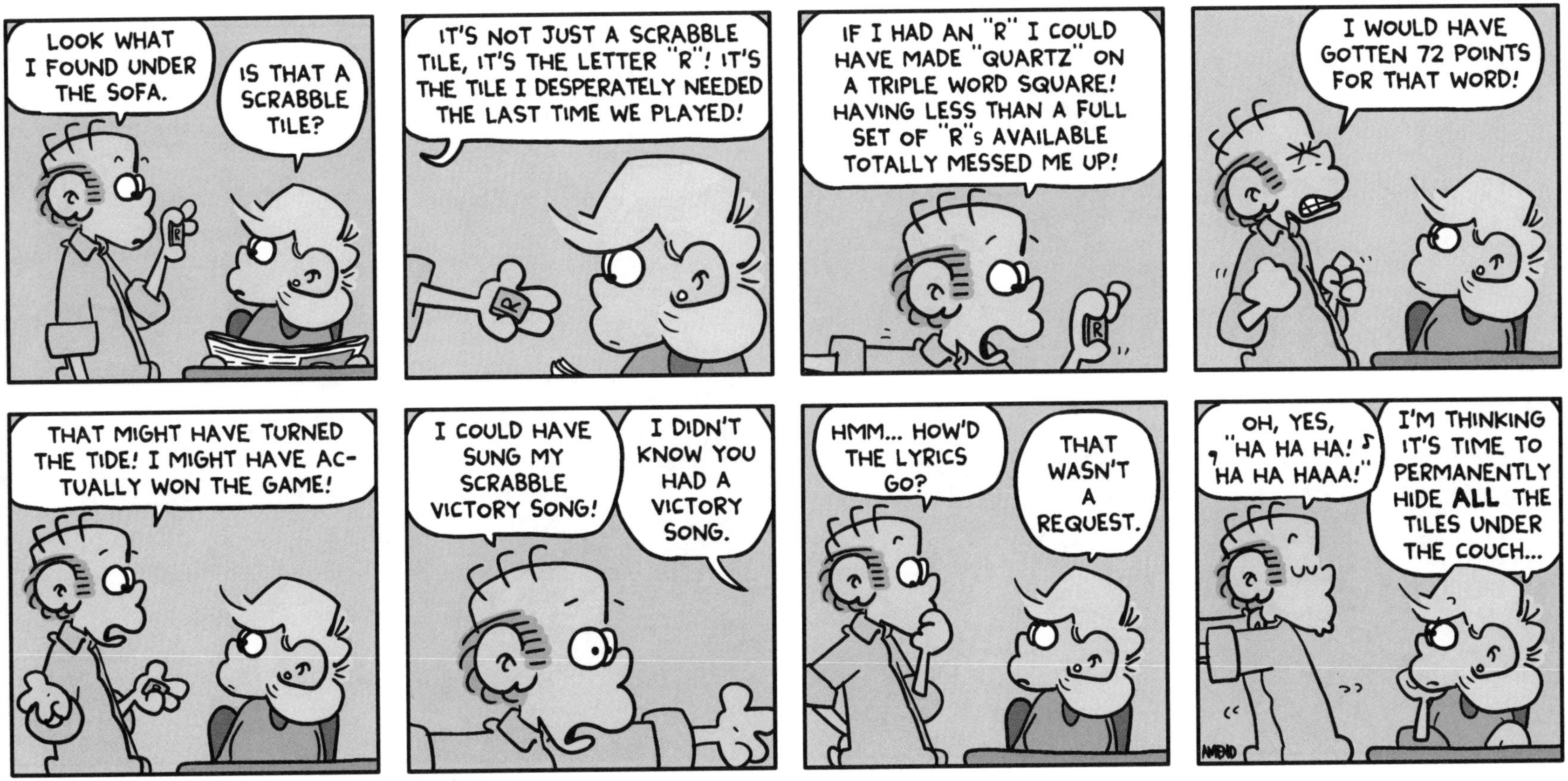
LOOK WHAT I FOUND UNDER THE SOFA.
IS THAT A SCRABBLE TILE?
R
IT'S NOT JUST A SCRABBLE TILE, IT'S THE LETTER "R"! IT'S THE TILE I DESPERATELY NEEDED THE LAST TIME WE PLAYED!
R
IF I HAD AN "R" I COULD HAVE MADE "QUARTZ" ON A TRIPLE WORD SQUARE! HAVING LESS THAN A FULL SET OF "R"s AVAILABLE TOTALLY MESSED ME UP!
R
I WOULD HAVE GOTTEN 72 POINTS FOR THAT WORD!
THAT MIGHT HAVE TURNED THE TIDE! I MIGHT HAVE ACTUALLY WON THE GAME!
I COULD HAVE SUNG MY SCRABBLE VICTORY SONG!
I DIDN'T KNOW YOU HAD A VICTORY SONG.
HMM... HOW'D THE LYRICS GO?
THAT WASN'T A REQUEST.
OH, YES, "HA HA HA! HA HA HAAA!"
I'M THINKING IT'S TIME TO PERMANENTLY HIDE ALL THE TILES UNDER THE COUCH...
AMEND

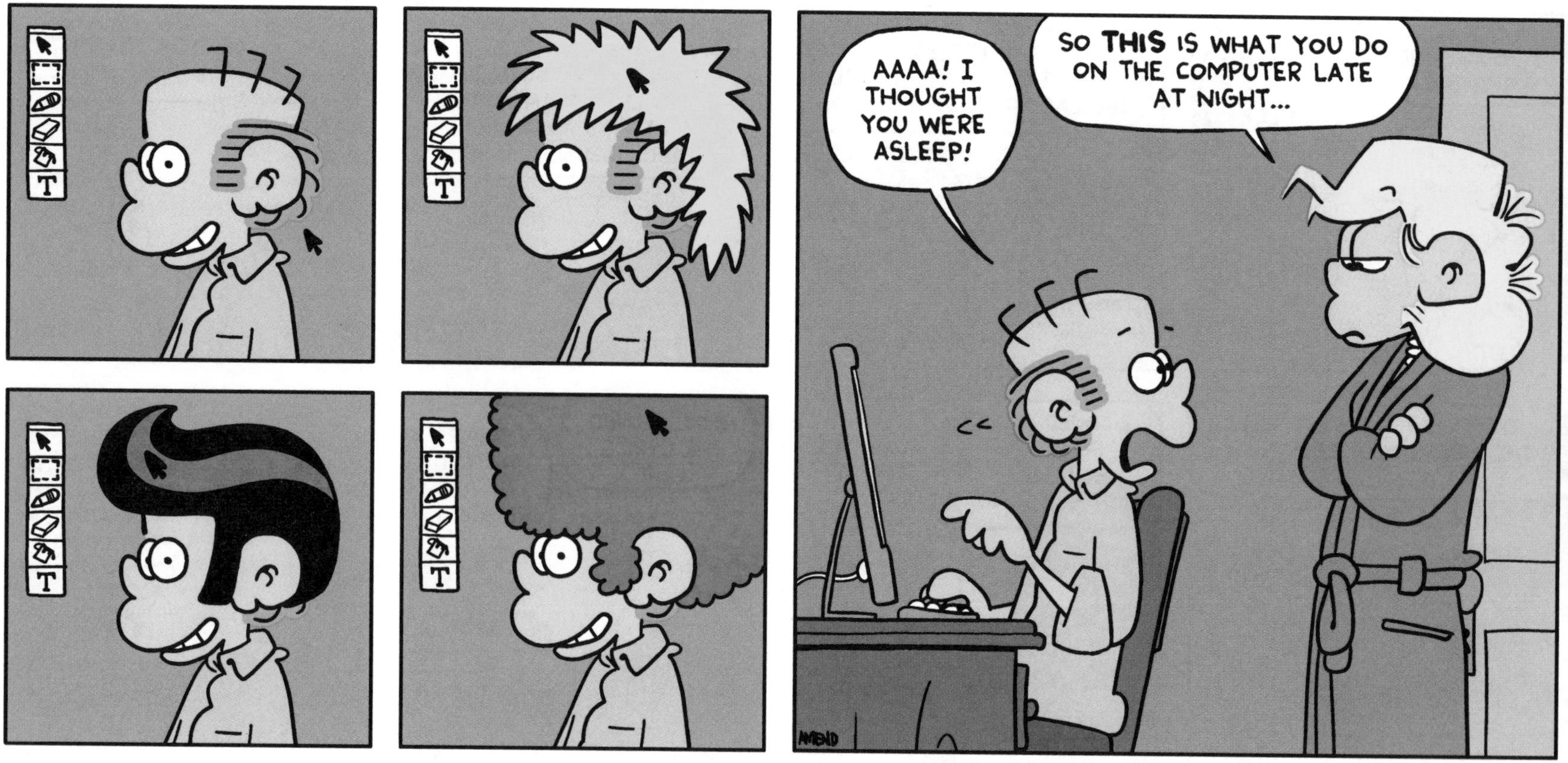
AAAA! I THOUGHT YOU WERE ASLEEP!
SO **THIS** IS WHAT YOU DO ON THE COMPUTER LATE AT NIGHT...
AMEND

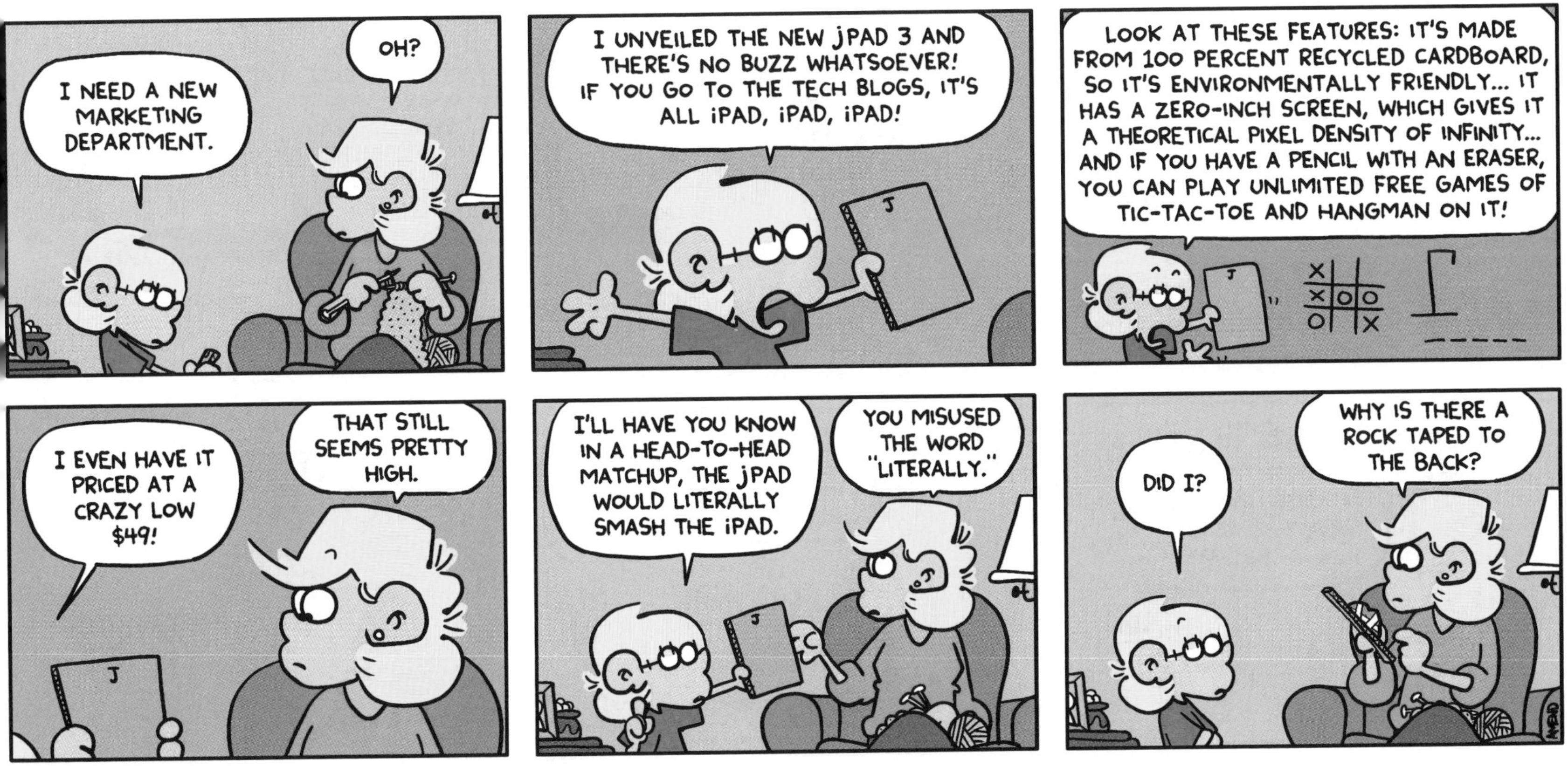
I NEED A NEW MARKETING DEPARTMENT.
OH?
I UNVEILED THE NEW jPAD 3 AND THERE'S NO BUZZ WHATSOEVER! IF YOU GO TO THE TECH BLOGS, IT'S ALL iPAD, iPAD, iPAD!
J
LOOK AT THESE FEATURES: IT'S MADE FROM 100 PERCENT RECYCLED CARDBOARD, SO IT'S ENVIRONMENTALLY FRIENDLY... IT HAS A ZERO-INCH SCREEN, WHICH GIVES IT A THEORETICAL PIXEL DENSITY OF INFINITY... AND IF YOU HAVE A PENCIL WITH AN ERASER, YOU CAN PLAY UNLIMITED FREE GAMES OF TIC-TAC-TOE AND HANGMAN ON IT!
I EVEN HAVE IT PRICED AT A CRAZY LOW $49!
THAT STILL SEEMS PRETTY HIGH.
I'LL HAVE YOU KNOW IN A HEAD-TO-HEAD MATCHUP, THE jPAD WOULD LITERALLY SMASH THE iPAD.
YOU MISUSED THE WORD "LITERALLY."
DID I?
WHY IS THERE A ROCK TAPED TO THE BACK?

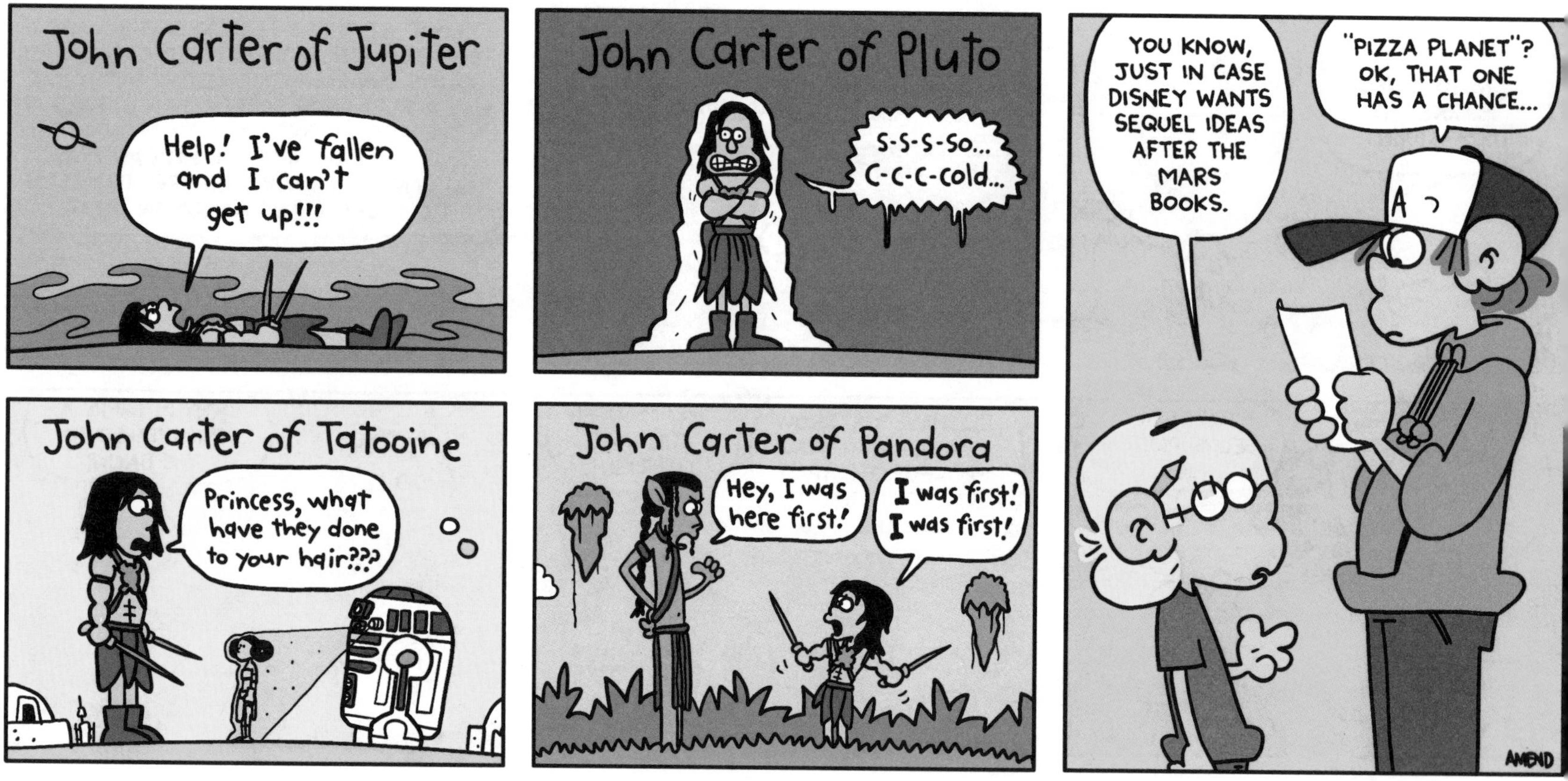
John Carter of Jupiter
Help! I've fallen and I can't get up!!!
John Carter of Pluto
S-S-S-So... C-C-C-cold...
John Carter of Tatooine
Princess, what have they done to your hair???
John Carter of Pandora
Hey, I was here first!
I was first! I was first!
YOU KNOW, JUST IN CASE DISNEY WANTS SEQUEL IDEAS AFTER THE MARS BOOKS.
"PIZZA PLANET"? OK, THAT ONE HAS A CHANCE...
AMEND

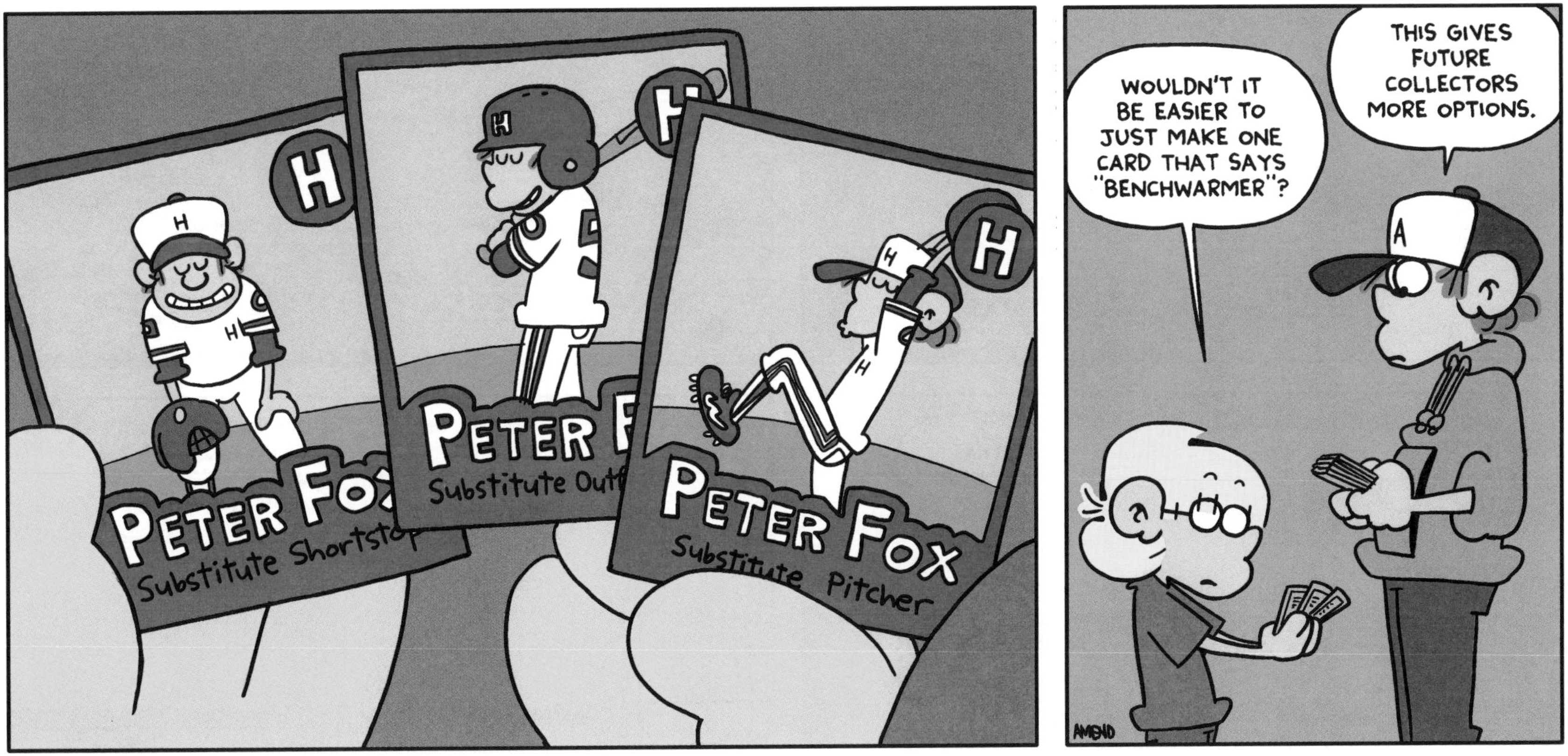
PETER FOX
Substitute Shortstop
PETER F
Substitute Out
PETER FOX
Substitute Pitcher
WOULDN'T IT BE EASIER TO JUST MAKE ONE CARD THAT SAYS "BENCHWARMER"?
THIS GIVES FUTURE COLLECTORS MORE OPTIONS.
AMEND

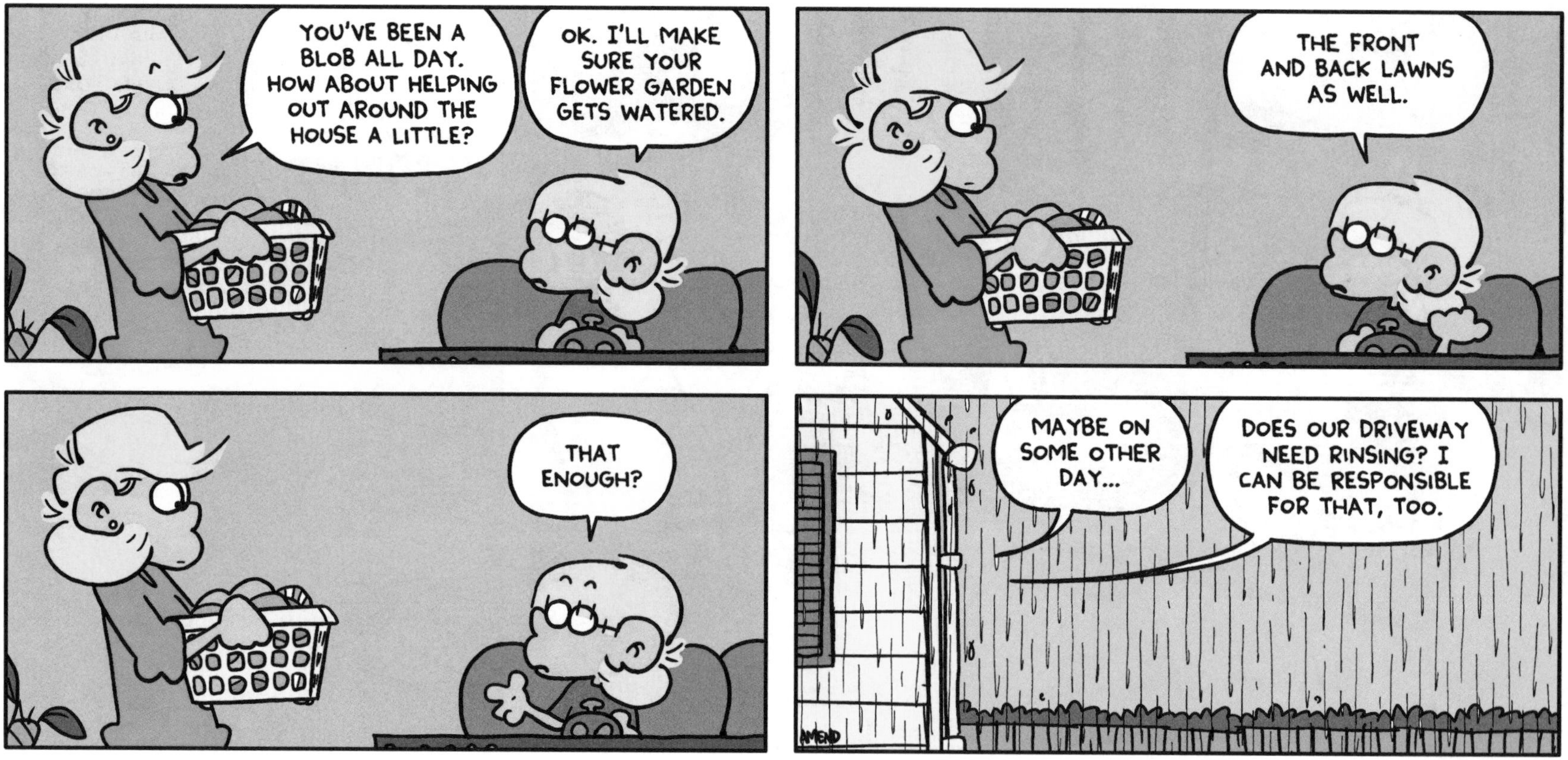
YOU'VE BEEN A BLOB ALL DAY. HOW ABOUT HELPING OUT AROUND THE HOUSE A LITTLE?
OK. I'LL MAKE SURE YOUR FLOWER GARDEN GETS WATERED.
THE FRONT AND BACK LAWNS AS WELL.
THAT ENOUGH?
MAYBE ON SOME OTHER DAY...
DOES OUR DRIVEWAY NEED RINSING? I CAN BE RESPONSIBLE FOR THAT, TOO.
AMEND

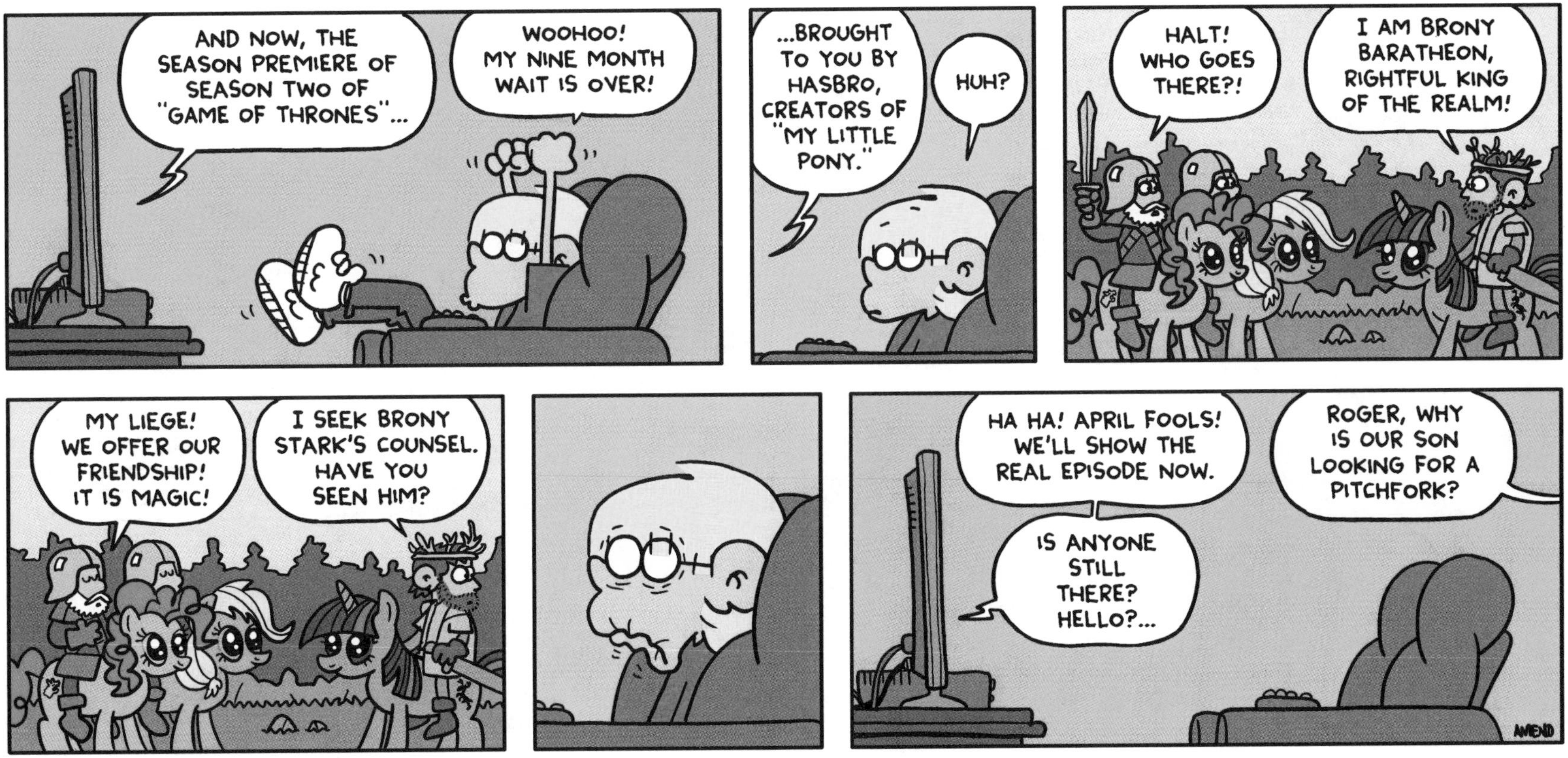
AND NOW, THE SEASON PREMIERE OF SEASON TWO OF "GAME OF THRONES"...
WOOHOO! MY NINE MONTH WAIT IS OVER!
...BROUGHT TO YOU BY HASBRO, CREATORS OF "MY LITTLE PONY."
HUH?
HALT! WHO GOES THERE?!
I AM BRONY BARATHEON, RIGHTFUL KING OF THE REALM!
MY LIEGE! WE OFFER OUR FRIENDSHIP! IT IS MAGIC!
I SEEK BRONY STARK'S COUNSEL. HAVE YOU SEEN HIM?
HA HA! APRIL FOOLS! WE'LL SHOW THE REAL EPISODE NOW.
IS ANYONE STILL THERE? HELLO?...
ROGER, WHY IS OUR SON LOOKING FOR A PITCHFORK?
AMEND

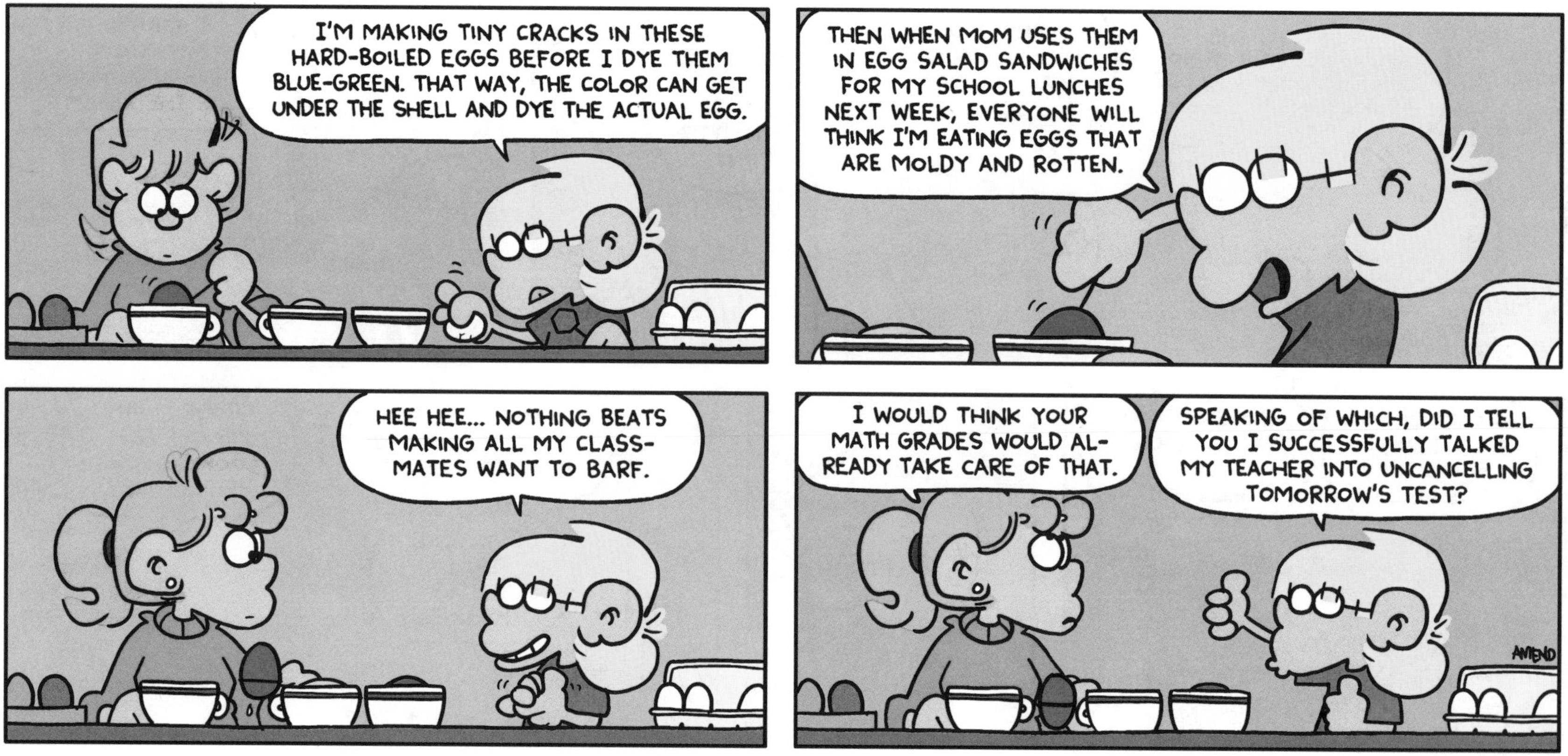
I'M MAKING TINY CRACKS IN THESE HARD-BOILED EGGS BEFORE I DYE THEM BLUE-GREEN. THAT WAY, THE COLOR CAN GET UNDER THE SHELL AND DYE THE ACTUAL EGG.
THEN WHEN MOM USES THEM IN EGG SALAD SANDWICHES FOR MY SCHOOL LUNCHES NEXT WEEK, EVERYONE WILL THINK I'M EATING EGGS THAT ARE MOLDY AND ROTTEN.
HEE HEE... NOTHING BEATS MAKING ALL MY CLASS-MATES WANT TO BARF.
I WOULD THINK YOUR MATH GRADES WOULD AL-READY TAKE CARE OF THAT.
SPEAKING OF WHICH, DID I TELL YOU I SUCCESSFULLY TALKED MY TEACHER INTO UNCANCELLING TOMORROW'S TEST?
AMEND

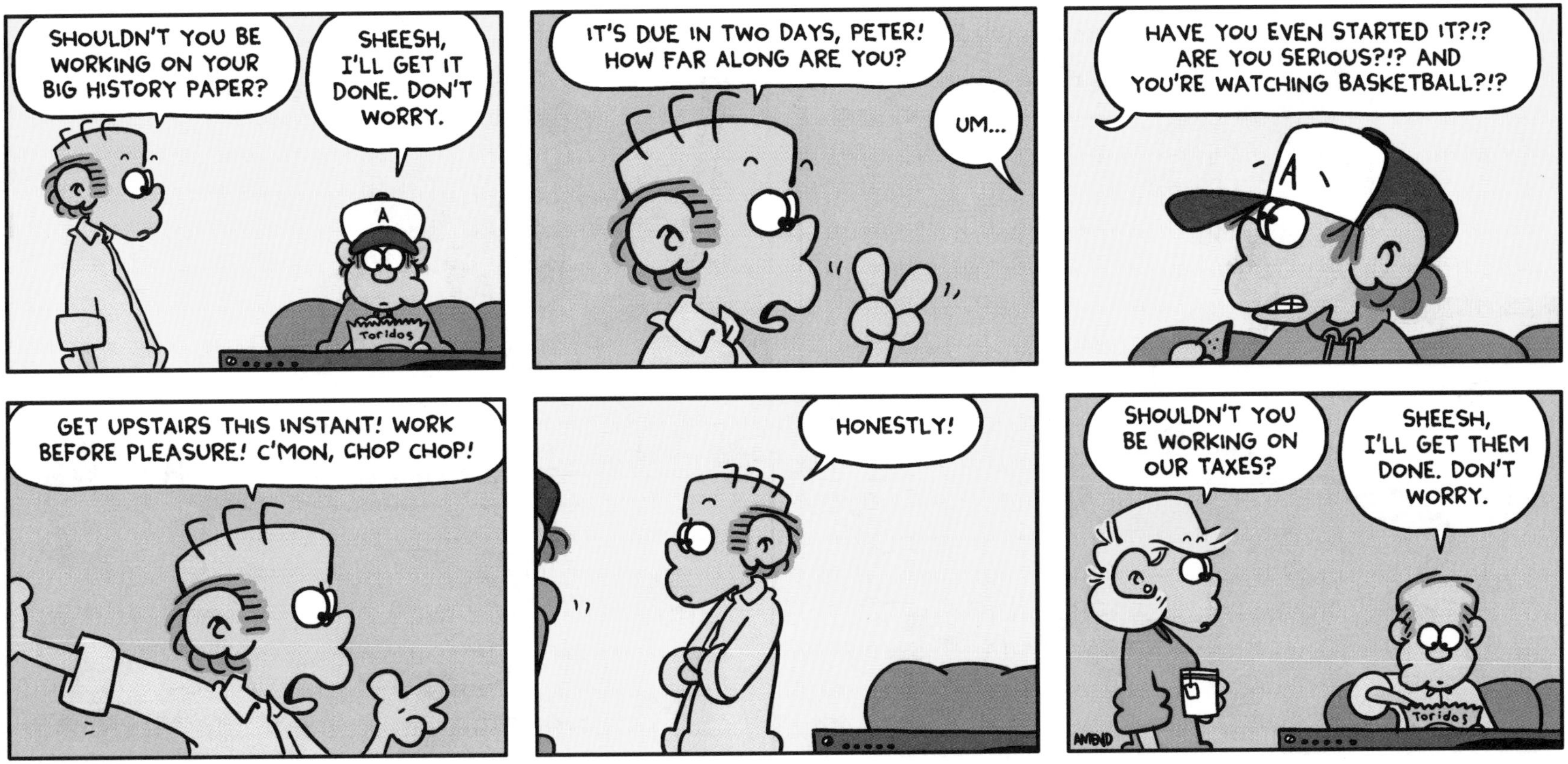
SHOULDN'T YOU BE WORKING ON YOUR BIG HISTORY PAPER?
SHEESH, I'LL GET IT DONE. DON'T WORRY.
Toridos
IT'S DUE IN TWO DAYS, PETER! HOW FAR ALONG ARE YOU?
UM...
HAVE YOU EVEN STARTED IT?!? ARE YOU SERIOUS?!? AND YOU'RE WATCHING BASKETBALL?!?
A
GET UPSTAIRS THIS INSTANT! WORK BEFORE PLEASURE! C'MON, CHOP CHOP!
HONESTLY!
SHOULDN'T YOU BE WORKING ON OUR TAXES?
SHEESH, I'LL GET THEM DONE. DON'T WORRY.
Toridos
AMEND

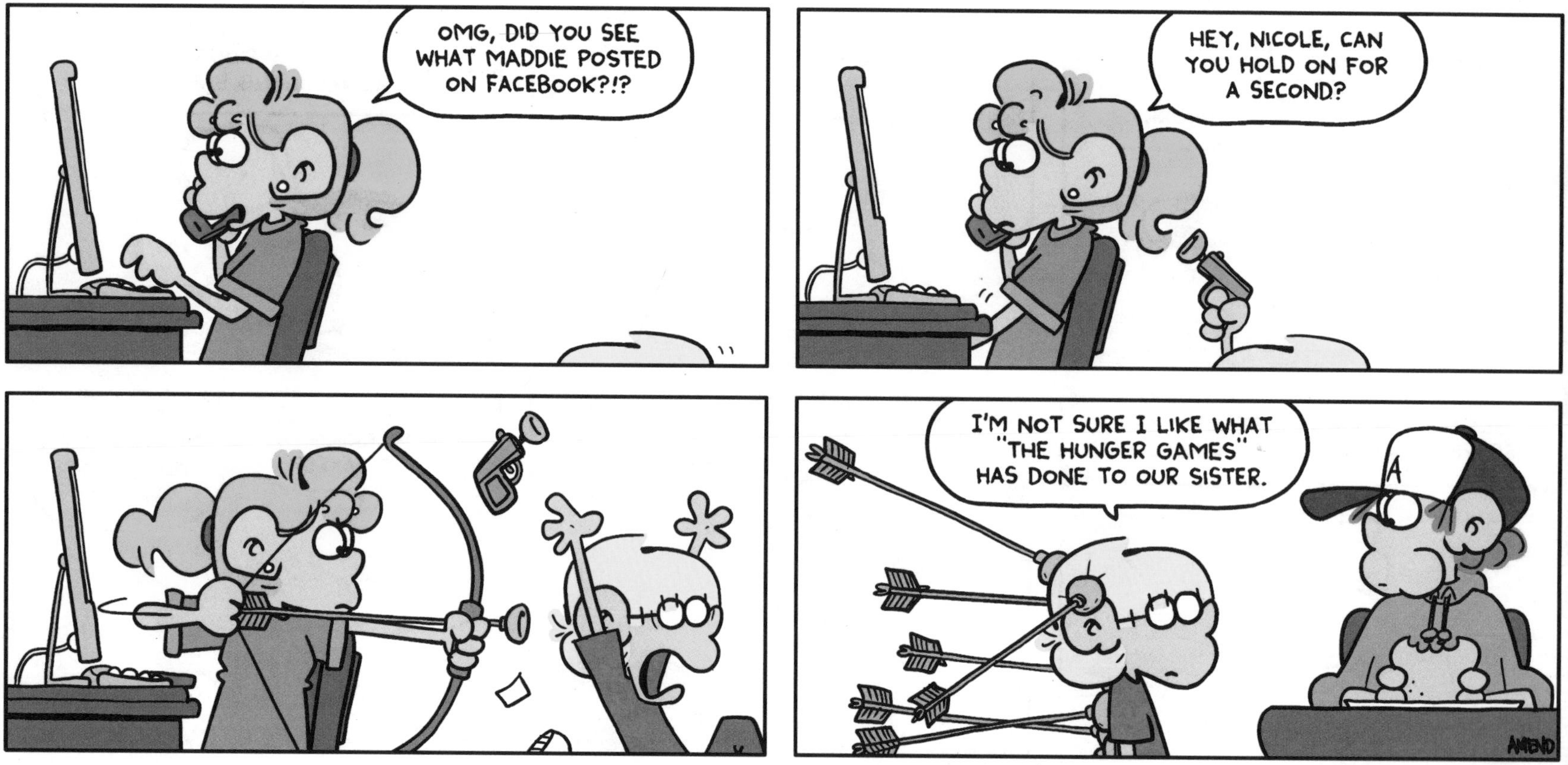
OMG, DID YOU SEE WHAT MADDIE POSTED ON FACEBOOK?!?
HEY, NICOLE, CAN YOU HOLD ON FOR A SECOND?
I'M NOT SURE I LIKE WHAT "THE HUNGER GAMES" HAS DONE TO OUR SISTER.
AMEND